Charandas Chor

and Other Plays

NEW INDIAN PLAYWRIGHTS

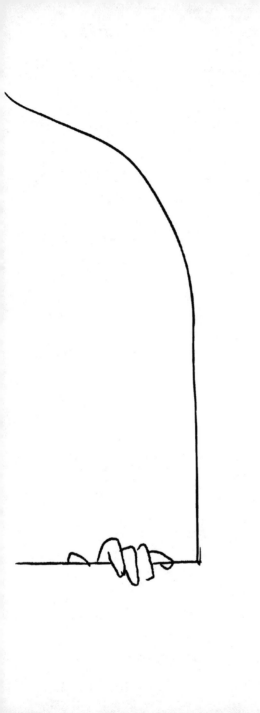

HABIB TANVIR

Charandas Chor
and Other Plays

LONDON NEW YORK CALCUTTA

Seagull Books, 2018

Original plays © Nageen Tanvir
Translation and introductory material © Seagull Books, 2004, 2005, 2006, 2018
This compilation © Seagull Books, 2018

ISBN 978 0 8574 2 495 2

British Library Cataloguing-in-Publication Data
A catalogue record for this book is available from the British Library

Typeset and illustrated by Manasij Dutta, Seagull Books, Calcutta, India
Printed and bound by Maple Press, York, Pennsylvania, USA

CONTENTS

THE RELEVANCE OF HABIB TANVIR

ANJUM KATYAL

A people's poet who, upon request, composes verses to help street vendors sell their juicy fruit; an irrepressibly honest thief who ends a lively career hoodwinking the authorities with choosing to die rather than break his sworn oaths; a beautiful damsel who brews the most sought after wine for miles around, and who ends up killing her only and beloved son; a tribal chieftain who struggles to deal with the demands of an administration system imposed by democracy. The four plays in this collection deal with all the above, covering the spectrum from broad comedy to deep tragedy, liberally seasoned with political and social commentary and critique. Signature Habib Tanvir.

It is impossible to discuss the theatre of independent India without the work of Habib Tanvir (1923–2009).[1] *The Oxford Companion to Indian Theatre* describes him as a 'Hindi and Urdu playwright, director, actor, manager, poet, and one of the most important theatre personalities of post-Independence India.[2] Indeed, his achievements were remarkable enough to justify the sobriquet 'renaissance man', which is what theatre activist and scholar Sudhanva Deshpande, in his obituary, calls him:

Habib Tanvir was a renaissance personality. There was nothing he could not do in theatre—he wrote, translated, adapted and evolved plays; he was a master director, a superb actor and a good singer; he wrote poetry and songs; he could compose music; he was a designer; he was manager of his company Naya Theatre, which he ran first with his wife Moneeka (and single-handed after her death) for exactly fifty years; he was a critic and theoretician; more, he was a seer, a guru for generations of younger theatre artistes. In all this, and through his prodigiously prolific theatre career spanning some sixty years, he remained an artiste with a deep social conscience and engagement, a public intellectual who never shied away from taking a stand and lending his name to progressive and secular causes.[3]

To me, Habib Tanvir embodied the ideal of the artist in today's India. Because in his artistic practice he drew on the rich multiplicity that is our true cultural heritage as a country, incorporating all the different strands, irrespective of religion or language, class or caste. Because his work combined high aesthetic standards with social commitment, growing out of his progressive, people-centric politics and his resolutely non-sectarian sensibility. And because he showed us a way of being contemporary, topical and relevant without excluding large segments of our populace who were part of an age-old oral culture.

Habib Tanvir's most important contribution to the Indian theatre scene, I feel, was his intervention in the fundamental discourse of modern and contemporary Indian theatre—its direction, and its form. Let me explain what I mean.

India had just gained independence when Habib Tanvir began his theatre practice. It was a period of nation building, not just in the areas of economy or the political arena, but also in the cultural field. Arts practitioners and theorists were deeply involved with the issue of what constituted Indian culture for our nascent nation-state. How was one to balance the heft of tradition and heritage with the needs and sensibilities of the current, the present-day? How could the arts be modern and contemporary and still remain distinctly 'Indian'? Theatre in India faced the same questions.

On the one hand there was the colonial legacy of Western-style proscenium theatre, which stylistically ranged from classic naturalism to the modernist and avant-garde, and in terms of content from pure spectacle to political plays with a strong message and social critique. This theatre was entrenched in the cities and urban centres, although popular Parsi and Company theatre groups toured extensively through the smaller towns and rural areas as well. Indeed, Habib Tanvir himself recalled being fascinated by such theatre in his hometown of Raipur, replete with backdrops, wings, sets, props, special effects and music from a live orchestra.[4]

On the other, thanks to the rediscovery of ancient Sanskrit texts and traditional performance forms instigated largely by the Orientalist-led exploration of ancient Indian culture, there was a strong interest in indigenous performance conventions and forms. Sanskrit theatre, as prescribed and categorized by the *Natyashastra*, was one such discovery: ancient texts were revisited and the conventions of performance re-activated. Another was the rich and colourful legacy of regional performative traditions and extant folk forms to be found all over the country, such as Maharashtra's Tamasha and Lavani, Gujarat's Bhavai, Karnataka's Yakshagana, the Therukoothu of Tamil Nadu, Jatra in Bengal or the Chhau of Orissa. Equally sought-after were various performer-training systems and martial arts disciplines like the Manipuri Thang-ta or Kalaripayyat in south India.

In the 1940s the Indian People's Theatre Association (IPTA), motivated by an interest in 'people's' culture, was perhaps the first group of artists to bring these 'folk' forms into their productions in a consistent manner. Soon, theatre directors in search of ethnic forms of expression started to seek them out, and this trend began to be seen as a 'roots theatre' movement.[5] Typically, 'theatre of the roots' employed aspects of these traditional forms to express the creative vision of an individual director, who would incorporate elements taken from regional performance forms into his or her work, most often as visual or stylistic accents.

While both these trends in modern Indian theatre—the 'Western-looking' and the 'ethnic-looking'—were being explored in the towns and cities, in the vast expanses of rural India a very different theatre and performance economy prevailed, traversing a separate circuit of its own. Part of centuries-old oral cultures, these were quintessential subaltern forms, irreverent, subversive, and very contemporary. Evolved over centuries, they continued to adopt from and adapt to popular trends from satirical skits on current affairs, to witty comments on local scandals, or the insertion of popular film dances and songs into their performances. However, as the age-old fabric of rural economy and society shredded and frayed, survival became a struggle for these performers and forms. 'Precious oral heritage slipped into oblivion as songs ceased to be sung, dances to be danced and rituals to be performed. Invaluable skills and indigenous knowledge, as important a part of India's cultural heritage as the Sanskrit scriptures the nation-state so zealously preserved, gradually grew extinct, largely unnoticed by the cultural mainstream.'[6]

Habib Tanvir's was one voice that spoke out in support of this valuable, and fast vanishing, oral cultural heritage:

> . . . the educated lack the culture which . . . the villages possess so richly though they are illiterate . . . being more than compensated by the rich oral tradition of our culture and who, therefore, are the more cultured. [. . .]

. . . the rural sophistication is not understood by the urban people and vice versa. But I find the villager much more sophisticated . . . in many, many instances. In the arts they are much more sophisticated.'[7]

Not only was he appreciative of this oral culture, he found it both relevant and viable. As theatre critic and scholar Javed Malick observes, at the time the term 'folk' was 'neither the fashion nor the passion of India's contemporary stage . . . it was a neglected and greatly devitalized category. Tanvir was one of those who pioneered the revival of interest in folk performance traditions and made it into a significant and influential category.'[8]

Habib Tanvir did not agree with the general trend of the time, which was to dismiss these 'folk forms' as backward looking and out of step with our modern age; charming, quaint, and colourful, perhaps, but unable to express the needs of contemporary living; at best capable of yielding stylistic features which could infuse a fresh energy into urban, sophisticated theatre, but in themselves inadequately contemporary. He begged to differ:

I believe in the viability of the rich forms of the rural theatre in which they have a tendency to incorporate the most topical, the latest local happening, the thematic and formal flexibility by which we cannot claim this is how it was performed 200 or 2000 years ago . . . I believe that it is possible to usher in progress without demolishing this cul-ture. This environment should be preserved, this . . . rural environ-ment most conducive to the fullest growth of the folk theatre form, because this community life which is so rich in its cultural expression can be transformed to a progressive community in which this expres-sion remains.'[9]

This, indeed, was the quest which consumed his creative career—how to bring these 'rich forms of the rural theatre' onto the mainstream stage, and how to demonstrate that they could hold their own as contemporary theatre. His solution was to create theatre with rural performers from Chhattisgarh, where the popular, lively, Nacha form attracted his professional attention. Finding the artistes highly talented, with an innate understanding of comic timing, he wooed them into working with him, thereby involving them in a demanding theatre practice far different from their habitual, short, loosely improvisatory skits laced with songs and dances. The result was a thoroughly modern theatre in a rural dialect and idiom. This was what he wanted. He said:

> If it is attempted to close this gap between the village and the town . . . above all in the realm of art, then we will begin to think in terms of a true indigenous form which is good enough for modern India whether in the cities or in the villages. After all we are trying to bridge this gap in terms of development in industry, agriculture. In terms of culture also we have to come to grips with what are the roots and not always remain in the urban vacuum which has been created in the last few decades.[10]

The plays in this volume demonstrate the extent to which he succeeded.

What made Habib Tanvir's approach different from that of his contemporaries, several of whom were also drawn to the folk performative traditions? Instead of using it, like they did, as a source of idioms and stylistic elements to be adopted into their own theatre projects, Habib elected to

> shape his own theatre around the presence of the folk performer, who is, literally, the embodiment and vehicle of oral performance culture. The folk performers are in themselves 'endangered archives'. He has said, time and again, that he was not running after folk forms as much as running after folk actors; with the actors came the forms. Another

way of saying that the owners of the tradition brought it with them; it was not taken from them for the use of others.[11]

Yes, he frequently used material such as folktales, folk songs and rituals in his productions, but as theatre critic Javed Malick says, 'Tanvir's fascination with the folk is not motivated by a revivalist or an antiquarian impulse.'[12] Habib Tanvir felt that 'you can do nothing worthwhile unless you went to your roots and tried to reinterpret traditions and used traditions as a vehicle for transmitting the most modern and contemporary messages. Which means intervening in the tradition creatively.'[13]

Consequently, he practised a modern theatre which yet made space for folk actors bringing with them a culture and aesthetic largely marginalized by mainstream India. This was the oral tradition; and it is this oral tradition that made Habib Tanvir's theatre unique. As he said, 'In my plays I take up the important issues of our times while working with people who are linked to the soil, people who are open minded and uninhibited. And it was the interaction of these two elements that gave birth to a new theatrical idiom.'[14]

Here, in my opinion, lies the greatest significance of Habib Tanvir's theatre legacy. His search for a satisfactory and meaningful theatre form can be seen as a 'sustained and serious exploration of how one could create a modern theatre integrated with an age-old yet equally contemporary oral culture, not just as an "exotic" imported element but as an integral part of its form and content.'[15] This is what his repertory Naya Theatre, with its Chhattisgarhi actors, achieved, creating productions that garnered both popular and critical acclaim, both within the country and internationally. And everywhere his productions were seen as modern, not folk, theatre. In a theatre environment divided between two dominant approaches, Habib Tanvir opened up a third way. This inclusive idea of Indian theatre was an intervention into the discourse xiv / ANJUM KATYAL

on the future direction of Indian theatre that forever proved that his third way was not just possible, but capable of being highly successful.

Today, several years after his death, his legacy assumes even greater significance as forces of exclusion gain ground throughout the country, bent on denying the ancient heritage of multiplicity India has celebrated since Independence. Habib Tanvir—brought up in a north Indian Muslim household, adept at Urdu, a language increasingly being marginalized as 'only a Muslim tongue' in contradiction to its history, working with tribal artistes belonging to the most downtrodden and disempowered segment of society, bringing them into focus with their language and culture which has otherwise vanished from the national discourse—embodied, both in his person and his practice, the composite India which is under attack by an aggressively narrow narrative of nation. His oeuvre covers classic Sanskrit dramas and local rural legends, contemporary Indian playwrights and international icons. In the content of his plays, Habib Tanvir's theatre foregrounded the voice and perspective of the people rather than the establishment: parodying, questioning, challenging, and exposing hypocrisy, oppression, and unjust discrimination, often through a robust humour that poked unabashed fun at hollow holy cows. His is an inheritance we cannot afford to disregard; a vision we must not forget.

We have spoken about the incorporation of oral culture into his theatre practice. What are these elements or features of oral culture—'typically collective, participatory, improvisatory and resistant to regulation'[16]— which find a place in his process and his productions?

To begin with, the element of collective or collaborative practice. Javed Malick talks of Habib Tanvir's collaborative approach in the way he 'fits and blends his poetry with the traditional folk and tribal music, allowing the former to retain its own imaginative and rhetorical power and socio-political import, but without in any way devaluing or destroying the latter'[17] as also in how he 'allows his actors and their skills to be foregrounded by eschewing all temptations to use elaborate stage design and complicated lighting.'[18] To me, Habib Tanvir's method of developing a scene with his actors also demonstrates this collaborative process: he would encourage them to improvise, prompting and exploring until he felt as a director that it was time to 'freeze' the sequence. He says:

> We work like this. I put a story across to the group members and they think it over. The next time round we go over the storyline and each one puts in a word for an elaboration or a nuance he thinks should be fitted in at such and such a point in the course of the play. This is something I've always tried to do—get the actors to move the play in certain directions.[19]

Secondly, there is language. His childhood in Raipur gave Habib Tanvir a close familiarity with the local Chhattisgarhi dialect. Language always held a particular fascination for him, especially language as used by the man on the street; and this interest was strengthened by his experience with the IPTA and Progressive Writers' Association (PWA).[20] 'Yet Tanvir did not just lift the language and use it to write dialogue, just as he did not just lift folk material and fashion plays from it.'[21] He chose instead, as already mentioned, to work with folk actors who brought in, along with the lively Chhatisgarhi language, a whole oral performative tradition.

Third, improvisation. Improvised theatre is collective in nature—another feature of the oral tradition, in which the performance belongs to all those who make it, with no fixed, authored script. This is basic to the folk oral performance forms, where the actor invents dialogue, contributes little bits of stage business, introduces topical references, and interacts with the audience. 'By incorporating two fundamental principles into his theatre—the native language, and the freedom to improvise—Tanvir ensured that the actors gained agency.'[22]

The fourth aspect of the folk oral culture in Habib Tanvir's work is the nonlinear treatment of time and space, very different from the classic, Aristotlean unities of time, space and action. He says:

> You see, I've learnt many things from watching Nacha . . . and learnt to have the stage set functional, very economical so that we remain mobile, for artistic as well as economical reasons. The architecture, set design, were also affected by the kind of awareness I gained in regard to the importance of the actor related to space and the relation of time to space and to actor and to action. All these things, I think, gave me very simple forms, like a rectangular platform with just one tree, to which I came after a few shows.[23]

He talks further of the 'magical simplicity' of an actor simply walking around the stage space to convey a journey or a new locale. In his theatre the actor's body defines space and time in performance, not sets, lights or scene divisions.

A fifth aspect of folk oral culture is the pervasive and subversive social critique, typically achieved through wit and humour. *Charandas Chor*, for example, highlights the greed and double standards of the wealthy and powerful, not sparing the false piety of priests and gurus. Even a stark tragedy like *Bahadur Kalarin* interweaves, with its Oedipal storyline, the issue of land acquisition by the wealthy and the steady disempowerment of the poor farmer.

Amongst the most noteworthy of the oral elements in Habib Tanvir's theatre is the use of song. His love of music and fascination with the many traditional songs which were part of everyday life in Chhattisgarh drove him to actively collect them and introduce them into his plays. Meanwhile the Nacha, responding to popular tastes, was rapidly replacing folk songs with Hindi hit tunes, causing their steady extinction. Due to their presence in his work several of these folk songs have been prevented from dying out altogether. Ditto for many of the life-cycle songs once sung during harvest, childbirth, weddings and so on. In his plays they are typically performed live both by a group of musicians and the actors, and contribute significantly to the narrative and over-all impact. Alongside the folk melodies he also introduced songs which, though based on traditional tunes and rhythms, had lyrics written specially for the play.

Let us now turn to the plays in this volume. *Agra Bazaar*, written and staged in Delhi in 1954, was his first major theatre production, and already shows, as we will see, markers of his later mature style. *Charandas Chor* (1975), widely considered to be the apogee of his theatre, is a lively romp with an unexpected twist at the end which lifts it from comic farce to something indefinable and deeply moving. *Bahadur Kalarin* (1978) is a tragic exploration of a local legend with Oedipal overtones, and further pushes the boundaries of his work with Chhattisgarhi actors, as we will discuss. And *Hirma ki Amar Kahani* (The Living Tale of Hirma, 1985), loosely based on a real Bastar tribal chief, is perhaps Habib Tanvir's most overtly political play. Together they provide an excellent overview of his oeuvre.

Although *Agra Bazaar* was Habib Tanvir's first major directorial venture, staged a whole two decades before the crystallization of his quest for a unique form, it exhibits certain distinctive characteristics which were intrinsic to his theatrical approach. This includes the fluid structure, for example, with its 'interwoven narratives, humorous sequences, live songs and music';[24] as also the clear 'local flavour in the setting and the language'.[25] He was already using folk tunes and Chhattisgarhi songs in this production.[26] His respect for the culture and language of the ordinary man on the street runs through this play. Another typical feature is the strong thread of socio-political commentary. We hear people discussing the changing cultural scenario as a feudal and monarchic order crumbles, and new ideas and practices emerge. His foregrounding of the subaltern, in the form of those who struggle for a livelihood, which he juxtapositions against privilege and the establishment, emerges insistently in this work, as in his later plays. He himself claimed that 'the genesis of what eventually developed into my characteristic style was there in *Agra Bazaar*' which, he states, was one of the three milestones in his theatre career.[27]

What drew him so strongly to the subject of Nazir the poet is clear to see: 'Here was a people's poet, an artist who put his creativity at the service of the common man, just as Habib himself had spent years trying to do, with both IPTA and PWA. His own interest in dialects and the language of ordinary people found an echo in the poetry of Nazir.'[28] He said, 'It was this aspect of Nazir's poetry that I wanted to focus on. So I chose it as the subject of my play . . . I wanted to highlight the fact that Nazir's love of the ordinary people has immortalized him.'[29]

This play also saw the birth of his distinctive fluid or flexible dramatic structure, which subsequently became central to his dramatic style:

It was just movement on stage—and the openness of the play, its form, the singing of the Nazir songs, came to me first as a feature. There was not enough material on Nazir to do anything more than just a feature. So I decided on collecting a few poems, the best, and making a feature of it with a thin narrative to describe Nazir; and I suddenly arrived at a dramatic form. Then I worked further on it, brought it to Delhi and it became a play. Now, that gave me great flexibility of form.[30]

Agra Bazaar was first presented on the Jamia Art Institute's open-air stage as a 40–50-minute show. Seeing the enthusiastic response, it was decided to present it in New Delhi at the Ramlila grounds; this time they played to an audience of thousands. Gradually it grew into a full-length play, with the introduction of more threads of plot: 'the *kotha* was introduced, a *goonda* (ruffian) was introduced, prostitutes and an inspector. At first it was a skeleton, then it developed into the full two-hour version in which Nazir is talked of, he's here, there, but never comes on stage.'[31]

The intervening twenty years between this and the next major milestone in Habib Tanvir's theatre career, *Charandas Chor* (1974-5) were rich with learning and experimentation. In these years Habib Tanvir studied abroad at RADA[32] and the Bristol Old Vic, travelled Europe on a shoe-string seeing theatre everywhere he went, spent time with the Berliner Ensemble just after the demise of Brecht, and returned to India convinced that his theatrical quest had to be rooted in the indigenous traditions of his country, albeit with all the ideas, concepts and learning evoked by his international exposure, not to mention his years with IPTA. He began to apply these straight away in *Mitti ki Gadi*, his version of the Sanskrit classic *Mrichhakatikam* by Sudraka. This, along with the many later productions leading up to the Eureka moment of *Charandas Chor*, marked one more stage on his long journey towards a theatre form that would fully express his vision.

Based on a Rajasthani folk tale, *Charandas Chor* is almost synonymous with Habib Tanvir and Naya Theatre, being both hugely popular, and critically acclaimed. It is also the best example of his mature theatre form at its most highly developed.

Charandas is an unlikely hero: an impudent Robin Hood figure, a thief with a kind heart. He gaily outwits policemen, grasping landowners, venial priests and other such worthy pillars of the establishment, but is eventually undone by his own innate honesty. His refusal to break the vows he has taken, including never to tell a lie, leads to his being put to death.

This most unexpected of tragedies turns the convention of a tragic hero on its head: our protagonist is a trickster whose success is his undoing, but whose fatal flaw is actually his innate integrity. A lighthearted romp with satirical overtones, brimming with slapstick moments, flips in the space of a moment into stark tragedy, leaving the audience stunned. 'Some didn't believe that he was dead, because I always used to get the actor to become very stiff. They thought it's a comedy and there'll be some trick and he'll come back,' says Habib Tanvir.[33] 'The very first night it was a stunning experience, in Kamani auditorium. He died. Total silence. Strange silence. People got up, thinking, when will the next line come? Disturbed. The restive, urban, Delhi audience was moved. And then, before going out, they stopped, turned and then stood for several minutes . . . watching from the door, uncomfortably.'[34]

Habib Tanvir decided to change the original ending of the comic folk tale to end with the death of Charandas. Why? I choose to read this as a political statement. In his own words:

Here is a common man—and that's why he must remain a common man—an unheroic, simple man who gets caught up in his vows and though he fears death, can't help it and dies. And the establishment cannot brook this. So for me the tragedy in the classical sense was perfect because tragedy has to be inevitable. There is an inevitability to his death because he didn't go the convenient way of saying yes to the queen, which would be a way out. That way was barred, it was not an option. The queen is not simply a tyrant, but a politician.

There is no way she can let him go free, because she entreats him not to tell anyone, and he says, but I must tell the truth; and as soon as she knows that the *praja*, the populace, will get to know, she fears for her position. As we have seen throughout history, such people are always eliminated.[35]

Along with being a political statement, it was also good theatre:

. . . this is, in the classical sense, a perfect tragedy. It makes you laugh till the last moment and suddenly you're silent. You're in the presence of death . . . Is it a tragedy? Yes. Is it a comedy? Yes. Is it a comedy? No. Is it a tragedy? No. I don't know what it is. It's difficult to put it in a category. And I think that's the secret of the success of the play. To this day I'm convinced that the death is the secret of its success.[36]

In terms of his dramatic trajectory, there are several reasons why *Charandas Chor* is considered a perfect example of Habib Tanvir's theatre. Let us cast a quick glance at what these are.

First, there is the pre-eminence of the Chhattisgarhi actor, moving confidently through a fluid performance space and speaking confidently in his and her native tongue. A simple set design, with time and space defined by the actor's bodies, is central to the play. This flexible, open space perfectly suits the agile folk actor, unused to blocking or prescribed movements. It also suits the choreographed group dances that intersperse the action. A change of locale is indicated through dialogue or simply by the actor making a round of the stage. Props are restricted to items that are essential to the plot—sacks of grain, the thief's bundle, the idol in the temple.

By this time Habib Tanvir the director had learned how best to work with a Chhattisgarhi cast. It involved jettisoning his Westernized training. He realised that their strength lay in a free, improvisatory approach to movement, and that they were inhibited by having to speak in an unfamiliar language, Hindi. These actors may not have been literate, but they were highly skilled at improvising in their own tongue. 'Once he adapted to the oral performance culture to which they belonged, and learnt how to work with it, he found his form.'[37] Habib Tanvir acknowledges:

> The actor's contribution in shaping the production was rich. It was mainly through improvisations . . . Improvisation has become quite my style of direction now. Not everything comes from the director, or from the actor, but a lot of it comes from this process of improvisation, interpretation of different imaginations and consciousnesses. In the process there is a lot of muck, a lot of repetitiveness, but also lots of gems. You clutch on to the gems and cut out the rest. Then I rush to my desk to write it all down.[38]

Charandas Chor marked the moment when his experiments with Chhattisgarhi actors suddenly came together. In his own words:

> I was doing things in Chhattisgarhi during 1970–73. But I didn't have a breakthrough until this time because I suddenly got the language of the body through improvisations . . . my vocabulary of the visual language of the Chhattisgarhi players had increased and so had my confidence in using it. It was simply that . . . Suddenly we broke all barriers and people who'd never come to see Chhattisgarhi plays during those three years started pouring in.[39]

Another typical feature which works powerfully in this play is the introduction of ritual in the dramatic action. About the use of ritual in his plays, Habib Tanvir explains: 'I find in this drama in an embryonic form and I'm presenting it . . . as good theatre which fascinates you. Its magic is felt. I visualize the beginnings of drama in India like this, a semblance of the kind of hymns chanted around the fire in Vedic times; and this is dramatic because religion is dramatic.'[40]

The presence and impact of live music, songs and dances is another typical Habib Tanvir feature. He used both traditional folk tunes and freshly composed songs with lyrics by folk poets Swaran Kumar Sahu and Ganga Ram Sakhet, set to traditional Chhattisgarhi melodies. The closing song is a tune composed by Habib Tanvir himself. In some songs, traditional choruses, chants or phrases are juxtaposed with words written for the play. Songs operate variously in this play as in the others. They play a Brechtian role of commenting on an action to bring out its larger moral and social significance, often contributing a sarcastic comment or ironic perspective. 'Songs also point to a conceptual development in the narrative—for example, "Charandas is not a thief, not a thief, no way" is sung at the point in the plot when he transforms from simple thief to people's hero by distributing the grain he has stolen from the corrupt landlord to the starving villagers. In Act Two, the panthi singers sing, "Oh Charandas don't try to rob Death of its due", thereby planting the thought of death in the audience's mind and subliminally preparing them for his assassination at the end of the play.'[41]

In addition to the above, live music and singing contribute a distinctive aural texture just as the rituals add a visual element, enriching the theatrical experience while simultaneously including an oral tradition that is increasingly ghettoized in contemporary performance.

And of course, like all Habib Tanvir's plays, *Charandas Chor* contains a heavy dose of sociopolitical critique. The honest thief stands in sharp contrast to the hypocrital and dishonestly exploitative policeman, guru, priest, and government official (munim): all supposedly servants of the people. Charandas exposes the corruption of the establishment—the forces of law and order, the landlord-moneylender, organized religion, the ruler and her henchmen; the

Queen would rather have an honest man killed than risk losing face in public. He also demonstrates solidarity with the poor, and a strong sense of social justice. We never see him cowed or subservient even in the face of authority.

Habib Tanvir also exposes the exploitative practices of so-called gurus and godmen—another facet of his work that renders it so completely topical and relevant:

> The guru's ashram is a den of gamblers, drunkards and addicts; and the guru himself is more interested in his dakshina than in the well being of his disciples. In the temple scene, even as devotees intone a hymn, Charandas and the policeman play an elaborate game of cat-and-mouse, undercutting the solemnity of the atmosphere with their antics. The priest is quite content to receive stolen loot as long as it enriches his temple.[42]

In a final political statement, the play ends by celebrating the quick-witted folk hero with his 'Utopian ideals of an equitable social system',[43] and the people's 'desire for truth and justice'.[44] It is this combination of elements, blending comic satire with tragic heroism and socio-political commentary with traditional music and ritual that, to my mind, gives this play the status of a modern classic.

Three years passed before he presented *Bahadur Kalarin*, which Habib Tanvir describes as 'a stark tragedy,'[45] but through those years the story germinated in his brain, fascinating him enough to work on it intermittently with his actors. He describes this process and its challenges in detail in his Introduction to the Hindi/Chhattisgarhi version, which is included in this volume, making it unnecessary for me to go over the same ground. Let us instead discuss some of the unusual and interesting features of this production.

From the moment he heard the local legend of Bahadur Kalarin the comely wine-seller, a single mother whose beloved and spoilt only son married 126 wives before confessing to his mother that he remained unsatisfied, having found no woman like her, thereby driving her to first kill him and then herself, Habib Tanvir was fascinated by the Oedipal nature of this tale. Turning it into effective theatre, however, involved a degree of psychological and emotional complexity that was wholly new to his actors. He managed to introduce these nuances through extensive workshopping and discussion with his troupe. In fact, the process of preparing his actors to enact *Bahadur Kalarin* is an excellent example of his psychological approach to actor training. Although their previous experience with Nacha did not require such in-depth or layered understanding of motivation and behaviour, ideas usually associated with contemporary theatre, he was sure that the actors would have no difficulty in understanding such supposedly alien concepts:

I would, even in the normal course of things, try to get the actor to relate himself to the reality around him, to his own experience; and knowing their experience as I do, I propel them towards that reality so that they can get the feel of what they are doing. And in this case, most of them being illiterate was quite an advantage because I talked them closer to the text and to the root of the matter. Whenever I came across any stumbling blocks such as this, I'd make it a kind of classroom in which exchange could take place. They'd narrate to me stories of incest and I'd analyse incest and tell them my way of looking at it; at least one additional way of looking at incest from a scientific point of view, a doctor's point of view, an analytical point of view, as a disease. They have the mental equipment to grasp it and to produce it in their acting . . . The thing is that sometimes, like in this case, there is an awareness. But I have to make them aware of their awareness.

They were aware of incest, but they weren't aware of the fact that incest can be analysed and dissected, reasoned out as an ailment, as a sickness.[46]

He was pleased with the result, with having achieved 'the wealth and the richness of the play and the texture which I wanted.'[47] This, of all his plays, stands out as a dark and intense work, albeit with some scenes of comic relief, and some lighthearted repartee.

An unusual feature of this play is that it is woman-centric. Naya Theatre boasted several woman performers of considerable skill and power, the outstanding Fida Bai amongst them, and they certainly held their own on stage; but most of the plays themselves were not centred on women characters, certainly not complex and layered woman characters. This is an exception. Played masterfully by Fida Bai, we first see Bahadur as a feisty teenage beauty who catches the eye of the king. She is far from shy or demure; rather she is impish, cheeky and totally unimpressed by his majesty, although her elders offer him due obeisance. He ends up dancing to her tune. Habib Tanvir introduced this strand into the plot, because the existing legend focused exclusively on the mother and son tale. By doing so, he was able to develop a more complete arc to the character of Bahadur, and also introduce the aspect of a feudal societal structure, which unfolds as the narrative builds. As the play progresses, we see her evolve and grow from a precocious adolescent into a young girl in love, then a woman abandoned, who suffers but is too proud to plead or seek out her absconding lover. Discovering that she is pregnant, she chooses to bring up her child alone. We next see her as a doting but uneasy mother, troubled by her hotheaded son's recalcitrance; and finally the tragic figure who is driven to murder her beloved only child. She is also shown as a shrewd and successful business woman who understands exactly how to run the most successful wine shop in the area and handle difficult customers, while warding off the unwanted male attention her single status inevitably attracts. She rejects offers of protection, even though this would make her life easier in some ways. Throughout, she walks her own path, living by her own rules, and refusing to submit to society's expectations, whether as a young girl or a grown woman. She has grit and courage, standing up to the villagers when they gang up against her. She has compassion too—she intervenes to save them from starvation when famine invades the area. Her decision to end what she sees as her son's unhealthy obsession is wholly her own; she faces the tragedy squarely, and chooses to act. No lynch mob drives her to it. Broken-hearted, she finally takes her own life, dying as she had lived, on her own terms.

Fida Bai played her part with a maturity and subtlety that delighted her director. Habib Tanvir comments: 'Fida Bai brought such sensitivity to the oiling of the hair and to the feeding of the meal to the boy, the sensitivity of the touching, the delicate way she did it.'[48]

Being Habib Tanvir, he is unable to resist introducing a political angle into the plot. This is a narrative strand which is wholly his own, not part of the original legend. The king, who has already seduced and abandoned one of his subjects, reappears with two princelings who are launched on a direct confrontational course with the peasant lads of the village, Bahadur's rebellious son Chhachhaan and his friends. The issue is the disenfranchisement of the local small farmer, whose fields are being bought up by the king and his agents. The politics of water is discussed in the play, as panchayats are held and generations clash over the loss of land. The final showdown between the king and Chhachhaan can be read not just as an extension of the Oedipal theme with the son literally killing the father but also as a direct clash between ruler and subject, the oppressor and the subaltern. Notably, Chhachhan's character is as free of subservience as his mother's.

It would be inappropriate to leave out mention of the use of song and dance in any discussion of this play. *Bahadur Kalarin* is stitched together with these, both traditional, and particular to the play. They comment on the action, help reveal layers and subtleties, and act as a narrative device. This last is evident in two particular instances. The first is in the depiction of one hundred and twenty six brides; and the second is when the mother forbids the villagers to give her son water: 'There's a song in which ritualistically I've shown the villagers condemning him, no water, not one drop to drink and he's becoming thirstier, in the middle of their circular dance.'[49] At the end of the play, after killing her son, Bahadur sings a poignant lament as she whirls in a dance, and at the climax, produces a dagger and dies. Song and dance here serves to deepen the tragic poignancy of the moment.

The last play in this volume, *Hirma Ki Amar Kahani*, is also a tragedy. Staged seven long years after *Bahadur Kalarin*, it marks yet another departure for Habib Tanvir's oeuvre, in that it is directly political in its discourse, in a way that is unusual for his work. Based on an actual event in Bastar tribal history, it is inspired by the life of Pravir Chand Bhanjdev, erstwhile ruler of Bastar, and deals with the friction between a tribal chief who is also the head priest of his people, and the newly established central government of a young nation: 'a clash of values, priorities, attitudes towards development, and friction over rival power bases and systems of governance.'[50] In 1985 the problematic tribal question was a pressing issue which this play addresses by attempting to show up the inherent ambiguities and complications of the situation. Explaining this, Habib says:

> As far as I am concerned, the play was a kind of tight-rope dance trying to strike a balance between feudalism and democracy—feudalism which would appear to be rather undefendable and yet might show some unassailable benign qualities; and democracy which needs

to be upheld, but which is also occasionally capable of carrying on a masquerade trying to conceal its fascist fangs underneath. I had tried to show a benevolent Raja of a tribe with some unaccountable personal kinks in confrontation with the democratic apparatus of the govt. which also carried more tyranny than the Raja was capable of.[51]

With Brechtian provocation, the play throws up challenging questions without easy answers, and Habib Tanvir insists that this is deliberate. It is up to the viewer to ponder on the dilemma of who is the victor and who the victim, the nature of development and the extremely contemporary question: 'Does development mean the same thing for all societies, including the tribals?'[52]

Habib Tanvir was conscious of the challenges of doing justice to this very political and controversial issue. He said:

> It was part of my intention through this production to tell some elements . . . that there are two distinct camps and that I'm certainly not in the rightist camp . . . Then the problem of the tribals which I have taken up in *Hirma* is such that to deal with it only in a spectacular or festive manner, which is what most people today are doing, would have been to turn my back to it. The subject, the script I wrote and the numerous misconceptions that surround the problem made it more or less imperative for me to confront it politically.[53]

Hirma is structurally reminiscent of *Bahadur Kalarin*: short scenes linked with songs that comment tangentially on the themes thrown up by the action, tribal dances interlaced through the narrative. But there are several features that set it apart from his other works. For example, this play has no humour in it, no comic asides to break the steady growth of tension. Instead, an air of foreboding pervades the text as it builds to the final showdown and Hirma's death. Another unusual feature is the Legislative Assembly scene of long speeches debating the adivasi issue, quite untypical of Habib Tanvir's Chhattisgarhi plays.

Taken together, the four plays in this volume offer a representative overview of Habib Tanvir's theatre, covering the important features of his *oeuvre*. As we consider them in terms of content, form, and style, it seems safe to reaffirm his claim that 'howsoever other people would like to characterize it, my theatre was, and still is, modern and contemporary'.[54] It is indeed. And very relevant.

Calcutta, August 2017

NOTES

1 For a comprehensive study of Habib Tanvir's theatre, see Anjum Katyal, *Habib Tanvir: Towards an Inclusive Theatre* (Delhi: Sage, 2012).

2 Ananda Lal (ed.), *The Oxford Companion to Indian Theatre* (Delhi: Oxford University Press, 2004), pp. 472–3.

3 Sudhanva Deshpande, 'Habib Tanvir and His Red-Hot Life' in *Pragoti*. Available at: http://www.pragoti.org/hi/node/3456 (last accessed on 17 August 2017).

4 Katyal, *Habib Tanvir*, pp. 5–6.

5 For a comprehensive study of 'theatre of the roots', see Erin Mee, *Theatre of Roots: Redirecting the Modern Indian Stage* (London: Seagull Books, 2008).

6 Katyal, *Habib Tanvir*, p. xviii.

7 Rajinder Paul, 'Habib Tanvir Interviewed', *Enact* 87 (March 1974). Reproduced in *Nukkad Janam Samvad*, 'Focus on Naya Theatre' [henceforth *Nukkad*] (April 2004–Mar 2005), p. 87.

8 Neeraj Malik and Javed Malick (ed.), *Habib Tanvir: Reflections and Reminiscences* (Delhi: SAHMAT, 2010), pp. 15–16.

9 Paul, 'Habib Tanvir Interviewed', p. 87.

10 Ibid., p. 86.

11 Katyal, *Habib Tanvir*, p. xix.

12 Javed Malick, Introduction to Habib Tanvir, *Charandas Chor* (Anjum Katyal trans.) (Calcutta: Seagull Books, 1996), p.7. Included here on pp. 113–31.

13 Habib Tanvir, 'In Conversation with Javed Malick' in Neeraj Malik and Javed Malick (ed.), *Habib Tanvir: Reflections and Reminiscences* (Delhi: SAHMAT, 2010), p. 104.

14 Ibid., p. 142.

15 Katyal, *Habib Tanvir*, p. xx.

16 Ibid.,p. *xxi*.

17 Javed Malick, 'Habib Tanvir: The Making of a Legend' in *Nukkad*, p.12

18 Ibid.

19 Habib Tanvir, 'The World, and Theatre, According to Habib Tanvir', *The Telegraph Magazine*, 17 April 1983, p. 6.

20 A progressive leftist creative organization that had a major influence on the formation of modern Indian arts and literature in the 1940s.

21 Katyal, *Habib Tanvir*, p. *xxii*.

22 Ibid.

23 Habib Tanvir, ' "It Must Flow"—A Life in Theatre', *Seagull Theatre Quarterly* 10 (June 1996): 29.

24 Katyal, *Habib Tanvir*, p. 26.

25 Ibid.

26 Habib Tanvir, 'Preface to the Revised Edition: Some Excerpts' in *Agra Bazaar* (Calcutta: Seagull Books, 2006), pp 18–19. Included here on pp. 17–35.

27 Ibid., p. 8.

28 Katyal, *Habib Tanvir*, p. 27.

29 Habib Tanvir, 'Preface to the First Edition' in *Agra Bazaar* (Calcutta: Seagull Books, 2006), p. 3. Included here on pp. 9–16.

30 Tanvir, ' "It Must Flow" ': 10.

31 Ibid.: 11.

32 Royal Academy of Dramatic Arts, UK.

33 Tanvir, ' "It Must Flow" ': 27.

34 Ibid.: 28.

35 Ibid.: 27–8.

36 Ibid.: 28.

37 Katyal, *Habib Tanvir*, p. 70.

38 Tanvir, 'In Conversation with Javed Malick', p. 114.

39 Tanvir, ' "It Must Flow" ': 28–9.

40 Ibid.: 22.

41 Katyal, *Habib Tanvir*, p. 71.

42 Ibid., p. 72.

43 Ibid.

44 Malick, Introduction to *Charandas Chor*, p. 15.

45 Tanvir, '"It Must Flow"': 11.

46 Ibid.: 35.

47 Ibid.: 32.

48 Ibid.

49 Ibid.: 34.

50 Katyal, *Habib Tanvir*, p.128.

51 Habib Tanvir, 'Janam Comes of Age' in Sudhanva Deshpand (ed.), *Theatre of the Streets: The Jana Natya Manch Experience* (Delhi: Jana Natya Manch, 2007), p. 72.

52 Habib Tanvir, 'A Dilemma of Democracy', Preface to *The Living Tale of Hirma* (Anjum Katyal trans.) (Calcutta: Seagull Books, 2005), p. 4. Included here on pp. 287–91.

53 Quoted in Safdar Hashmi, 'Habib Tanvir's Latest Play *Hirma ki Amar Kahani*', *Nukkad*, p. 200.

54 Habib Tanvir, 'In Conversation with Shampa Shah' in Neeraj Malik and Javed Malick (ed.), *Habib Tanvir: Reflections and Reminiscences* (Delhi: SAHMAT, 2010), p. 142.

AGRA BAZAAR

Translated by Javed Malick

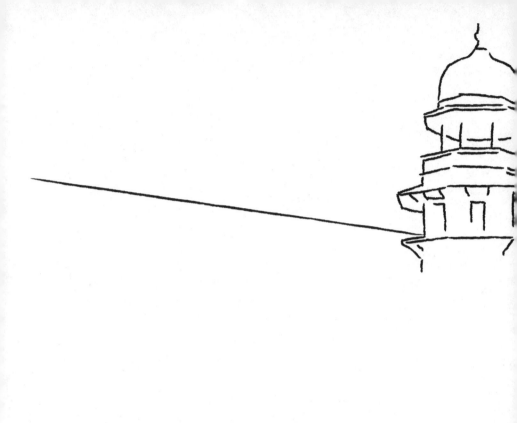

TRANSLATOR'S NOTE

JAVED MALICK

It was the late J. N. Kaushal who first suggested that I translate Habib Tanvir's *Agra Bazaar* for an anthology of Indian plays in English translation that the National School of Drama was planning to publish. My first response was to say a polite but categorical no. I was quite familiar with the text and knew that it was full of Nazir's poetry. And translating poetry, as someone once remarked, is a metaphysical impossibility. It is even more of an impossibility when the language of the original and that of the translation are culturally as far apart as Urdu and English. What further compounded the difficulty was the fact that Nazir employed a great deal of colloquial and idiomatic expression and drew much of his vocabulary from several different linguistic registers.

It was the thought of these difficulties that lay behind my initial refusal to even brook the proposal. Nevertheless, somewhere deep in my subconscious, I must have found the idea of translating Tanvir's play into English quite tempting. For it was not very long before my categorical no turned into a tentative yes. All it needed was another call from Kaushal and some persuasion from Tanvir himself for me to agree to give it a shot. Once I had started, I enjoyed the challenge so much that I did not stop until it was nearly half done.

It was, I remember, in the February of 2003 that Kaushal first approached me. Later that month I had a talk with Tanvir. In May, I was in Raipur spending a part of my summer holidays with my ailing mother. By that time, I had already translated some of the poems and I read these out to her. She knew the Urdu original but did not follow much English. Nonetheless, she seemed to like the sound of my translations. Encouraged further by this, a month or so later I sent the draft of the first act to Tanvir who had recently returned from a visit to Europe. His first response was encouraging and confirmed my resolve to go on with the project.

The first draft was ready in just a few months; more precisely, by January 2004. But it took nearly another year and a half to revise it and make it ready for publication. One of the most time-consuming things was reworking the text and making it correspond with Tanvir's authorized version. I had translated the play from the only available printed version, published in 1970, which had been out of print for some years. This version had several serious textual errors which had remained undiscovered until then. It was only during the latter half of 2004, when the persuasive powers and resourcefulness of Sanjna Kapoor made him take time off from travelling to prepare his plays for publication, that Tanvir detected these errors and corrected them for the new edition. He drew my attention to the flawed nature of the existing print version and asked me to wait for the revised manuscript. This revised manuscript, a photocopy of which was eventually sent to me, was in fact no more than a photocopy of the previous print version with Tanvir's handwritten notes in the margins. The corrections were so complicated and confusing that it seemed more sensible to wait for the new print version which was finally released at the Prithvi Theatre Festival at the end of November 2004. It was only then that I began to carry out the required changes, which not only involved several instances of textual rearrangement but also extensive revision and some additions.

Another thing that slowed me down was the difficulty in deciding how exactly to render Nazir's poetry in English. I do not claim to be a poet and I am sure the verses in this translation are not free from defects. Right at the outset of this project, I found myself faced with a severe dilemma that took the form of several nagging questions. Should I remain close to Nazir's semantics and attempt a more or less literal translation (perhaps in prose) of what he says in his poems; or should I focus on his style and aim at reproducing the formal aspects of his poetry? Nazir wrote rhymed verse and, even within a verse, employed verbal rhythms that gave a kind of musicality to his lines. How can one reproduce this quality in English without sounding silly and ridiculous? Isn't it enough—and more sensible—to merely communicate a sense of the versatile and democratic character of Nazir's poetry and the dramatic interest of Tanvir's use of it? These puzzling questions seemed to entail yet another—and, from my point of view, more fundamental—question, i.e. who is the implied reader of this English translation? I agonized over all this for a while and eventually decided that my translation should mainly, though not exclusively, aim at those non-Urdu knowing people who might have already seen the play in performance and would like to follow the text better with the help of a translation. Meanwhile, it was also my duty as the translator to do full justice to Nazir as a poet as well as to Tanvir as a playwright.

In translating Nazir's poetry I exercised a certain degree of flexibility and occasionally departed from strict adherence to the rules of prosody. While Nazir's ghazals, in keeping with the technical requirement of this form, followed the same rhyme scheme throughout a poem, his *nazm* was usually made up of several four-line stanzas interspersed with a refrain. Each stanza was rhymed and although the metre remained unaltered throughout, the rhyme changed from stanza to stanza. When I began working on this translation I had to decide between rendering the poems in free verse or, in keeping with

Nazir's poetic style, in rhymed verse. I chose the latter mainly because it made the process of translation more playful and thus more pleasurable—for me certainly but, I hope, for the reader too. But this self-imposed obligation to rhyme my lines while also remaining faithful to Nazir's content was not easy at all. It sometimes required me to change the metre in the middle of a poem. This lack of uniformity in the length of my verses was something I was not really happy about but there seemed nothing that I could do about it.

In some of his poems, Nazir, in a style somewhat reminiscent of Walt Whitman, includes long lists of ordinary everyday things or activities. This is particularly true of his long poems such as the 'Banjaranama' with which the second act in this play begins or the 'Adminama' with which it ends. In my translation I have tried my utmost to be faithful to the original but it has not been possible to translate every item in these lists. I have often had to find some other way of conveying Nazir's ideas. For example, the first stanza of the 'Banjaranama' reads like this in Urdu:

> Tuk hirs-o-hawas ko chhor mian, kyoon des bides
> > phire mara
> Quazzakh ajal ka lootey hai din raat bajaa
> > kar naqquara
> Kya badhiya, bhainsa, bail, shutur, kya goi palla
> > sar bhara
> Kya gehun, chawal, moth, mattar, kya aag, dhuwan
> > kya angara
> Sab thhaat pada rah jayega jab ladd
> > chalega banjara.

The third and the fourth lines of the stanza list animals and foodgrains respectively. I have not found it possible to translate the list in all its particulars.

Instead I have resorted to more general, generic names. Consequently, my translation of these lines reads thus:

Why do you wander restlessly, why this envy and greed
Death'll follow wherever you go, a truth you better heed.
All your wealth and possession your cattle of every breed,
Those heaps of rice and lentils, every grain and every seed,
As you pack your bag to leave, there's nothing you'll need.

Whether and to what extent I have been able to communicate the singular richness and power of Nazir's poetry, is for the reader to decide. On my part, I can only say that the entire experience has been highly enjoyable and rewarding. And if my translation is able to convey even a part of that experience I will consider it a success.

Rather than write an introduction to this volume, I have included the two prefaces that Tanvir wrote for two different editions of the play—the first edition of 1954 and the recent revised edition of 2004. These, to my mind, are immensely useful texts. They document the play's genesis, the processes of its creation and revisions and the long history of its staging. In translating them, I have tried to retain Tanvir's anecdotal style. However, I have also had to tighten his text here and there a bit for the sake of brevity and coherence. Hence, certain details which, to my mind, did not seem of much value for the readers of this translation had to be jettisoned.

A word by way of acknowledgment. I wish to put on record here the contribution of Neeraj, a fellow academic who is also my wife. Without her active assistance this work could not have been completed. She was associated with it from the beginning; she not only read and corrected my first draft but often significantly improved upon it. There are parts of this text which she has virtually co-authored.

The publication of this translation would have made my mother Bilquees Jamal, and Moneeka Mishra Tanvir, Habib Tanvir's wife and partner in theatre for nearly five decades, very happy. Unfortunately, they did not live to see its completion. My mother was an ardent lover of Urdu poetry and had a deep interest in Tanvir's work. As I have mentioned earlier, it was she who provided the initial encouragement which helped me to take up this project. Monica Tanvir was so enthused by the idea of an English translation of the play that she had even started making her own translations of Nazir's poems.

I wish to dedicate this work to their memory.

2006

PREFACE TO THE FIRST EDITION

HABIB TANVIR

Much pain although being in love has meant
It also brought pleasure to the heart's content

Nazir

Athar Parvez phoned to say that on 14 March the Jamia Millia chapter of the Progressive Writers' Association was observing 'Nazir Day' and that it would be nice if I helped prepare a play for the occasion. I have been interested in Nazir's work for a long time but I had never thought of writing a play about him. I had sometimes thought that it should be possible to write an interesting tragedy on Insha, that highly talented but unfortunate Urdu poet [Syed Inshaullah Khan, a prominent Urdu poet of the eighteenth century]. However, on reading Nazir's poetry more carefully many poignant images of our society emerged before the mind's eye. The liveliness of these images would make not only Insha but also the work of the biggest Urdu poets pale in comparison. In Nazir's poetry I heard echoes of optimism and social relevance. I was inspired by Nazir's voice which was different from any other poet's but was also the voice of humanity and no one else could achieve this all-embracing quality.

I got hold of whatever material I could find on Nazir and settled down to study it. While this increased my interest in Nazir's poetry, it also brought home to me the difficulties of writing a play on him. I was searching for a dramatic conflict around which to build my play. It was during my research into the poet's life and historical sources that I suddenly found the most dramatic chapter in the history of Urdu poetry.

It is commonly believed that the period between Mir [Mir Taqi, 1722–1819] and Ghalib [Mirza Asadullah Khan, 1797–1869] did not produce a poet equal to these two great masters. Whenever they looked back in time, Ghalib and his contemporaries said in one voice: There was a stalwart called Mir who lived in times gone by. After Ghalib, the next poets who claim our attention are Iqbal [who belonged to the twentieth century] and Hali [Altaf Hussain, poet and reformer of the eighteenth–nineteenth century]. These poets represent significant milestones in the history of Urdu poetry and their works tend to absorb all our attention. The truth, however, is that the works of Hali and Iqbal, and then Josh [Shabbir Hasan Khan, of the twentieth century] and the other modern poets, are indebted above all to the poetry of that most unassuming 'humble poet' Nazir who emerged in the period before Ghalib and after Mir.

Nazir does not find a mention in the histories of Urdu literature. Or, if mentioned at all, it is as if the critic were doing him a great favour. If we look closely at his work, we will find that even today his poetry represents a significant example from which contemporary poetry can learn a great deal. Despite all the changes in form and content, our poetry continues to be deeply influenced by the ghazal. And the Urdu ghazal to a large extent is influenced by the Persian tradition. Consequently, Urdu poetry today is burdened with those ancient poetic constructions and images, those tired and faded phrases and idioms, from a bygone era. However, one can still learn how to use the people's language and colloquial Hindustani from Nazir. For he was undoubtedly Urdu's most Hindustani poet. He deserves the same importance in the history of Urdu poetry that Ratan Nath Sarshar (Pandit Ratannath Dar, nineteenth-century Urdu essayist and publisher) and Munshi Premchand [twentieth-century Urdu-Hindi novelist] enjoy in the history of Urdu prose.

Nazir lived for about one hundred years. During his life no writer cared for him and, for more than a century after his death, no critic ever mentioned him. But he was kept alive by the common people for nearly two hundred years and his poetry, transmitted orally from generation to generation, continued to survive. People preserved their inheritance with great love and care. Even today Nazir's poems can be found on the lips of mendicants, vendors and others in streets and bazaars throughout India. This is the greatest drama of Nazir's life and work, as well as the most interesting chapter of our literary history.

It was this aspect of Nazir's poetry that I wanted to focus on. So I chose it as the subject of my play. The difficulties that I faced in researching the poet's biography proved to be a blessing in disguise for they played an important part in determining the play's theme and structure

Much of the information found in books about Nazir's life tends to be quite unreliable. There is no agreement among writers even about the date of his birth. The only thing we know for certain is that his contemporaries refused to regard him as a poet and dismissed him as a mere versifier. But the common people loved and revered him. And this is the most important fact that we know about him. So whether one is writing a critical essay or a play, this is precisely what deserves to be underlined. But the problem was, how to do so in a play? It was this difficulty which eventually directed me to the form of my play. I had initially contemplated writing a short play which would either deal with various aspects of this poet's life and work or focus on some specific aspect of it. But this is not what I really wanted to do. I wanted to highlight the fact that Nazir's love of the ordinary people has immortalized him and that he continues to be popular with the fakirs and dervishes of this country even today. Thus, his own poetry gave me the idea of a chorus of fakirs which became the play's main structural component.

I also wanted to show that in contrast to the plebeian sections, the educated elite of Nazir's time praised him as a person but totally ignored him as a poet. This gave me the idea of the Book-seller and the Kite-seller who help the play move forward and whose shops become the two opposing poles of the marketplace. I had read that Nazir would create poetry almost spontaneously at the request of small traders, vendors and beggars. Whether this was true or not, I liked the idea as it was helpful in the development of the play. After reading his works, I was quite ready to believe it too. Thus emerged the character of the protagonist, the Kakri-seller. It also provided the basic plot of the play, its *mise-en-scéne* and the title.

With regard to the plot, the play is fictional. It revolves around an invented, brief and simple story. My chief concern was to present the show in a way that allowed what I wanted to say about Nazir to get across effectively and entertainingly.

I was trying to understand and place Nazir's poetry in its historical context. I found that it was possible to reconstruct the entire socio-cultural history of that period on the basis of his work. I also realized that it is difficult to fully appreciate his poetry without its political and social context. And this realization gave birth to a new character, the Madari, and to his dialogues.

Our books on literary history tend to leave out the political conditions of a period entirely or, at best, make perfunctory references to them. Similarly, our political histories do not tell us much about the literary and cultural aspects of life. It is wrong and misleading to see these two aspects of our collective existence as two absolutely separate categories. So I had to make my own connections between the literary and political histories and calculate the relevant dates by keeping both types of books before me. From this exercise, emerged the character of the Horse-trader as well as several related speeches in the play. It also helped in locating the action against a specific historical backdrop.

The period of the play is around 1810. If one goes by the common understanding of the year of his birth as 1735, he would have been 75 years old at the time. He had another 20 years to live. He died in 1830. I chose to locate my play in this period for various reasons.

Nazir was witness to the entire period from Khan Arzoo Shah Hatim, Sauda [Mirza Mohammed Rafi, early eighteenth century] and Mir to Ghalib. With Mir, an important period of Urdu poetry ends. He died in 1810 when Ghalib was 14 years old. I had wanted to discuss Nazir in relation to the poetry of a major Urdu poet like Mir. The aim was also to indicate that it was this period that witnessed the birth of Urdu's most popular poet, later to be known as Ghalib.

This was the period when the foundations of the system based on individual rule were being shaken. Mughal rule had ended. Akbar-e-Sani who occupied the throne in Delhi was only a ruler in name. British dominance was in the ascent and there was widespread plunder and anarchy in the country. Delhi and Agra had frequently witnessed large-scale destruction due to internal and external attacks. Urdu poets were fleeing Delhi and Lucknow was fast emerging as an important literary centre. The ruler of Lucknow was Nawab Sa'adat Ali Khan. The process of the decline of Urdu poetry, which is associated with this period, had already set in. At the same time, Urdu prose was registering remarkable growth. In Calcutta's Fort William College, recently established by the British, the work of translating and publishing was proceeding in full earnest.

In other words, even in that period of decline there were tendencies in our social environment which had the potential of developing into progressive currents. The old social structure was crumbling. There was anarchy and political turmoil everywhere. The economic condition of the common people was steadily deteriorating. A few years later, the reaction to these conditions would take the form of the War of Independence of 1857, an event which influenced Ghalib's poetry. One can understand the depth and authenticity of Nazir's poetry better by viewing it in the context of these social and political developments. This is why I found it more appropriate and meaningful to set the play in the early nineteenth century.

I wanted to make Nazir's poetry, not Nazir himself, the basis of my play. It also occurred to me that it would be better not to bring Nazir personally into the play. This strategy not only took care of many of my difficulties but also had a positive effect on my technique, making its connection with the subject stronger. I did not want to make Nazir's mysticism my main concern. I wanted instead to focus on his liveliness, hope and humanism. Bringing a 75-year-old Nazir onto stage would have impeded the clear articulation of what I wanted to say and directly affected the implication of my play. Besides, I wanted to present him and his poetry as immortal. I also wanted to preserve the legendary aspect of Nazir's personality. Therefore, it was only by keeping him offstage that I could establish him as the greatest hero of Urdu literary history. It would have been very difficult for any actor to convincingly represent this character on the stage.

Now the difficulty was: how could I establish a sense of Nazir's presence and that of his personality in the hearts of the spectators without bringing him onstage? This made me devise various strategies, one of which was the character of Nazir's Granddaughter. The idea of this new character had its basis in the fact that most of the information about Abdul Ghafoor Shahbaz [Nazir's first biographer] was obtained from his granddaughter Vilayati Begum. I had also toyed with the idea of presenting Mir on stage but gave it up. Instead I resorted to representative characters like the Tazkiranawis, who not only represents contemporary and later critics but also has something of Mir in him. He should be seen as a blend of Abdul Quasim Mir Qudratullah, Shefta [Nawab Mohammed Mustafa, Urdu poet, and Ghalib's friend] and Mir. I also decided to present the decline of traditional poetry through the character called Poet and the contradictions in the sensibility of the middle stratum of society through the character of the Companion.

Other characters, like the vendors, the Potter, the Kite-seller, etc., were easily derived from Nazir's poems. The dramatic quality of these poems proved to be helpful in this regard. I even found some of the speeches of the Kite-seller and the Madari in Nazir's poems.

After a month of research, I wrote the play in a week's time. Members of the Jamia Millia worked with me and we had the production ready after only one week of rehearsal. Those who participated included not only the teachers, students and children of Jamia but also some persons from the city of Delhi, and men, women and children from surrounding villages. Local groups from Tughlaqabad, Badarpur and Okhla, together with a goat and donkey, also participated. Altogether, some 75 persons were on stage at the same time. It was a result of their hard work that the play was so well received by everyone. Most felt that the play should also be shown in the city. So it is now being staged in New Delhi on behalf of Jamia Dramatic Society. In particular, it is through the encouragement and the efforts of Begum Qudsia Zaidi, Begum Anis Kidwai, Mrs Elizabeth Gauba and Professor Mohammed Mujeeb that the play is being staged in the city on 19, 20, 24 and 25 April. A cast of about 50 to 60 people is busily preparing for the event these days.

Jamia Nagar, Delhi, 16 April 1954

(Translated from Urdu by Javed Malick, 2005)

PREFACE TO THE REVISED EDITION

Some Excerpts

HABIB TANVIR

Agra Bazaar (1954), *Mitti ki Gadi* (1958) and *Charandas Chor* (1975) are the three milestones in my career in the theatre. They represent major turning points in the evolution of my work. In other words, each of these productions has contributed significantly in shaping the style which has now come to be recognized as my signature. Interestingly, all these plays were fiercely attacked by the critics but the spectators loved them and, instead of declining, their popular appeal has continued to grow over the years. Besides, these plays have also helped me the most in realizing the dream of a professional theatre.

By professional theatre I do not mean a commercial theatre driven solely by profit but one which provides sufficient income to its artists and thus leaves them free from the worries of livelihood to devote themselves entirely to their work in the theatre.

In 1954 when I produced *Agra Bazaar*, I was neither familiar with classical Sanskrit drama nor with Bertolt Brecht. Nor did I possess a deep enough understanding of folk styles of performance. Even so, the three plays mentioned seem to have something fundamental in common with one another. Thus it seems that the genesis of what eventually developed into my characteristic style was there in *Agra Bazaar*. It is a different matter that the production that paved the way for *Charandas Chor*, and indeed for all my subsequent plays, was *Gaon ke Naam Sasural More Naam Damaad*. But this has more to do with unschooled village actors, their dialect and the ways of working with them than with that fundamental feeling which has been active in my theatre from the outset.

My endeavour to establish a professional theatre had already begun with *Agra Bazaar*. It was with this idea in mind that I had moved to Delhi after spending nine years in Mumbai, which included seven years of theatre work with the IPTA. The success of *Agra Bazaar* on the Jamia Millia stage further intensified this desire and I actively began to look for ways of realizing my dream. Professor Mohammed Mujeeb was vice-chancellor, Jamia Millia, at that time. He was himself a fine playwright and used to direct plays. He had founded the Jamia Drama Society and created a tremendous enthusiasm for theatre among students and teachers. When he learnt of my obsession with theatre he came forward and readily offered his full support and help in every possible way. Kalam-sahib, director of Jamia's Arts Institute, was already helping me. The play could not have been undertaken without his cooperation. The rehearsals were held on the Arts Institute's open-air stage where the play's first show was also presented. Nevertheless, Jamia Millia also had gentlemen with long beards who wielded considerable influence and power. These mullahs and maulvis were opposed to theatre and even Mujeeb-sahib had to often keep quiet in front of them so that the play could be staged. Kalam-sahib was an important ally. However, for some unknown reason even he turned against me. A whimsical person by nature, he was suddenly overcome by the strange suspicion that I was trying to replace him as director of the Arts Institute. Thus, a valuable supporter and ally turned against us and became our enemy. This made me give up the idea of establishing a theatre in Jamia and instead I founded Okhla Theatre. M. S. Sathyu even designed an impressive monogram, and we had a seal made. Okhla is situated on the banks of the river Jamuna and Jamia Millia is adjacent to Okhla village. This proximity made Kalam-sahib object to Okhla Theatre too and I had to give up that idea as well.

That was when Begum Qudsia Zaidi offered help and it was her endeavour that led to the formation of Delhi's first professional theatre group, the Hindustani Theatre. This was the culmination of a long endeavour which had started with *Agra Bazaar*. It was for the Hindustani Theatre that I produced *Mitti ki Gadi* in 1958 which marked the second stage of that endeavour. Finally, in 1959, Naya Theatre was established and became a professional group in 1972–73. The success of *Charandas Chor* in 1975 strengthened it further. Thus, this play became the third and final stage in this long journey.

LAWRENCE OLIVIER AND ECKARD

Professional theatre needs trained actors. This training can be acquired through formal schooling or through the experience of regular work in the theatre. However, sometimes, in the absence of either of these, one's experience of life comes in handy.

I had seen Lawrence Olivier act the part of a millionaire businessman in a film. As the plot progresses, he is bankrupt and forced to beg. He stands in a dark corner behind parked cars near a building, holding his hat in his hand and saying to the passersby, 'I am hungry.' These three simple words, spoken in an embarrassed and broken voice, sent a chill down my spine. They were remarkably effective in communicating a terrifyingly intense and painful hunger.

I am sure Olivier had no firsthand experience of this. What he built upon was his observation of life, his training as an actor and his experience of the stage. He also drew upon his remarkable natural talent.

Similarly, I saw Eckard playing Azdak in the Berliner Ensemble production of *Caucasian Chalk Circle*. Eckard was Bertolt Brecht's son-in-law. He was very wealthy and quite bourgeois in his lifestyle. Extremely arrogant and proud, he did not mingle with other theatre artists and was, in turn, disliked by them. In spite of all this, Eckard played the role of the hungry and poor Azdak with such skill and conviction that one found it difficult to believe that this man had never experienced poverty. He is one of the world's finest actors. It is a measure of his success as an actor that I still remember his Azdak so vividly.

THE IDEA OF A REPERTORY THEATRE

In other words, to be a good actor one either needs training and stage experience or the experience of life and some skill. In the Naya Theatre, there have been actors who did not have any formal training or acting experience. What they had was the experience of life and natural talent. That is why in *Shajapur ki Shantibai*, my adaptation of Brecht's *Good Woman of Schezuan*, these unschooled and inexperienced actors, including Fida Bai, played their roles so effectively. They drew upon their own experience of how poverty and deprivation degrade a person and breed selfishness, greed and opportunism.

In 1954, while preparing *Agra Bazaar*, I had neither kind of actors. All I had were some teachers and students of Jamia Millia and an immense enthusiasm which enveloped us all. Rehearsals on the open-air stage often attracted the curiosity of not only the Jamia children but also men and women from the village of Okhla. Some villagers would stop by with their goats on their way to the Yamuna. I told them to come closer to watch the play. The women immediately brought their goats onto the stage and settled down. Later, the men and the children, too, started to sit on the stage. Kalam-sahib had made the set, and the play took shape. I did not have to do anything special about the costumes of the village spectators. There has been hardly any change in the cloth-ing style of the Indian villager over the years. The men wear dhotis, pyjamas, kurtas and *salukas* while the women wear colourful skirts, blouses and chunris. What else did one need? If we lacked a professional theatre, at least, there was enough 'atmosphere' for the play.

The same villagers appeared on stage when the play was performed at the Ramlila Grounds in front of thousands of spectators. Jamia's real paan-seller in the role of the Paanwala, the real tailor in the role of the Tailor, and the silent presence of a donkey in front of the Potter's shop throughout the play was very effective. An addition to the realistic atmosphere of the performance was pro-vided by the quiet and patient donkey who produced a whole lot of dung on stage. Now the stage had both the colours and the smell of a traditional bazaar. It reminded me of Stanislavsky's production of Chekhov's first play for the Moscow Art Theatre which had rooms, doors and windows. The innovative-ness of this realistic setting, which also had the appropriate smell, impressed the theatre-goers.

The performances of *Agra Bazaar* continued. If they were interrupted, it was never because of lack of audience but because of the unavailability of the urban actors needed for this production in addition to the Chhattisgarhi artists of my group. The play was in great demand and we travelled to different cities in India, from Kashmir to Calcutta. To Kashi, Lucknow and Kanpur in Uttar Pradesh as well as to several places in Punjab. When the play stopped, it was again because of the same compulsion. After a few years, when it was again in demand, we changed the cast and prepared the production afresh. Once again, it went through a long circuit and then stopped. With it ended my dream of a professional theatre.

MOHARRAM ALI

I was talking about love of theatre. Sometimes after the first exposure to the stage, a person falls so obsessively in love with it that it becomes difficult to control. I remember a tragic instance of this in 1954 during the first production of *Agra Bazaar* in Jamia. I had selected a simple lad of 15 or 16 for the role of the Madari. Moharram Ali was very dark, pockmarked and with only one good eye. He might not have been an attractive man but his face had character. He played the Madari with great elan. When the season of shows was over, he disappeared and we often wondered where he had gone off to. One day, somebody reported that he was in Mumbai doing the rounds of film studios in search of roles. We laughed at this. Some time later, we learnt that he had died of severe diarrhoea. We were stunned at this news and, for days, could not get him out of our minds. Our conversation frequently turned to him and to his youthfulness, his childlike innocence and his simplicity. Even today, whenever I think of him, his face vividly appears before my mind's eye.

GYARSA AND SANGEETA

I met Gyarsa in Delhi in 1989. He was a Rajasthani street artist who lived in Shadipur Depot. His daughter Sangeeta, a slim girl of 12 or 13 years of age, used to give acrobatic performances. Reclining on the floor, she would place a glass of water on her forehead. Then she would put her feet through a small metal ring and slowly push it up her legs and waist, finally slipping it out over her head. And all this while neither would the glass fall from her forehead nor a drop of water spill. When Gyarsa and Sangeeta appeared in the village fair scene in *Agra Bazaar* the entire auditorium was spellbound. The only sound was that of Gyarsa's drum as the audience watched Sangeeta with bated breath.

As soon as she slipped the ring over her head, the hall broke into a long and thunderous applause.

Sangeeta is now married and has children. Whenever Gyarsa meets me he only has one complaint: that nobody cares for the traditional acrobats and their performances any more. He wants me to take him into the drama troupe. I don't know how to explain to him that every production cannot use acrobatic performances. However, now that *Agra Bazaar* is being revived in December 2004, I have been thinking of Gyarsa and of where to find him. I want to ask him if he has any other performer like Sangeeta who can accompany us to Mumbai.

AUTHENTIC, SMELLY FAKIRS

Agra Bazaar has been revived in almost every decade. Every new reincarnation has involved changes in the cast, in the structure, in characters or in incidents. As far as the chorus of fakirs is concerned, originally in the Jamia Millia production, I used two brothers, Ashfaq Mohammed Khan and Ishtiaq Mohammed Khan, who were both associated with Jamia. Years later, I found two real fakirs, Jogaram and Lalchand, who sang and begged in the streets of Ajmer. I liked their singing. That was the time when we used to live in Ber Sarai village opposite the Jawaharlal Nehru University campus in New Delhi. I invited them and gave them a poem of Nazir's to sing. Their Urdu pronunciation was all right. I sang for them some of the tunes that I had heard from fakirs in my childhood. They learnt the tunes and memorized the poems. I gave them a short rod and thick iron bangles. In my childhood, I had seen fakirs going around the streets of Raipur during the month of Ramadan, singing and striking such a rod against their iron bangles in order to wake up Muslims for the pre-dawn meal and prayers. For years subsequently, I continued to see such fakirs in almost every town from Delhi to Bangalore. But the number of such fakirs had been declining and now they are extinct. To strike the rod against the bangles to the beat of a song may sound easy but in fact it is very difficult. The fakirs who were expert in this art not only played the beat but also during every refrain moved the rod over the bangles with such skill that it made a pleasant sound. Jogaram and Lalchand had no expertise of this kind but they could follow the beat by rhythmically striking the rod against the bangles.

These were real, authentic fakirs in every respect. They did not have the traditional cloak and the begging bowl, which we had to provide for them. But their singing style and their body odour were quite true to form. We realized this during a visit to Srinagar. This was when the village artists from Chhattisgarh had already joined Naya Theatre. After the show, when we returned to the big hall where we were to sleep, the folk actors promptly found places for themselves and spread out their bedding. Only one corner of the room was left and our fakirs lay down there. Now there was no place left for Monica and me, except for a narrow space very close to Jogaram and Lalchand. That is when we discovered that our fakirs were authentic, smelly fakirs.

Our fakirs were heavy drinkers too. Once we performed in Delhi's Air Force Auditorium. The show was sponsored by the Indian Air Force. At the end of the show, there was food and liquor. Jogaram and Lalchand were drinking continuously, gulping down large pegs of neat rum. Jogaram, who had already had some eight pegs, was standing quietly in one dark corner. An Air Force man approached him with a bottle and asked: 'More?' Jogaram silently nodded and had his glass filled to the brim. He brought the glass to his mouth and drank it all up like water in one breath. We were amazed, but apparently, he was still not drunk. He had become very quiet but remained quite steady on his feet. There were no visible signs of drunkenness. It was probably this heavy drinking which eventually killed him at a relatively young age.

Once I had found two brothers who earned their living by singing and begging in the streets of Bhopal. I invited them to Delhi and kept them with us in Ber Sarai. I made them rehearse the part and used them as the chorus in several subsequent shows. One of them suffered from a chronic cough which refused to subside despite all medication. A thorough check-up revealed that he had tuberculosis. Instead of rehearsals we got busy getting him proper medical treatment. As soon as the shows were over, we sent them back to Bhopal with the required medicines. In 1996, when we moved base to Bhopal, they came to see us. They again wanted to act with us but I did not have the time then to revive *Agra Bazaar* and I did not think they were suitable for any other play.

In short, I either encountered urban middle-class amateurs who could not work in the theatre regularly due to the compulsions of their jobs or other personal problems, or I found ordinary people who would have liked to stay on but whose skills were so limited that I could not use them in more than one play.

Once, the famous singer of Bhatinda, Khalili, and his partner, Deshraj, played the role of the fakirs in *Agra Bazaar*. For a long time they continued to participate in all our shows. They were very good singers and made an excellent chorus. Khalili too died of excessive drinking. For the next revival of *Agra Bazaar* I cast Ram Dayal Sharma and his son Devendra in the role of the fakirs. They were good singers and Ram Dayal used to act in *nautankis*. He also worked in Delhi's Bal Bhavan as a music teacher. These two made a good chorus and participated in all our shows at that time. Now, in 2004, when the play is being revived once again by popular demand Ram Dayal will again play the fakir. Devendra is presently studying in the USA. I am looking for someone else to play the other fakir.

THREE STRANDS OF THE PLOT

I have mentioned already that whenever this play has been revived I have made some changes in the plot and the characters. The first Urdu edition of the play published in 1954 by Azad Kitabghar offered the original 50-minute version that was staged in Jamia. In that version the plot was entirely centred on the Kakri-seller who finds it difficult to sell his kakri until he gets Nazir to write a poem on it. He sings this poem and does brisk business. Gradually, another strand was added to the play which concerned a prostitute and a Police Constable. This also produced three other characters—the two cops and the Rake. The character of the Horse-trader Manzoor Hussain survived but all his dialogues were jettisoned. He became dramatically more effective as a mute figure who had lost his mental balance after being robbed by highwaymen and who was passionately in love with the courtesan. However, a new character, Beni Prasad, was needed to tell Manzoor Hussain's tale. The two eunuchs, Kariman and Chameli, were also added later. They arrive at the Potter's door to sing and dance to celebrate the birth of his son. This becomes the excuse for bringing in Nazir's poem about Lord Krishna's childhood days. New and appropriate dialogues had to be written for the two eunuchs which perhaps made the scene even more interesting.

The third strand of the plot is located in the conversations at the Bookseller's shop. It relates to major changes that were taking place in the nineteenth century in printing and publishing, and in the language of public and literary discourse. It also focuses on the implications of these changes for the material conditions of the Urdu and Persian poets, writers and publishers. A new character, Ganga Prasad, was added to represent these changes more fully. This hectic activity of the marketplace forms the backdrop against which Nazir wrote. His poetry, his life, the source of his livelihood, namely tutoring, was closely connected with this environment and his poetry reflects this. The play is nothing but a portrait of all those aspects of that marketplace. My purpose was to provide a comprehensive picture of Nazir's work.

SELECTION OF POEMS

During a second reading of the play, certain changes were made in the selection and the location of some poems. Nazir's opus is full of good poetry. It is one thing to make a selection of his poems on the basis of their poetic merit but quite another to select them in keeping with the play's requirements and the limitations of performance time. At the same time, it was also necessary to ensure that Nazir's most significant poems do not get left out. So his 'Banjaranama', which was not included in the first version, was brought in. As for 'Shahar Ashob', it has always been the opening poem of *Agra Bazaar* because of its connection with the play's central theme of widespread unemployment.

Originally Act Two used to open with Nazir's 'Akbarabad'. It was later replaced with 'Banjaranama' which deals with the theme of man's mortality. One cannot find another poem of such power on the topic of death in any language. The play ends with 'Aadminama' as before because the one message that comes across powerfully through Nazir's poetry is his humanism, love and goodwill for the common people. In later productions we changed the order of his poems.

The biggest weakness of the 1954 production was that the poems on the kakri, watermelon, and laddoo were followed by poems on the Potter's wares, the kite, a bear cub and Holi, with 'Aadminama' coming at the end. The play's logic, however, demanded that nothing should intercede between the first three poems listed above and 'Aadminama.' The play starts with the difficulties faced by the street vendors because of lack of business. The Kakri-seller hits upon the idea that he will be able to sell his wares if he has an appropriate song to go with it. This makes him run after every person who seems to him to have the potential to write verses on his kakri. After repeated disappointments, he finally hears about Nazir, goes to him and gets a poem written by him. As he sings it to hawk his kakris, people start to approach him and buy them. The Watermelon- and Laddoo-seller also follow his example. Before the Kakri-seller completes his song, they enter one after another with their songs. Since this very simple and fragile storyline is the basis of the play, this was the best point at which to end the play. If, in 1954, the play was successful even without this arrangement of the songs, the credit goes to Nazir. His writing has such power that if one were to merely present his poems on stage, that too would be received well by the spectators.

The first version did not have the erotic triangle involving the Courtesan, the Police Constable, and his rival (the Rake). And as already mentioned, this was added in the revised version. It was necessary to take this story to its logical climax. In the course of working out this problem, yet another difficulty got sorted out which had to do with the aesthetic and semantic impact of the music. I had already arranged the vendors' songs into one sequence. The three songs are sung one after another in quick succession. Each has a different tune. To make the transition from one tune to another dramatically effective, a musical bridge was needed. I obtained this bridge by using a Chhattisgarhi folk song as a recurrent orchestra. The problem now was that these songs were immediately followed by the 'Aadminama' which had an entirely different tune. The poem could not be shifted anywhere else because it provided a perfect ending for the play. What helped was the scene that I had written as the culmination of the story of the rivalry between the Police Constable and the Rake which shows how through duplicity, falsehood, brute force and misuse of his position, the Police Constable has the Rake arrested on trumped-up charges and thus achieves a victory over him. To solve my musical problem I placed this brief scene between the vendors' songs and the last chorus (the 'Aadminama'). This solved my problem regarding the musical transition as well as completed the story. In fact the scene helped to deepen the impact of the last chorus on the subject of 'Man'. The arrogantly victorious Police Constable cannot even abide Manzoor Hussain's quiet and selfless love for the Courtesan and, after rudely driving him away from her chamber, lets out a loud guffaw. Just at that point the fakirs enter singing Nazir's 'Aadminama'. The entire cast joins in this last chorus, the last verse of which is:

> Man is the best of the best that we have
> And the worst and the meanest too is man.

TUNES FOR THE SONGS

The songs in the play were mostly set to the tunes that I had either heard during my childhood or had composed for my own poetry. Only the tune of 'Banjaranama' was composed by Khalili of Bhatinda. During a visit to Agra, my old friend from the IPTA days Rajendra Raghuvanshi, pointed out that Holi was traditionally sung differently in the region of Agra and Mathura. Since Nazir was from Agra and my play is set in Agra, it was appropriate, he felt, that I employ authentic local tunes. Raghuvanshi was my senior in age and was actively associated with the IPTA since 1942–43. IPTA had eventually broken up. In 1957, or even earlier than that, there was no IPTA anywhere in the country. But its Agra unit continued to survive, thanks to Raghuvanshi's efforts. In subsequent years when IPTA revived, under a new name or its own in some parts of the country, it offered plays that were not really different from what the mainstream drama groups were staging. In other words, IPTA was no longer presenting the kind of radical political drama that it used to. But Ranghuvanshi did not change his style and continued to present revolutionary plays of the old kind. Now the Agra unit of IPTA is being run by his son. How could I tell a man as respectable as he that, as far as authenticity was concerned, it was not there in my dialogue either? Agra has its own specific idiom which I do not know and which I have not even found it necessary to know. In *Agra Bazaar* as well as in my play on Ghalib titled *Mere Baad* I have used the language of Delhi while in *Shatranj Ke Mohre* I have employed the speech that is specific to Lucknow. I have drawn upon the works of Khwaja Hasan Nizami [Urdu stylist of the early twentieth century] and Mirza Farhatullah Beg [essayist, humorist of the early twentieth century] for Delhi's language and upon Pandit Ratan Nath Sarshar's writings for the speech of Lucknow. I have fashioned the hawkers' speech from Delhi's language. I could not find any reliable source for the kind of language that was spoken in Agra. I said nothing of this to Raghuvanshi and instead, expressed a desire to hear the traditional Agra tunes of Holi. I found the tunes very appealing and later on, receiving an audio cassette of them from him, I selected a couple and wove them into my Holi scene without altering the basic tune of Nazir's song. Since it was difficult to fit Nazir's lines to those tunes, I accommodated them together with their traditional words alongside my original tune with some alteration in the sequence of its words.

FLAWS IN THE FIRST EDITION

Keeping the duration of the performance in mind, I had selected only some parts of Nazir's poems. However, in the printed version whole poems, sometimes running into nine or 10 stanzas, were reproduced. This was not done to increase the bulk of the printed book but to make it possible for any future producer of the play to make his own selection. By the next edition, the changes in the plot as well as the sequence of poems had already been completed. By 1970, and even before that, the play was already being produced with this revised text. Despite this, the first Hindi edition was not free from flaws. My journalist friend Manish Saxena was proficient in Urdu as well as Hindi and could read and write both scripts. He possessed a refined literary taste and wrote in Urdu as well as Hindi. In preparing the first Hindi edition, he diligently helped me and our very dear friend Om Prakash of Radhakrishna Prakashan. I did not even have the time to check the proofs. So Manish had to do that too. He consulted me and Nazir's complete works in order to remove verbal errors from the text. But the sequence of poems in the play continued to be flawed and the list of characters incomplete. And when Radhakrishna brought out their second edition in 1992, all these errors were reproduced. In 1998, Mohammed Hassan published an anthology of Urdu plays titled *Urdu Drame ke Intikhaab*, in which he also included *Agra Bazaar*. But the text that he reproduced was taken from the first Urdu edition published by Azad Kitabghar in 1954. In the present edition, I have tried to oversee the entire process from the manuscript to the page proofs in order to make it, as far as possible, error-free.

NAZIR, AN URDU OR A HINDI POET?

There has always been a considerable amount of Hindi vocabulary in Urdu just as Hindi has always included a large number of Urdu words. When Hindi was made the national language and Urdu was systematically suppressed, it not only hurt Urdu but had an adverse effect on Hindi too. For, the shared idioms of colloquial Hindustani have either been entirely removed from the standard Hindi or have been replaced with stilted literal translations. I am speaking of simple words and expressions such as *na sirf* which is replaced with *na keval* which sounds awkward, at least, to my ears. Besides, some speakers and writers of Hindi pick up certain favourite Urdu words and, without fully understanding their meaning, employ them wrongly. It is depressing to hear such misuse of Urdu words. Take for example the word *khilafat*. The word is often misused, even by educated persons, to mean opposition, for which a perfectly good Hindi word, *virodh*, is available. *Khilafat* refers to what in English is called the Caliphate. The widespread familiarity with this word in India dates back to the Khilafat Movement led by the Ali brothers, Mohammed Ali and Shaukat Ali, for the restoration of the Turkish Caliphate during the British Raj. The Urdu word for opposition is *mukhalifat*. If this word seems too heavy or difficult, or if its Persian construction does not appeal to you, or if you simply do not like its sound, why not leave the word alone and make do with the beautiful Hindi word, *virodh*? Why should one impose one's own ignorance on to a language? The situation with the Urdu writers and speakers is somewhat similar. In reaction to the official Hindi, they often reject simple, colloquial Hindi words in favour of heavy Persianized words. Consequently, the distance between the written language and the language of everyday communication is increasing. One does not find such a rift between the written and the spoken language anywhere else in the world. What is worse is that the written language is fast becoming the spoken language. This sets a bad example for our young people whose speech is already so influenced by the TV that one would like to plug one's ears rather than hear them speak. For example, when a pre-recorded young female voice tells one on the telephone '*aap ki call intizaar par hai*', one feels like banging the phone down. This is the influence of English which generates literal translations of English phrases into Hindi.

As far as Nazir is concerned, it will not be wrong to describe him as a Hindi poet either. Poems like his 'Mahadev ka Byaah', which in keeping with the topic are in Hindi. Besides, there are poems that are in Urdu (like the song of the Courtesan) but which also use a rich admixture of constructions and vocabulary not traditionally associated with Urdu.

FOREFATHER OF THE URDU NAZM

It is difficult to pinpoint the uniqueness of Nazir's poetry. The description of specifically Indian flowers, plants, birds and animals is available either in classical Sanskrit literature or in Nazir's poetry. In the works of classical Urdu poets one does not find any mention of the flora and fauna that we in India are so familiar with. Instead, deriving its imagery predominantly from the Persian cultural environment and tradition, it contains references to flowers and birds that are found neither in the Hindi-Urdu heartland nor anywhere else in India, except of course Kashmir. The scores of different kinds of kites that the Kite-seller in this play lists were obtained from Nazir's two poems on kite flying titled 'Patang' and 'Patang Baazi'. I talked to several kite-sellers and found that they had not even heard of most of these names. Only some of the kites named by Nazir are still made; the rest have become extinct.

In India, a large variety of festivals are observed. Apart from Nazir, no Urdu poet ever paid attention to this fact. Similarly, no poet except Nazir and the classical Sanskrit poets has written about the distinct Indian seasons and their specific qualities. In Urdu prose we do find praises of various seasons in the writings of Farhatullah Beg. Not only has Nazir written about the seasons, but each of his poems is also distinct in quality and full of artistic appeal and interest. Every rhyme has impact and every couplet is well constructed. Nazir tried his skill on every poetic form, whether it is be the ghazal, the *na'at*, the *quata*, the *musaddas*, the *geet*, or the *bhajan*, except the *quasida*. Nazir also wrote about various religious communities and about the sacred icons of their creed. He wrote about Guru Nanak, Baldevji, Mahadev, Lord Krishna and so on. He wrote about each with utmost respect. Each poem carries a sense of its spontaneity and simplicity and yet each is rich and imaginative in poetic terms.

A whole variety of poetic forms, including the ghazal, the *quasida*, the *marsia*, etc., had long existed in Urdu. But the form that we today recognize as the *nazm*, the form developed by Iqbal, Josh and several other poets of recent times, did not exist before Nazir's time. It is not wrong therefore to describe Nazir as the forefather of the Urdu *nazm*. As for themes, Nazir has dealt with subjects that did not draw the attention of any other poet either before or after him. In any case, it is not easy to write on the kind of subjects that Nazir addressed in his poetry. A whole flood of verses seemed to flow out of him spontaneously, otherwise it could not have been possible to write such skilful poems on such humble subjects as vegetables, fruits and utensils. Take, for example, the poem on the kakri; the kakri which is curved is like Heer's bangle and the one that is straight is like Ranjha's flute. What is more, these beautiful similes pour into the poem with complete ease and seemingly without any effort:

> Like Farhaad's liquid eyes or Shirin's slender mould,
> Like Laila's shapely fingers, or Majnu's tears cold.

All this praise is for the kakris of Agra. How passionately Nazir must have loved his town! This poet was remarkably close to the life and concerns of the common people. He not only wrote poems on subjects like money, poverty, sycophancy and food but also wrote in a simple and spontaneous style without compromising on poetic quality. Nazir's vocabulary is full of words that are either very common and humble or traditional but rarely used by poets. The names of foodgrains, spices, condiments, etc. are traditionally regarded as unpoetic. But Nazir uses these very words with a dexterity and skill in his masterpiece 'Banjaranama' on the theme of life's transience, that it is unparallelled in world literature.

It is difficult to list all that is unique in Nazir's poetry. Take his portrayal of himself. Many other poets have captured the portrayed physical appearance of the beloved. Nazir has drawn his own portrait in just a few verses with such succinctness, simplicity and humility. This humility neither stems from a sense of inferiority nor does it signify that false humility about which Jesus had warned when he said, 'beware of the pride of humility.' This self-portrait in words is the only authentic portrait of Nazir that exists. There are no paintings or photographs. Artists have imaginatively drawn his sketch using this poem as their source. The poem possesses the same economy of representation that one associates with good painting. It begins with:

I'll sing of Nazir the poet, please do listen to me

and ends thus:

God to him was very kind, and though he had no luxury,
His basic needs were always met, and he lived with dignity.

Translated from the Urdu by Javed Malick

The earliest version of *Agra Bazaar* was staged at Jamia Millia in Okhla, Delhi, on 14 March 1954. The cast included:

FAKIR 1	Ashfaq Mohammed Khan
FAKIR 2	Ishtiaq Mohammed Khan
KAKRI-SELLER	Abdul Sattar Siddiqui
MELON-SELLER	Asghar Hasan Islahi
LADDOO-SELLER	Noman Lateef
KITE-SELLER	Mohammad Iqbal
BOOK-SELLER	Zia-ul-Hasan Farooqui
MADARI	Rajkumar
POET	Mohammad Zakaria Ansari
COMPANION	Wali Shahjahanpuri
TAZKIRANAWIS	Rashid Nomani
KITE-BUYER	Rais Mirza
HORSE-TRADER	Syed Hassan
BEAR-TAMER	Moharrram Ali
STRANGER	Shakil Akhtar Farooqui
BOOK-BUYER	Junaid-ul-Haque
BOY (HAMID)	Liaquat Ali Khan
GIRL	Saadia
ICE-SELLER	Pandit Barafwala
TAILOR	Hafiz Mohammed Ishaque, Tailor Master
PAAN-SELLER	Munne Khan Paanwala
MONKEY	Mohammad Nafees
BEAR	Fayyaz Ahmed

PASSERSBY, CHILDREN, SINGERS AND QAWWALS, EUNUCHS, ETC.

STAGE DESIGN	Abul Kalam
COSTUMES AND MANAGEMENT	Abdul Rahman
MAKE-UP	Akhtar Hassan Farooqui,
	Jameel Akhtar M. S.
PROMPTER	Azhar Parvez, Masood-ul Haque
CURTAIN	Sajjaad Ali, Habib Ahmed
SCRIPT AND DIRECTION	Habib Tanvir

In the first production, nearly 75 persons were on stage simultaneously. These included street performers, singers and ordinary folk from the nearby villages of Okhla, Badarpur, Faridabad and Tughlaqabad, as well as students and teachers of Jamia Millia Islamia, Delhi. However, the play can be successfully staged with a cast of about 20 people.

PLACE: A busy intersection of Kinari Bazaar in Agra
PERIOD: Around 1810
TIME: One day
DURATION: About two hours

The script has been considerably revised since this first production and contains some extra characters who do not appear in this cast list.

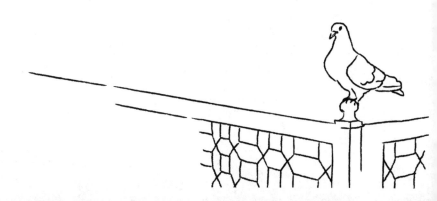

SCENE ONE

Two fakirs enter the auditorium singing Nazir's 'Shahar Ashob'. The fakirs are dressed in the traditional kafni *and carry the customary begging bowl and beads in one hand and a short wooden rod in the other. They strike the rod against the metal bands round their wrists to the rhythm of their song.*

FAKIRS. My words no longer have their usual grip,
My speech has begun to falter and trip;
I am always in a sad thoughtfulness caught,
And my poetry has virtually come to a halt.

Why shouldn't my tongue lose its eloquence
And my words retreat,
When everyone in Agra finds it hard
To make two ends meet.

All around—only suffering, deprivation,
Who should one weep over, who should one mention?
The times are barren of any sustaining breeze
And the tree of life withers, without a single leaf.

Jewellers, traders and other wealthy gents,
Who thrived by lending, are now mendicants;
The shops are deserted, dust on counter and scale,
Desolate shopkeepers wait like captives in jail.

Poverty has destroyed what was once a lovely city,
Every street, woebegone, every mansion arouses pity;
A garden needs a gardener in order to grow and thrive,
But Agra waits in vain for a tender, caring eye.

Call me lover or doting slave, I am Agra's native,
Call me mullah or learned knave, Agra's where I live;
Call me poor or call me fakir, I am Agra's native,
Call me poet or simply Nazir, Agra's where I live.

Fakirs exit, singing. The curtain rises briskly, revealing a market-place. A pall of gloom shrouds the scene. Various vendors—including the sesame-seed Laddoo-seller and Kakri-seller—are desperately trying to hawk their wares. They call out to passersby in vain. In the background, the sound of a woman singing a ghazal to the accompaniment of tabla and sarangi. Prostitutes seem to have their quarters above the paan shop. The kite shop is still closed. A couple of customers browse through books at the bookstore. As Kakri-seller approaches them, they move away to the paan shop. Book-seller busies himself with the accounts book.

LADDOO-SELLER. Six for half a pie . . . sir, six for half a pie. You won't get it any cheaper anywhere else. Six for half a pie, sir, six for only half a pie. (*To a child*) Try some, little master. Sesame-seed laddoos! Sweet as sugar! Come on, try them.

The child turns away.

MELON-SELLER. Watermelon! Sweet and cool melon. Pleases the eye and cools the heart. Like a bowl of sweet red sherbet, my melon! Drives out the heat and quenches the thirst! Watermelon, sweet cool melon!

People continue to pass by without paying any attention to the vendors.

ICE-SELLER. Ice! Buy my ice! Sweet creamy ice!

KAKRI-SELLER. Fresh kakri! Come, it's really fresh! Crisp, green and juicy kakri. Four for a damri! Taste it, sir! Soft as silk and sweet as sugarcane. Fresh kakri from Iskandara. Fresh kakri!

EAR-CLEANER. Pick your teeth or have your ear cleaned . . . just one chhadam! Two services for just one chhadam! Two birds in one stroke! I'll clean your teeth and the wax from your ears! Only one chhadam!

PAAN-SELLER. Masters, come and taste my tender Banarasi paan! Take a bite and see how red your tongue becomes! Large-sized paans specially for you. The fragrance of the cardamoms will knock you over. Come, masters, try my paan!

KAKRI-SELLER (*to Laddoo-seller*). Hey, you're sitting in my place again!

LADDOO-SELLER. No wonder. No one is buying my laddoos. (Calls out to the passersby) It's going cheap, will be gone before you know it. Already sold 200 since the morning. Only a few left. Be quick, buy them before it's too late!

KAKRI-SELLER. Sitting in my place and lying so brazenly—(mimicking him) 'Sold 200 since the morning!'

LADDOO-SELLER. What else should I say? That I haven't sold a single laddoo in the last 10 days? This is business, my love. Here you're paid for how well you talk. Six for half a pie, sir! You can't find laddoos cheaper than mine! Sir, six for only half a pie!

KAKRI-SELLER. Move! Get out of my place.

LADDOO-SELLER. Get lost.

KAKRI-SELLER. Hey, don't act so smart.

LADDOO-SELLER. Shut up! Don't you take that tone with me. Driving me bloody mad! Your parents must have given birth to you so that you could be a constant pain in other people's you-know-what.

KAKRI-SELLER. You shut up, you skinny bag of bones! Don't make my blood boil. Lay off.

LADDOO-SELLER. Go away, you blackface! Where have you erupted from? Get out! Can't you see that the customers turn away when they see something black?

KAKRI-SELLER. Very funny! Do you fool around with your father too? (*Calling out to the customers*) Four for a damri . . . Soft as silk and sweet as sugarcane. Especially from Iskandara. Four for a damri. Fresh kakri, sirs, fresh kakri. Four for a damri!

Some people enter. Kakri-seller goes towards them and stands in their way. Meanwhile, a madari, who has entered with his monkey from the right, begins his show. Hawkers, children, youth and passersby gather around him. The noise stops and, for the first time, The madari's words can be heard clearly.

MADARI (*to the monkey*). Come, show them your dance. Let us dance for the people of Agra. Children, give him a hand—can you clap with one hand? (*To the monkey*) Show us how you play *mridang* in Holi. (*Monkey mimes playing the* mridang) And how do you fly a kite? (*Monkey mimes*) And how will you go to the fair of Mahadev dressed like a dandy? (*Monkey puts on a cap at a slanting angle and swaggers*) And if it starts to rain? (*Monkey pretends to slip and fall*) You'll slip and fall? Very good. And what if you feel cold? (*Monkey mimes the shivers*) And when you are old? (*Monkey bends over a stick and walks*) And when you die? (*Monkey lies down motionless*).

Gentlemen, I ask the Hindus in the name of Ram and Muslims in the name of Quran, please move back a little. (*To the monkey*) All right, now show us how Nadir Shah attacked Delhi. (*Monkey strikes Madari with his stick*) Oh! Oh! You'll destroy the entire city of Delhi! Stop it, stop it, man! All right, how did Ahmed Shah Abdali invade Delhi? (*Monkey strikes again*) Oh! Oh! Enough now! You will flatten the entire country. Now tell us, how did Surajmal Jat attack Agra? (*Monkey repeats the act*) Oh! Oh! You'll kill me! Stop it! Stop it, man! All right, tell us, how did the British enter India? (*Monkey mimes begging*) And what did the Laat Sahib do in the battle of Plassey? (*Monkey holds the stick like a gun and mimes firing*) Oh! He opened fire! And what happened in Bengal? (*Monkey slaps his stomach and mimes weakness*) There was a famine! (*Monkey lies down*) People died of hunger! And what is our condition today? (*Monkey slaps the stomach again*) And what will happen to us tomorrow? (*Monkey falls down*) So what should we do? (*Monkey approaches those watching the show and prostrates itself at their feet*) Salute them! (*Monkey salutes; people start to slip away*)

KAKRI-SELLER. Kakri from Iskandara. Four for a *damri*!

LADDOO-SELLER. Sir, six for half a pie! Six for only half a pie!

MELON-SELLER. Beat the heat! Buy watermelon, cool watermelon!

MADARI. Salute!

Monkey moves to the paan shop—which is on the right—and salutes a customer.

KAKRI-SELLER (*to the same man*). Fresh kakri! Yes, yes, fresh kakri! Try it! Taste it, sir! Green, juicy, crisp! Soft as silk and sweet as sugarcane!

The man moves away. Upset at losing a probable patron, Madari pounces on Kakri-seller and, snatching the basket from his hand, throws it down, scattering the kakris.

MADARI. Damn you! One blow from my stick and you'll forget all kakri selling!

KAKRI-SELLER. You bloody monkey!

MADARI. I'll make a monkey of you, if you don't shut up! Bloody idiot, trying to sell kakri! His kakri drove away all my patrons.

LADDOO-SELLER. Hey! What's happening?

MELON-SELLER. Let's bash up this bloody madari!

MADARI. He drove away all my patrons.

KAKRI-SELLER. I was only trying to sell my kakri.

MADARI. Sell your kakri! You couldn't find another place to sell your wretched kakri?

LADDOO-SELLER. Why are you hell bent on ruining the little chance you have of some earnings? How can he drive away your customers? Don't you know, these days people vanish the moment you mention money?

MELON-SELLER. As God is my witness, brother, I have not sold a single watermelon in ten days!

MADARI. That man was about to pay me but this fellow shoved in his kakri.

LADDOO-SELLER. All right, enough of this now! Go your own way.

MADARI. Why? Does this street belong to your father?

LADDOO-SELLER. You mind your language, eh?

MADARI. Why? Who do you think you are?

MELON-SELLER. Let's thrash the bastard!

KAKRI-SELLER (*from the right corner*). People here don't have money to buy food and he thinks they'll pay to see his monkey.

LADDOO-SELLER. Don't mess with me, you rascal, I'll skin you alive. You better watch out!

MELON-SELLER. Go, get out of here! Get lost.

MADARI (*from the left corner*). God! What a crazy town! (*Exits*)

KAKRI-SELLER. Son of a bitch!

Enter fakirs, singing.

FAKIRS. An eyeless fakir was once asked:

Of what stuff are the moon and stars.
The fakir smiled and shook his head:
Bless you, sir, the answer's bread.
the poor know not planets nor the stars,
The thought of food our vision mars.

On empty stomach, nothing feels good,
No taste for pleasure, just craving for food.
The hungry can't live the pious way,
Food prompts people to worship and pray.

For food some go strangely dressed,
Some let their hair to grow unchecked,
Some wear a 'kerchief around their head,
All such stratagems only for bread!
Hundreds of forms fashioned by bread,
God too is worshipped, only for bread.

Exit fakirs.

REWRI-SELLER. Rose-flavoured rewri. My rewri is sweet and syrupy. Sir, buy some for your family! Rose-flavoured rewri!

EAR CLEANER. Double service, single price! Pick your teeth and clean your ears! Only one *chhadam*!

MELON-SELLER. Watermelon, sweet and cool!

LADDOO-SELLER. Sir, six for half a pie!

CHANA-SELLER. The chana I have got
So spicy and so hot!
Agra's fame runs far and wide,
My chana is the city's pride,
The price I ask is not too high,
You can afford it, come and try!
It helps adults' stomachs clear,
Sends kids to school without a tear!
This chana I have got
So spicy and so hot!

KAKRI-SELLER. Wow! What a clever idea!

LADDOO-SELLER. What are you talking about, blackface?

KAKRI-SELLER. Something absolutely novel.

LADDOO-SELLER. You aren't thinking of committing suicide, are you?

KAKRI-SELLER. Only fools think of suicide. There are better alternatives for the wise ones.

MELON-SELLER. What clever idea have you had? Let's hear it too.

KAKRI-SELLER. Those who can't think, won't be able to understand either.

LADDOO-SELLER. We'll try our best.

KAKRI-SELLER. Now you'll see how my kakri sells!

MELON-SELLER. Why, are you going to turn into a monkey-tamer?

LADDOO-SELLER. How can he afford a monkey? He'll have to dance himself to sell his kakri.

MELON-SELLER. What is it? It won't harm you to tell us, will it?

KAKRI-SELLER. It isn't wise to reveal one's business secrets to all and sundry.

LADDOO-SELLER. Don't you put on such airs! Why won't you tell us what you're thinking of? (*Grabs Kakri-seller by the arm.*)

KAKRI-SELLER. I won't tell you. Do what you like!

LADDOO-SELLER. You watch out! I'll give you one in the neck!

KAKRI-SELLER. Give me one in the neck? You? I'll smash your mug before that!

LADDOO-SELLER. Hey, mind how you speak to me. You think you're Aflatoon's brother-in-law? All right, stop fighting and tell us your secret.

KAKRI-SELLER. Let's see who wins today—you or me! Bloody fool! Thinks he's Alexander the Great himself!

LADDOO-SELLER. Why're you bent on courting death? A couple of hard punches from me and you'll turn into a bloody laddoo yourself.

KAKRI-SELLER. Oh yes? You better watch out or I'll beat you to a pulp!

LADDOO-SELLER. You little bag of bones, I'll grind you to powder!

KAKRI-SELLER. Let's see, I challenge you! Says he'll turn me into powder!

LADDOO-SELLER. I'll re-arrange your face!

KAKRI-SELLER. I'll demolish you. One blow and your mouth will collapse into your throat! Your tongue will drop out! Don't be under any illusions!

LADDOO-SELLER. Hey, darky! You better guard your dental works!

MELON-SELLER. Hey! What are you two up to?

LADDOO-SELLER. He's acting bloody haughty.

KAKRI-SELLER. Who's acting haughty, me or you?

MELON-SELLER. Ok, friends, now stop this quarrel.

LADDOO-SELLER. You'll be on a stretcher when I'm through with you.

MELON-SELLER. All right, all right! Now calm down, friends!

KAKRI-SELLER. You shut up! Eh?

LADDOO-SELLER. Yes, shut up and don't meddle. I can handle this blackface myself.

MELON-SELLER. Snapping at everyone! Didn't get enough to eat at home today?

LADDOO-SELLER. Quiet!

MELON-SELLER. You think you can shout everyone down!

LADDOO-SELLER. Will you shut up or do I give you one too?

MELON-SELLER. Crazy fellow! Who do you think you are?

LADDOO-SELLER. Your father!

MELON-SELLER. What did you say?

LADDOO-SELLER. Want me to repeat it?

MELON-SELLER. You scoundrel! I'll carve you into slices!

LADDOO-SELLER. Laddie, I can eat you raw! I can chop you into pieces!

ICE-SELLER. Keep quiet, you fools! Blasting our ears with your tongues snipping like the tailor's scissors!

LADDOO-SELLER. Oh, are you asking for it too? Come on then! I can flatten you both in no time!

REWRI-SELLER. Why must you wrestle so foolishly? Just shut up!

KAKRI-SELLER. Don't you talk to me about wrestling! I've been trained by Haji Sharifuddin! One throw and that's the end of you.

LADDOO-SELLER. Who's this bird, Sharifuddin? Sharifuddin's student, my bloody foot!

KAKRI-SELLER. Now, don't push me too far. You're making my blood boil.

LADDOO-SELLER. Ha! I'll reduce you to rubble, you coxcomb!

KAKRI-SELLER. Just try. I challenge you!

They come to blows. The rest join in the fray leaving their wares. A few idlers and urchins use this opportunity to help themselves to rewri, kakris and laddoos, etc. This further aggravates the situation. In the melee, some of the potter's wares are destroyed. Shopkeepers pull down their shutters. The fakirs enter, singing.

FAKIRS. Only the poor know the pain of poverty!
They know no polite formality,
They fall upon food with alacrity,
'Tis bread they seek, for food they moan,
And fight like dogs o'er every bone.
The poor become mean in adversity,
Only the poor know the pain of poverty!
Famed scholars, of themselves so sure,
Lose heart on becoming poor,
Confused by hunger, they begin to see
Day as night and A as B,
And those who tutor poor men's wards,
Find survival especially hard,
Forever they live in dire adversity,
Only the poor know the pain of poverty!
However good a man, but if he is poor,
He's often insulted and called a boor,
Clothes torn, hair unkempt, unoiled,
Mouth parched, body badly soiled.
Uncomely and grim is the face of adversity,
Only the poor know the pain of poverty!

Exit fakirs.

POTTER. What a fight! Just wouldn't stop. What harm had I done to any of you? The bastards have broken two of my pots. As it is, business is down, and now I have to suffer this.

KAKRI-SELLER. I'm sure you still have a few pots intact. I've been rendered bankrupt. The rain spoiled all my kakris yesterday. I'd borrowed money to buy this lot. And now half of it is gone.

LADDOO-SELLER. It's you who started the quarrel. Now sit quietly!

MELON-SELLER. Don't start all over again. Otherwise, there'll be neither a single laddoo left with you nor a single melon with me.

KAKRI-SELLER (*going after a passer-by*). Sir?

PASSER-BY. Yes? What is it?

KAKRI-SELLER. I want to ask you something. I hope you don't mind.

PASSER-BY. Go on.

KAKRI-SELLER. Do you write poetry?

PASSER-BY. I have not felt competent enough to, as yet. But why do you ask?

KAKRI-SELLER. Just like that!

PASSER-BY. What crazy people one meets!

Passer-by leaves. Poet enters with Companion.

POET. He writes and how he writes!
'Mir, mingle not with the wealthy any more,
It is their wealth which rendered you poor.'

COMPANION. Excellent!

KAKRI-SELLER (*moving closer*). Excellent! Beautiful, sir, very beautiful! I too have a small request, if you don't mind.

POET. I don't want it, brother!

KAKRI-SELLER. No, no! There's something else I want to say, if you would kindly walk this way with me.

POET. What is it?

KAKRI-SELLER. Sir, it's a question of my livelihood. I will be able to sell my kakri and bless you for the rest of my life! If only you . . . Please excuse me, but I'm struck by a thought. I hawk through the entire city from morning to evening. I have not sold a pie's worth of kakri during the past few weeks!

POET. As I have already told you, I don't want your kakri.

KAKRI-SELLER. But, sir, I am not asking you to buy kakri. In fact, you can have them all for free.

POET. What a pest! What is it then? What d'you want? Why don't you just say it?

KAKRI-SELLER. It has occurred to me that if I were to hawk my kakri by singing, my business would pick up!

POET. Very good! Congratulations!

KAKRI-SELLER. I will be very grateful to you if you kindly write a few verses on my kakri!

POET (*guffaws*). Sir, I am too small a poet for this job! If you wish, I can get a great master to write an entire ode on your kakri.

COMPANION. What's the matter?

POET. This gentleman wants me to write a few verses on his kakri. So I told him that if he wished I could ask the great master Zauq to write a poem on this rare subject.

COMPANION. Absolutely right! Brother, have you heard Zauq's name?

KAKRI-SELLER. I am a poor uneducated person, sir! What do I know about poets and poetry?

POET. But you sound clever enough! How can an unschooled person come up with such a bright idea!

COMPANION. He is tutor to His Majesty, the Emperor! His praise can make a mean particle of dust glow like the sun itself.

KAKRI-SELLER. Such a great poet, why would he want to write on this humble kakri.

POET. Why not? He is a poet after all!

KAKRI-SELLER. How can I have access to the royal court!

POET. If you wish, we could forward your request.

KAKRI-SELLER. You're making fun of a poor man, sir.

POET. Frankly, brother, only an established poet can do justice to a subject as beautiful as kakri. It's not something that a novice like me can handle.

Still laughing, Poet and Companion approach Book-seller's shop.

MELON-SELLER (*waylaying them*). Watermelon! Cool watermelon! Cools the heart, satisfies the eye, gives new life to the summer day, red bowl of pure sherbet, beats the heat and quenches the thirst! Try it, sir, cool, sweet melon!

POET. Listen, brother, you will not be able to sell your melons like this. You, too, should get a Mirza or Mir to write a few verses on your watermelons. Then we will also buy them if only as a tribute to their poetry. (*Laughs and moves on.*)

MELON-SELLER (*going to Laddoo-seller*). Do you know what the secret was? He wants a poet to write verses on his kakri!

LADDOO-SELLER. Why doesn't he memorize the couplet that the madari used:
'Come, buy my kakri and be quick!
Or you'll get one blow of my stick!'

MELON-SELLER. Yes, quite right! (*They both laugh.*)

LADDOO-SELLER (*laughing*). If poets were to start writing verses on kakris and melons, they might as well give up poetry and start selling fruit.

MELON-SELLER. Or better still, why don't we give up selling fruit and take to writing poetry instead? If we have to starve, we may as well starve as poets. What do you say?

POET (*at the bookstore, looking through a book*). Now look at this. He writes:
'Now even alms are denied to them in Delhi town,
Who till yesterday dreamt only of sceptre and crown.'

BOOK-SELLER (*settling in his seat*). Wonderful! I hear that Mir- sahib suffers from bouts of insanity these days?

POET. It's remarkable he's still alive. He's above eighty.

COMPANION. And the times Mir-sahib has seen in this life! In this very town, he saw the unfaithfulness of his own dear ones. Left home, left his native town. Even left Delhi which was once the ultimate destination of every sensitive and accomplished person. Wandered from place to place, witnessed the attacks by the Persians and the Turks. Witnessed the oppression of the Afghans, the Ruhelas, the Rajputs, the Jats, the Marathas. Saw a river of blood flow through Delhi with human heads floating like bowls. In front of his own eyes his house was destroyed:

'My house burnt before my eyes and there was
nothing I could do.'

He went through all this. And now he lives in Lucknow and is witness to the havoc caused by the English.

BOOK-SELLER. You are right, these are turbulent times. When I look at it, what I see is not the Mughal Empire but a big, powerful lion being attacked by hundreds of cats and dogs. Seeing it wounded and helpless, vultures and other birds of prey have also gathered to tear it to pieces. And the lion has neither the leisure to moan nor the luxury to die.

POET. Very good, Maulvi-sahib! Only you can speak like this. What language, what style! I am a poet in name only. But you talk poetry in everyday conversation!

BOOK-SELLER. This is only because I keep company with persons like you!

COMPANION. You are both being modest.

POET (*sitting near Book-seller*). Call it our modesty or your own graciousness. In any case, I feel my verse should be published only he who is a connoisseur of poetry.

BOOK-SELLER. And I believe that if I am to publish poetry, it must be the work of a genuine poet. I don't like to publish all and sundry.

COMPANION (*to Poet*). Your collection must be ready by now?

POET. A poet's collection is complete only with the termination of his life. However, I do have a sufficient number of verses to make up a book.

BOOK-SELLER. And you didn't even mention it to me.

COMPANION. He's so laidback. A poet, after all.

POET. I thought there was no formality between us. That I could give you my manuscript at any time and let you decide what to do with it.

BOOK-SELLER. Don't be so unfair. You must send me your manuscript first thing tomorrow.

Fakirs enter.

FAKIRS. All the world loves a flatterer
God loves one too.

Flatter to serve your own interest,
Flatter even if you have none,

Flatter God, saints and prophets,
In short, flatter everyone.

All the world loves a flatterer
God loves one too.

Flatterers get whatever they want,
Those who can't, live in poverty and want,
Flattery brings house, land and crown,
Turns white to black, black to brown.

All the world loves a flatterer
God loves one too.

Flatter the good, flatter the bad,
Flatter the happy, flatter the sad,
Flatter the holy, and unholy,
Flatter the dog, the ass, the rat.

All the world loves a flatterer
God loves one too.

BOOK-SELLER. Gentlemen, just before you arrived, the whole place was rocked by such a din as though doomsday itself was at hand.

POET. Why?

BOOK-SELLER. There was a dispute among some low-class persons. Before we knew, it turned into a full-fledged brawl. Looting and rioting!

POET. I hope nothing happened to your shop?

BOOK-SELLER. Perhaps one should feel thankful that there is no great demand for books in the world.

COMPANION. Why, they can always be sold as waste paper.

BOOK-SELLER (*laughs*). The mischief was started by a kakri-seller.

POET. That man sitting out there?

BOOK-SELLER. Yes. That's the one.

POET. He approached me a while ago and requested me to write verses on his kakri.

BOOK-SELLER. Really?

COMPANION. But isn't it possible for a poet to capture this entire milieu in words?

POET. What do you think Mir's work is all about if not a profoundly moving picture of these tragic times? 'Troubled livelihood, a troubled heart'—this single phrase encapsulates a whole world of meaning.

COMPANION. No, sir, he is only expressing his personal difficulties.

POET (*interrupting*). Why should the poet carry the burden of the whole world's woes?

COMPANION. No, what I meant was that perhaps the ghazal as a form lacks that broadness of scope which would allow all kinds of subjects and ideas to be written about.

POET. You are attacking a centuries-old tradition of great Persian and Indian masters. In which other culture can you find a thing as beautiful as the ghazal?

COMPANION. I am not disputing its beauty, only commenting on its limited scope.

POET. What you cannot write about in a ghazal, you can always say in a *quasida*.

COMPANION. Besides encomiums for kings and rulers, what else can you write in a *quasida*?

POET. But the *mathnavi* allows you the freedom to write about anything you please.

KAKRI-SELLER (*seeing Tazkiranawis*). Sir, you are a person of eminence, I am a small man. Your mind is like the very sun in the sky and I am no more than the dust under your feet. It may sound like audacity on my part but please forgive my impudence. Kindly listen to a small request.

Tazkiranawis looks towards him, frowns and moves on.

TAZKIRANAWIS (*on reaching the bookstore*). Assalam Alaikum!

BOOK-SELLER. Walaikum Assalam! Please come in, Maulana! (*Gives his seat to Tazkiranawis and sits on a stool.*)

POET. The poor man has been waiting for you since the morning to request you to write a couple of verses on his kakri. And you didn't even bother to answer him.

TAZKIRANAWIS. I don't want to pollute my speech by talking to riff-raff.

BOOK-SELLER. It seems you are following in Mir-sahib's footsteps. It is said that on his way from Delhi to Lucknow, Mir-sahib shared a horse-carriage with a man from Lucknow but did not utter a word throughout the journey lest it corrupt his speech!

TAZKIRANAWIS. Sahib, it is these traditions which will probably keep the language and literature alive in the times to come. Otherwise, everything is all but ruined! Look at the kind of language spoken in Delhi these days. I just shut my ears . . . I understand that an Urdu translation of the Holy Book is available now.

BOOK-SELLER. Yes, Shah Rafiuddin's translation is already out. But if you want Maulvi Abdul Quadir's translation, it will be available in a week or two.

POET. These are times of progress, Maulana.

BOOK-SELLER. Call it progress or call it decline. The fact, however, is that times are changing very fast. Machines have arrived and there are printing presses everywhere. There are translations of the Holy Book, as well as of the Bible. I have heard of an Englishman in Calcutta who is an expert in Sanskrit, Persian, Urdu and several other Indian languages. He has started a school called Fort William College. Various Indian languages are taught there and now I understand that they will also hold *mushairas*.

POET. I have heard that a college will open in Delhi as well where they will teach English, Chemistry and Physics.

BOOK-SELLER. This is the age of atheism. We need a crusader to alter the course of the times. There are many who feel concerned but what we lack is a crusader.

COMPANION. What the age really needs, Maulana, is not crusaders but human beings. But, unfortunately, there is no sign of them.

POET (*standing up*). What are we then? Beasts? (*They all laugh. Poet sits down.*)

COMPANION. I believe that this new system of education will also give birth to human beings. These are difficult times. Every person one meets complains of the lack of jobs. Hopefully, these new colleges will at least be able to provide employment to some people.

BOOK-SELLER (*to Tazkiranawis*). I don't think, Maulana, that there is much future for writings like your *Sharah-e-Hadith*, *Tabsira-o-Tanquid* and *Tazkira Naweesi*.[1] I think you should also explore new avenues now. (*Rises and sits next to Tazkiranawis.*) There is a rumour that a publishing house is coming up in Delhi and that soon, there will be journals and newspapers in Urdu. I think I should also shift my bookstore to Delhi and join newspaper publishing.

TAZKIRANAWIS. These are tough times! Truly tough times! Only yesterday I met Nasrullah Beg-sahib at Abul Fatah-sahib's clinic. We talked about how Delhi and Agra have been ravaged by the rapacity of some people. We went on to discuss poetry and literature . . . Beg-sahib told me the tragic tale of Mir Amman Khan. It seems Surajmal Jat has destroyed his home and seized his property. Mir-sahib is now living in the English madarasa in Calcutta and writing *Kissa Chahaar Darvesh*.[2] He wants me to come to Calcutta and says that I can earn a living there teaching Persian. I have received a similar message from Rajjab Ali Suroor. Nasrullah Beg is also of the same opinion.

BOOK-SELLER (*rises to go out*). Now look at Suroor himself. He is a risaldar in the British Army and living in comfort. (*Goes out through the left.*)

POET. It is said that his nephew Asadullah has married?

TAZKIRANAWIS. That's right. An unusually bright boy, this Asadullah! Even at this young age he writes poetry in Persian. And such poetry that, frankly, even I cannot fully comprehend it.

COMPANION. He's only thirteen or fourteen years old, isn't he?

POET. Yes, but what's so surprising about it? Take Sheikh Mohammed Ibrahim 'Zauq'. He couldn't have been more than eighteen or twenty when he went to the court of Akbar-e-Saani.[3] He challenged and overthrew the dominance of veterans like Shah Nasir and now he is the tutor to the Emperor. He is held in high regard by everyone in Delhi.

TAZKIRANAWIS. Mian, which Delhi are you talking about? Which court and which Akbar-e-Saani? After Akbar and Alamgir and other great rulers, Alamgir-e-Sani, Shah Alam Saani and Akbar-e-Saani are like the recurrent motif on the tablet of Mughal rule. And in that frightfully lonely place in the devastated city of Delhi which was once known as *quila-e-mualla*,[4] a rag-tag court is established. Sounds of poetry and literature are heard for a brief moment before a terrifying desolation takes over again. People have started escaping to Awadh and the Deccan. Delhi's royal cemetery is once more home to dogs and owls.

A customer enters from the right.

BOOK-BUYER (*mistaking Tazkiranawis for Book-seller*). Sir, would you have a copy of Munshi[5] Mirza Mehdi's *Nadirnama*?

Book-seller enters briskly from the left, tying the string of his trousers.

VOICE (*from the left, in anger*). What is this, mister? Every day you just sit down in front of the shop! The place stinks to high heaven!

Stranger, who had been strolling about in the market, peeps out of the lane and listens attentively to all this. Looking at Book-seller, he bursts into loud uncontrollable laughter.

BOOK-SELLER (*to the customer*). Sorry, I do not have *Nadirnama*. However, an Urdu translation titled *Tarikh-e-Nadiri* is available.

BOOK-BUYER. What about *Quissa Laila-Majnoon*?

BOOK-SELLER. Amir Khusro's *Quissa Laila-Majnoon* is also out of stock. However we have just received Haidri-sahib's translation of it.

BOOK-BUYER. Could I see it?

Book-seller and the customer enter the shop. A group of villagers, dressed colourfully, enters from the left, singing about Baldevji's fair. A group of Sikh devotees enters from the opposite side, singing in praise of Guru Nanak. There is tension in the air as the two groups seem about to clash and swords, spears and lathis are brandished. Eventually all bow before Guru Nanak's portrait. They all sing together and then leave, peacefully.

SIKH DEVOTEES. Nanak Shah is a learned saint, our revered Guru,

Lights our way like a brilliant star, our revered Guru,
Makes all our hopes come true, our revered Guru,
Giver of peace and happiness, our revered Guru,
Generous, kind and all loving, our revered Guru,
All worship him and bow their heads
And hail our revered Guru!

HINDU DEVOTEES. New faces, so beautiful, so fair,
    Prompting all to stand and stare;
    Disciples walking in masters' care,
    The scent of flowers filling the air;
    Families, friends and loners who
    Include townsfolk and villagers too;
    All kinds of money, lost and won,
    Performers, acrobats, amusement and fun;
    A surge of humanity, almost an endless one!

All this colour, beauty and pleasure,
Baldevji's fair has 'em in good measure.

There's Ram and there's Lakshman,
Kachh-machch and Ravan,
Varah and Madan Mohan,
Baldev as well as Lord Kishan;
In each form His incarnation
Of Narsimha and of Narayan.
There he walks so natty and proud,
Here he chants or sings aloud.

All this colour, beauty and pleasure,
Baldevji's fair has 'em in good measure.

Men and women seek their pleasure,
In sensuous pursuits or lively leisure;
With words like arrows, and eyes like darts,
Ready to conquer all young hearts;
Comely lasses in colourful attire,
Set all ablaze with love and desire.

All this colour, beauty and pleasure,
Baldevji's fair has 'em in good measure.

Joy and merriment, Jai Baldev!
Happy engagement, Jai Baldev!
Constant excitement, Jai Baldev!
Everywhere evident, Jai Baldev!
Rejoice every instant, Jai Baldev!
Shout every moment, Jai Baldev!

All this colour, beauty and pleasure,
Baldevji's fair has 'em in good measure.

*The groups exit to the right, singing. Benazir, an attractive young woman,
enters. She is wearing a tilak on the forehead and a bracelet of flowers. She is
being pursued by a young rake.*

RAKE. My heart-warmer, my darling sweet, when and where can we meet?

BENAZIR (*smiling*). What do you want?

RAKE. To bare my heart.

BENAZIR. Go ahead.

RAKE. As Lord Rama conquered Lanka, your heroic beauty has conquered the
fort of my heart—
'My heart was always like Ravana, and Ravana alone.
Conquered by a pretty idol I am now all for Rama.'[6]

BENAZIR. Who will bear witness to it?

RAKE. Hanuman. (*The young woman laughs and the two of them move on, talking.*) Dear matchless beauty! Bird of radiant colours! Lovely and desirable destroyer of hearts! By what name shall I call you?

BENAZIR. My humble self is called Benazir. May I have the honour of learning the gentleman's name?

RAKE. This insignificant creature is called Badre Munir. Where do you dwell?

BENAZIR. In Beauty Colony. And the gentleman?

RAKE. On Desire Street.

They exit.

POET. Maulana, I hear that you are writing a tazkira of Urdu poets?

TAZKIRANAWIS. Yes.

POET. At what stage is it now?

TAZKIRANAWIS. Well, sir, it is stumbling through one blind alley after another. The late Soz-sahib was my friend and companion. It was he who encouraged me to write. There was a time when one frequented Delhi and its environs. Apart from Soz-sahib, one often had the pleasure of the company of such figures as Mir, Khwaja Mir Dard, Sauda, Mir Hassan and Fughan.[7] We used to meet often. But their departure has put an end to all that.

BOOK-SELLER (*stopping a village lad*). Boy, come here a moment. (*The boy does not respond.*) Hey, you scoundrel, come here! (*The boy comes to him.*) These idiots don't understand simple prose unless one uses abusive words. (*Giving him money*) Go and get four paans from that shop there!

The boy goes to the paan shop.

BOY. Can you make four paans, brother?

PAAN-SELLER. Yes sir, sure. Large Banarasi leaves with lots of cardamoms.

TAZKIRANAWIS. Mir-sahib returned to his birthplace, Delhi, after a gap of some thirty years. He met scholars and intellectuals. He received honour and recognition. But he did not meet anyone who could provide succour to his restless soul. 'Oh God,' he thought, 'Is this the same town in which one could find distinguished poets, scholars, munshis and intellectuals in every lane and bylane? Today there is not a person here who can provide pleasurable and edifying company.' Saddened by the experience, he went back, having spent only four months in his dear homeland.

(*The boy returns with the paans*).

'"Mir" he entered the room, that's all I remember
And then all was dark as the lamps went out.'

In other words, sahib, tazkira and tazkiranawis are things of the past now. However, a golden page from the old times continues to twinkle in some remote corner of my mind. If the gloomy shadows of the present era do not snuff out that light too, I just might be able to leave something behind for posterity. Otherwise, it is enough that I am still alive.

A man enters briskly through the back door and goes out to the left. Kakri-seller, calling out, runs after him.

POET (*referring to Book-seller*). Maulvi-sahib here insists on publishing my collection. If you would look it over, it will help me improve it. It may also provide you with a fresh breakthrough in your idea of writing a tazkira of Urdu poets.

TAZKIRANAWIS. Well, there is hardly any chance of a new breakthrough. However, I am happy to be of service to you at any time.

The same man enters from the right and goes out through the left. Kakri-seller also enters, pursuing the man, but stops on reaching the centre of the stage. His voice grows faint. He slowly walks towards the paan shop and sits down on a bench near it.

BOOK-SELLER (*to the customer*). No, sir. The Persian text of *Laila Majnoon* is not in stock. I had informed you earlier too.

The customer leaves.

TAZKIRANAWIS. Do you see how depressing the times are? These days you cannot find Persian books in bookstores. Now even prose is written in Urdu. So what commentary can one write and to what purpose?

BOOK-SELLER. Oh, that reminds me! Recently, a disciple of Nazir came to me with a poem of his and inquired if I would use my influence and have it published. Now, you tell me, who would want to read Nazir's poetry?

Three or four men walk across the stage, laughing. Kakri-seller runs after them. The men exit. Kakri-seller is disappointed.

POET. In times to come only these vulgar things will be read. Anyone who can write a few cheap rhymes on Holi or Diwali will be thought to have scaled the heights of scholarship and creativity. After all, that is what popular taste demands these days. A little while ago, this kakri-seller came running up to me and requested me to write a poem on his kakris. Now what would you say to that!

A VOICE OFFSTAGE. I've told you a hundred times, I don't want your kakris. Have you gone mad or what?

KAKRI-SELLER (*offstage*). No, sir, no . . . It's like this . . .

VOICE. Just lay off. I've told you I don't want your kakris. Nor can I write poetry. Driving me crazy when I myself am in such dire straits!

People have begun to gather at Potter's shop. A group of eunuchs—which includes Kariman and Chameli—enters.

KARIMAN. May God save you and the saints protect you! The proud father of the new baby boy! Accept my love and my blessings, dear soul! May God save you and the saints protect you!

TAILOR. Ramu, hey, Ramu! How long are you going to be closeted with your wife? Come out and sit with your friends for a while. (*Ramu, the potter, comes out laughing.*) Silly shy fellow! Won't you offer us sweets?

KARIMAN. May God save you and the saints protect you! On this happy day, I must have a new dress. I will settle for nothing less. May God bring you prosperity!

POTTER. Hey, why are you all barging in like this? Move, make way!

KARIMAN. May you live long and may Allah protect you! Hey, Chameli, why are you sitting there like a statue? Come here, Miss Lost Soul!

POTTER. Get out, all of you! Go away! Will someone drive these bloody eunuchs out of here!

CHAMELI. Why do you shout and scold us on this happy occasion? I'll call you such names that you'll see stars, be swept off your feet. Hey, Kariman! Where the hell has she disappeared, the fool! (*Spotting her*) There you are! I'm hoarse from calling out for you! Don't just stand there gaping, sing a song!

KARIMAN. May Allah grant long life to the baby boy! May he flourish and replenish the earth! May God save you and the saints protect you! How can I refuse to sing on such an auspicious day! Come on, start the *seeties*.[8]

POTTER. Shut up! Don't you dare sing *seeties* here!

CHAMELI. Hey, Kariman! You silly woman, why are you inviting trouble? Sing something decent and leave the bloody *seeties* alone!

GROCER. Ramu, why don't you sing first?

ALL. Yes, good idea! Come Ramu, you begin.

POTTER (*sings, playing the rhythm on a pitcher*).

> Behold the splendour of my pots of clay!
> Like a bed of flowers on a sunny day,
> That freshen your heart and brighten the way;
> Useful for storing milk, curd and whey,
> By tapping on it like this you can play
> Any old rhythm, either sad or gay.
> Behold the splendour of my pots of clay!

TAILOR. Now, you sing something devotional.

KARIMAN. As you wish, sir! Come, Chameli. Pick up the *dholak*.

EUNUCHS (*singing*). Milkmaids away, the little one had a field day!

> He stole into houses like a thief much skilled,
> Climbed on a cot and brought down the pot
> That with cream or butter was freshly filled;
> He ate some and wasted some,
> And some he simply spilled.

> Fabulous were Krishna's childhood days,
> So many tales of his naughty ways!
> Caught red-handed by a returning maid,
> He looked innocent and sweetly said:
> I wasn't trying to steal from you!
> Believe you me, it's really true!
> Shooing off flies, keeping out ants,
> Is all I was really trying to do!

> Fabulous were Krishna's childhood days,
> So many tales of his naughty ways!

Women marched up to Jasoda, his mother,
We've come about Kanha, none other!
He breaks our pots, he calls us names,
And when we catch him, it's us he blames!
Whatever he says, whatever he claims,
You have to stop his naughty games!

Fabulous were Krishna's childhood days,
So many tales of his naughty ways!

Jasoda's response was sharp and quick,
She turned to Krishna, picking up a stick,
Feigning innocence he pleaded his case:
Mother, these charges are false and base;
In spite of this, if you must insist,
Your punishment I am ready to face.

Fabulous were Krishna's childhood days,
So many tales of his naughty ways!

Once caught by Jasoda with his mouth full of butter,
He widened his eyes and smiled at his mother,
She wasn't amused and made him sit,
Opened his mouth and peered into it;
What she saw was a vision, a miracle to wit,
She saw the whole universe brightly lit.

Fabulous were Krishna's childhood days,
So many tales of his naughty ways!

Enter Constable. Seeing him, people melt away. Shopkeepers mind their shops.

CONSTABLE (*goes to Book-seller*). Maulana, do you know what caused the rioting in this bazaar?

BOOK-SELLER (*respectfully rising to his feet*). Sir, my greetings to you. Constable-sahib, rioting has now become a daily occurrence. Some incident or the other takes place every day in this town. There was a fight between some street vendors, that is all.

CONSTABLE. I have received a report that there was rioting among the shop-keepers here.

BOOK-SELLER. Sir, it was entirely the fault of a kakri-seller. The poor shop-keepers were unnecessarily dragged into it.

CONSTABLE. Anyway, it has been decided to levy a fine of one rupee on each shopkeeper.

BOOK-SELLER. Kindly sit down. (*Calling out to Paan-seller*) Hey, Munney Khan, will you please make one of your best paans for constable-sahib. Sir, what do I have to do with fights and quarrels? As I have already submitted, it was a fight among the low-class street vendors.

CONSTABLE. Yes, yes. They too shall be fined.

BOOK-SELLER. Please do accept the paan.

CONSTABLE. Some other time. (*Moves away.*)

BOOK-SELLER. How very unfair!

TAZKIRANAWIS. What exactly happened here?

CONSTABLE. (*to Melon-seller*). Who was this kakri-seller and where is he now?

MELON-SELLER. He must be somewhere around, sir. Should be here any moment. It was he who started it all.

CONSTABLE. Ay, ay! I know all that. All of you are to blame and all of you will be fined. Go to the police station and deposit the fine.

LADDOO-SELLER. Sir, why should we all have to suffer because of one man? He is the one who provoked us and started a fight for no reason at all.

CONSTABLE. We shall soon find that out too. Investigation is on.

Picks up a melon, assesses its weight and carries it away with him.

LADDOO-SELLER. What a cruel joke. It was just getting peaceful when this fellow marched in. Now, the innocent will suffer along with the guilty.

MELON-SELLER. Brother, it's our fate! We can't escape it.

Nazir's granddaughter, a girl of 9 or 10 years, enters, singing to herself.

GIRL. 'Fabulous were Krishna's childhood days.
So many tales of his naughty ways!'
(*Reaching the grocer's shop*) Uncle, grandpa has asked for some mango pickle.

GROCER. Where is Mian Nazir? Great injustice has been let loose upon the town. Tell him to write a poem on it. We are all being forced to pay a fine of one rupee. And through no fault of ours.

GIRL. Grandpa is with the Rai-sahib.

GROCER. Rai-sahib must have persuaded him to stay for dinner.

GIRL. You know what! Rai-sahib has had besan roti made specially for grandpa.

GROCER. I see! That's what the pickle is for. Tell him to drop in for a while. (*Giving her the pickle*) Here.

GIRL (*running off*). 'Fabulous were Krishna's childhood days.
So many tales of his naughty ways!'

COMPANION. Maulana, how would you rank Nazir as a poet?

TAZKIRANAWIS (*browsing through a book*). A very lively man—good-natured, soft-spoken, greets everyone with a smile, does not hurt anybody. In other words, a man probably without a parallel anywhere in the world. But poetry? That's an entirely different kettle of fish. I could never accept vulgarity, cheap nonsensical rhymes and a shoddy and common kind of humour as poetry. To regard Nazir as a poet will be a gross injustice both to him and to poetry. There is no room for him in the list of poets.

Melon-seller gets up and exits, still hawking. The girl returns.

GIRL. 'Fabulous were Krishna's childhood days . . . ' (*To the grocer*) Uncle, grandpa has sent the pickle back.

GROCER. Why?

GIRL (*suppressing a laugh*). Read this. (*Hands him a paper.*)

Grocer takes the letter from the girl and reads it silently. Then he peers into the pickle container and bursts into loud laughter. The girl runs away.

POTTER. What's the matter, Lalaji?

GROCER. Listen to this. Mian Nazir has written a new poem.

'Again, there is a market for rats these days,
I too have prepared them in various ways;
I chop and I pound and I mash three or four
And make such a mix you'll ask for more!
My rat pickle is the pride of any store!
The rats I choose are large and fat,
Each frog I add is the size of a cat,
Deliciously crisp and spicy and hot,
Judge for yourself how well they have rot!
Its price is rising, is sure to rise more,
My rat pickle is the pride of any store!'

(*Laughs uncontrollably. Pulls out a dead rat from the container.*) Bloody rats! So fond of pickle!

Other shopkeepers laugh.

POET. See? The level of Nazir's poetic imagination!

BOOK-SELLER. What is surprising is that Mian Nazir belongs to a respectable family. It's a shame his poems are being sung in streets and marketplaces by illiterate and uncultured people. He should show some regard at least for his family's reputation, if not for his own.

TAZKIRANAWIS. Sir, what shame or self-regard can you expect from a fellow whose entire life is spent in flying kites, in enjoying the pleasure of fair-grounds, in vagrancy and gambling!

POET. That's right. Though, now, in his last years, he has started living a life of piety. Otherwise, it is said that in his youth he used to roam the streets singing and visiting brothels in the company of other young men. Play Holi with great fervour, participate in every ritual.

BOOK-SELLER. Now, look at these mystical songs that the beggars sing in the street. Won't it be a great injustice to the sublime art of poetry to dignify these songs as verse?

It is evening now. Courtesan's chamber has started showing signs of activity. Rake enters from within, followed by Benazir. A couple of persons are already waiting in the room. Several more come in during the song. A fakir with a long beard, dressed in a green kafni, enters. He is carrying burning incense on a plate with which he moves around the room to spread its smoke. Placing the plate on the floor, he sits down unobtrusively in one corner. Another man enters carrying garlands of fresh flowers on a short wooden stick. He goes around the room tying the garlands on the visitors' wrists and receives baksheesh from them.

RAKE. My sweet rose, my beautiful fairy princess! Now that we know each other properly, how about singing something?

BENAZIR. As you wish! What should I sing?

RAKE. Rarely does one come across such silvery loveliness. You are matchless in beauty. I am sure you are also matchless in the art of singing.[9] Sing anything. How about something scintillating, something close to your own experience?

NEW GUEST (*entering*). Greetings!

BENAZIR. How are you?[10]

GUEST. 'The other day, she asked me in the language of Punjab,
Tell me how you are these days. Has life been soft or hard? I stood there with folded hands, and said, why do you ask? Nothing's hidden from you, you know it all, sweetheart.'

BENAZIR (*laughing*). All right, I'll sing something of Nazir's. You could regard it as my own experience and it won't be altogether incorrect. (*Sings*)

'Cruel, uncaring tormentor, playful and lively,
Heart hard as stone, words so soft and sugary.
Demeanour like a drawn bow, eyes glowing darkly,
Heady cups of wine, bright in part and dark partly;
Beguiling eyes, deceiving looks, her ample bosom, heavenly.

An embroidery of jewels on that fair and delicate breast,
Flower bud, diamond necklace, waistband, anklet,
Inflaming hearts with desire, inviting glances to trip,
The flat and silky belly, sparkling navel, chiselled hip;
Her open flirtation, her frivolity, her coy modesty, heavenly.

Forever alert, forever keen, quick to follow every word I say,
Scolds, cajoles and sulks, playful by night, stern by day,
That frivolity, that zest, forever present, forever at play,
Flirting, evading, that gait seducing with it swing and sway;
The teasing veil, the seductive show of body and face, heavenly.

During the song, Constable enters. Benazir greets him by gesture. Constable says, 'Bless you' and sits down.

RAKE. Excellent! This describes you beautifully! This poet Nazir is quite a miracle worker. Does he visit you often?

BENAZIR. Yes, but he hasn't quite a while now. Do you know him?

RAKE. No, my dear. But this poem makes me want to meet him. Anyway, at this moment, I am so full of the joy of meeting you that I cannot think of anything else in the world.

Receiving hints, guests begin to leave. Constable beckons Benazir to one side.

CONSTABLE. Listen—am I not allowed to come in today?

BENAZIR. You are welcome. Except that I feel slightly unwell at the moment.

CONSTABLE. I'll gladly massage your head, if you have a headache. If it is your heart that aches I can find a cure for it. If the ache is somewhere else I can apply balm there too.

BENAZIR. Please come tomorrow.

CONSTABLE. I'd prefer it right now.

BENAZIR. Now, don't insist, constable-sahib. This is not the time for it. Come some other time.

CONSTABLE. Are you trying to fool me? Who is that evil-faced rival there? If you want, I can have him thrown out of here.

RAKE (*rising*). How dare you?

CONSTABLE. Who the hell are you? You seem to be a new bird in here. Young man, you don't know who I am!

RAKE. I am beginning to have some idea. Give me a chance and I'll get to know you better. Shall we step out?

BENAZIR. Please! What is this? That's not the way to talk to my guests.

RAKE. I apologize. I beg your forgiveness, my lady.

BENAZIR (*to Constable*) Now tell me, when will you visit me next?

CONSTABLE. I'll come a thousand times, if only you'd call me!

BENAZIR. I'll call you a million times, if only you'd come! I think I'll have to use bait.

CONSTABLE. You don't need any bait with 'This fair visage, these long dark tresses.'

BENAZIR. The gentleman seems to be a bird!

RAKE (*to Constable*). Okay. Goodbye!

CONSTABLE. Who cares about birds here? This place specializes in clipping wings. Goodbye!

BENAZIR. Farewell.

Constable goes downstairs.

RAKE (*turning towards the inner chamber*). Strange creature!

BENAZIR. Don't you know? He's the chief constable of this city. You're incredible!

RAKE. Chief constable, so what? He can't eat me up!

BENAZIR. All right, now come inside.

CONSTABLE. (*to Kakri-seller in the market*) Where were you all this while?

KAKRI-SELLER. I was doing my rounds, master.

CONSTABLE. You have all become lumpen now.

KAKRI-SELLER. Sir, it was not my fault at all. It was the laddoo-seller who tried to assault me.

CONSTABLE. My men are investigating the cause of the quarrel. Meanwhile, go to the police station and deposit the fine.

KAKRI-SELLER. Constable, sir, I haven't done any business since the morning. If I manage to sell kakri worth a *chhadam* or two we shall have food, else it will be another day of fasting.

Constable goes out.

POET. How many copies should one print of the first edition?

BOOK-SELLER. About 500.

POET. However, I have certain personal difficulties. So if I could get an advance of a few rupees it'll free me from these problems.

BOOK-SELLER. Oh, sir, don't you know? These days the authors publish books at their own expense. There are three new texts—*Karima, Ma-Muqueema,* and *Aamadnaama*[11]—that I am keen to publish but am unable to do so for lack of money. Why don't you do one thing? Chowdhary Ganga Prasad is your acquaintance as well as an admirer of your work. Why don't you arrange to have the book published in partnership with him?

POET. Don't you think it will be better if you talked to him yourself? He knows me and he won't say no to you. And even if he refuses, the matter will be known only to the three of us. You can give me five rupees from whatever money you receive from him.

BOOK-SELLER. The difficulty is that once when I asked him for money, he ignored my request. You will be approaching him for the first time and he will not say no to you. That is why I suggest that you mention your book to him. Ideally, if he agrees to lend you the money, you should let me have my share of it so that I could print your book as well as mine. My books are not likely to cost more than ten or twelve rupees.

POET. All right.

Fakirs enter, singing.

FAKIRS. Money is what the rich desire,

Money is what the poor require,
Of power and glory money's the sire,
Makes the world spin and go haywire;
To colour and beauty money gives birth,
The penniless have no value, no worth.

Heaps of money makes one rise above all,
Bestows greatness where none exists at all,
Brings name and fame with many mansions tall,
Without it man is weak and small;

To colour and beauty money gives birth,
The penniless have no value, no worth.

Money can make you tame a wild bear,
Without it even a mouse fills you with fear,
With money you're 'master,' and even 'dear,'
Without it, a leper whom no one comes near;

To colour and beauty money gives birth,
The penniless have no value, no worth.

Wherever money sits and spreads its wings,
It is visited by angels, heroes and kings,
Beautiful damsels from far off it brings,
And lissome fairies dancing in rings;

To colour and beauty money gives birth,
The penniless have no value, no worth.

It's money that leads to bloodshed and wars,
Invents guns, daggers and scimitars,

It peeps from soldier's wounds and scars,
And makes them die for medals and stars.

To colour and beauty money gives birth,
The penniless have no value, no worth.

Charity exists on the strength of money,
Religion persists on the strength of money,
Hell is shunned on the strength of money,
Paradise earned on the strength of money.

To colour and beauty money gives birth,
The penniless have no value, no worth.

Money is the reason for name and fame,
It leaves only credit, removes all blame,
Controls all bodies and the souls they frame,
It's man's god, his master, his guiding flame.

To colour and beauty money gives birth,
The penniless have no value, no worth.

Kakri-seller has entered during the song and listens to it with rapt attention.

KAKRI-SELLER (*with great wistfulness*). Why won't somebody write a poem on my kakris? (*Begins to leave but, suddenly struck by a thought, calls out to the fakirs*) Shah-sahib![12] (*Still calling, runs out through the right but comes back soon and runs out through the left*) Shah-sahib! Shah-sahib!

Fakirs re-enter, singing. Kakri-seller enters calling out to them but they go out. Dejected, he sits down, holding his head in his hands. Fakirs' song continues to be heard as the curtain comes down.

SCENE TWO

Once again, the fakirs enter through the auditorium singing and stand in front of the curtain which rises during the last stanza.

FAKIRS. Why do you wander restlessly, why this envy and greed,
  Death'll follow wherever you go, a truth you better heed!
  All your wealth and possessions, your cattle of every breed,
  Those heaps of rice and lentils, every grain, every seed,
  As you pack your bag to leave there's nothing you'll need.

  Yes, you are a big trader and your stakes are very high,
  But, beware, there's another, a bigger one, close by,
  All your sugar and saffron from lands far and nigh,
  Sweet condiments, hot spices that bring tears to the eye,
  As you pack your bag to leave there's nothing you'll need.

  Time will empty your saddlebag and deflate it as it must,
  Your fabulous wealth and rosy health will also gather rust,
  And you will lie all alone in the wilderness of dust,
  Quite forsaken and forgotten by all you love and trust,
  As you pack your bag to leave there's nothing you'll need.

  Why crave for worldly goods, why pine for Midas's touch?
  Where you're headed, silly man, you won't be needing much,
  All this velvet, all this silk and glittering brocaded stuff,
  Fancy saddles and gilded howdahs won't add up to much,
  As you pack your bag to leave there's nothing you'll need.

  Your sole thought is of profit which makes you slog like mad,
  But don't forget you're stalked by an enemy vicious and bad,
  None can help, not family nor friends nor mum nor dad,

No prayer you made, charity you gave, nor succour to the sad,
As you pack your bag to leave there's nothing you'll need.

Death'll drive you to yonder shore leaving the body in tatters,
Others'll claim your worldly goods and everything that matters,
You'll be alone in a dark grave as your dust in the wind scatters,
None will look in, no bird no insect nor the cricket which chatters,
As you pack your bag to leave there's nothing you'll need.

Fakirs leave. It is early morning. Some shopkeepers, having arrived early, are busy opening their shops. Vendors' cries can be heard.

KAKRI-SELLER. Why are the policemen patrolling the market so early in the morning today?

MELON-SELLER. Where? I didn't see any policeman.

LADDOO-SELLER. They must be looking for you, blackface, to arrest you.

Poet and Companion come to Book-seller's shop.

KAKRI-SELLER. Let them come. How does it matter to you? It won't be such a bad thing if the bastards arrest me. At least I'll get to eat. I starve the whole day and break my back in the bargain. Much better to sit in the lock-up, eat in comfort and not have to worry. Let the jealous go green with envy!

BOOK-SELLER. Didn't Chowdhary Ganga Prasad-sahib say anything else to you?

POET. He spoke obliquely. I realized that it was not an appropriate moment to talk to him.

BOOK-SELLER. But he must have said something?

POET. I told you. The moment I mentioned you in connection with the publication of my collection, he interrupted me and said he'd first like to clear certain old matters with you before considering any new book.

BOOK-SELLER. Why did you mention me at all?

POET. What else could I do?

BOOK-SELLER. Dear sir, I have been in his debt for a long time now. That is why I had asked you to talk to him about the book yourself.

Kite-seller enters carrying a caged parrot and humming a song and goes on to open his shop.

KITE-SELLER (*hums*). The poor, the lowly, and persons of high degree,
Everyone in Agra swims and swims wonderfully.

Congratulations, Ramu! I am told you are the proud father of a son now and that there was much celebration here?

POTTER. Where had you disappeared, brother?

KITE-SELLER. I went with Mian Nazir to the swimming fair. On my return, I find my shop has incurred a fine. This penalty was the last thing I needed.

POTTER. You should just tell them your shop was closed. There are witnesses. I'm willing to vouch for you.

KITE-SELLER. Who listens to our complaints and grievances here? (*Seeing tazkiranawis approaching Book-seller's shop*) Behold, there he comes sporting a beard that looks as though it's made of jute! (*They both laugh.*)

POTTER (*taking sweets to Kite-seller*). Here, some sweets for you. Come on, have some. They're really nice. Did you take the parrot along while swimming?

KITE-SELLER. Of course! I swim across the river with cage in hand, what do you know! God, how the Yamuna was packed with people! All the way from Chhatri to Braj Khoti and Dara, even beyond that. Everywhere you saw only heads! Like floating melons. Really, friend, the people of Agra are remarkable! There were men who crossed the river with nightingales perched on their heads! Amazing, these people!

BOOK-SELLER. Have you heard, sir? Mian Nazir had gone to the riverbank to watch semi-naked mermaids. Old age has made no difference to his tastes.

TAZKIRANAWIS. Old age cannot alter a man's character. Old habits die hard. When he had the strength, he used to participate in the swimming. Now he goes to the Yamuna with old memories and desires and derives vicarious pleasure from seeing others perform what he can no longer accomplish himself.

COMPANION. But, sir, this swimming festival is really quite remarkable! And it is peculiar to Agra. What a splendid, poetic sight it is! To tell you the truth, even I feel a strong urge to participate, even to write a poem on this beautiful subject. But I don't know how to.

POET. It's simple. Just start rhyming like this:

'Some swim with tears, some swim with glee,
Everyone in Agra swims and swims wonderfully.'

All laugh.

COMPANION. But it should be possible to write a proper poem on this subject.

POET. On swimming?

COMPANION. Why not?

POET. How?

COMPANION. If I knew I would have written it.

POET. What is the point of glorifying as 'poetic' a subject on which you cannot write poetry?

COMPANION. I only said I wish I could write on the subject. I never said it was easy or even possible.

POET. How sensible, do you think, is it to want to write on a subject on which it is impossible to write verse?

LADDOO-SELLER. You barging in again? Go and sit beside your favourite friend.

KAKRI-SELLER. Are you out of your mind? Always tilting against windmills!

Two policemen come to the paan shop to eat paan.

MELON-SELLER. Don't you start quarrelling again. Otherwise there'll be nothing left of us or our wares.

Hamid, a young lad, enters and goes to the kite shop.

HAMID. Where were you yesterday?

KITE-SELLER. I had gone to the swimming fair.

HAMID. I thought you had quit selling kites.

KITE-SELLER. Who, me? I give up kite flying or kite selling? Impossible! Which kite do you want? I have them in every colour, every shape, every style, every character, every humour—which one do you want, Sir? *Do-dharia, gilahria, dowaaz, lalpara, ghayal, langotia, chand-tara, bagula, dopanna, dhir, kharbuzia, pendipaan, dokonia, kalsara, kakri, chaughara, bajra, kajkulaah, chamchaka, tawakkul, jhanjar, maangdar* . . .

HAMID. Please, stop! I've never even heard the names of these kites.

KITE-SELLER. What kind of a kite flyer are you if you don't even know their names?

HAMID. Well, never mind that. I am a small flyer. Just give me the simple *dodharia*.

KITE-SELLER. Here!

HAMID. How much?

KITE-SELLER. Twenty-five *kauris*.

HAMID. Here. (*Takes the kite and leaves.*)

BOOK-SELLER (*To Hamid*). Come here, lad! (*Hamid goes out. Book-seller leaps after him.*) Boy, come here a moment! (*Returns to the shop followed by Hamid.*) Sit down. (*Points to a place close to himself but the boy sits away from him.*) You are called Hamid, aren't you?

HAMID. Yes.

BOOK-SELLER. Maulana, you should listen to the works of the classical poets sung by this boy. Believe me, his voice is as silky and sweet as his face!

TAZKIRANAWIS. Really!

HAMID. What would you like to hear, Maulana?

BOOK-SELLER. You know the works of the great masters by heart! Why do you ask us? Just choose something yourself.

TAZKIRANAWIS. That's right, boy.

HAMID. I will sing a ghazal.

'Messenger, go tell her without mentioning me,
The one who loves you is dying, so sick is he.
The moment, in anger, she went away from me,
Why didn't lightning strike and I cease to be?
It must be she who goes out dressed up at this hour,
From her radiant face alone can issue the light I see.
No one shed tears as I wandered in the wilderness,
Except the blisters on my feet which wept openly.
When others fell, she rushed to help them up again,
But when I fell there was neither help nor sympathy.
Ah Nazir, we advised you but you listened not,
You perused the book of love too keenly.'

POET (*surprised*). Is this Nazir-mian's ghazal?

COMPANION. How wonderful! I hadn't heard this before.

BOOK-SELLER. If one continues to try throughout one's life, one is bound to stumble upon a good piece of verse once in a while. There is nothing surprising about it. Come on, boy, sing something else.

COMPANION. But, sir, don't you see, the poem employs the metre and rhymes that have been used by great masters.

BOOK-SELLER. One can find any number of third-rate poets who are presumptuous enough to tread on the path of the inimitable masters.

COMPANION. But one has to admit that Nazir's poem is very sophisticated and refined.

TAZKIRANAWIS. See how Mir uses this metre and rhyme scheme:

'Mir, he looks at me with eyes of raining fire,
Alas, this poisoned cup, was meant just for me.'

And listen to this too. What wonderful use of the 'weeping blister' image!
'Thorns in that wilderness are still bathed in blood,
Where blisters on my feet had burst and wept openly.'

This is how the great masters write!

POET. No doubt. Insha too has played creatively with this image. Listen to this:

'Make me wander so through the harsh wilderness of love
That blisters of tears on the feet of my eyes may flow openly.'

COMPANION. But my dear sir, Nazir's couplet is also not without interest:

'No one shed tears as I wandered in the wilderness,
Except the blisters on my feet which wept openly.'

POET. Sauda too used the same rhyme pattern.

COMPANION. Mister, do you know any of Syed Inshallah Khan's work?

BOOK-SELLER. There is no parallel anywhere to the polemics in Insha and Mushafi's poetry. Particularly the argument between them in that ghazal— 'the neck of the pitch dark night . . .' Nawab Sa'adat Ali Khan's court must have been a wonderfully lively place!

TAZKIRANAWIS. Friend, you are talking of a time long past. The time of 'the neck of the pitch dark night' is now over. Now even a witty and good-humoured person like Inshallah Khan is lamenting—

'We are all set to go whenever comes the call,
Many have gone ahead, the rest await the curtain's fall.'

COMPANION. And now, one hears that Aatish and Naasikh have taken Lucknow by storm and even Insha and Mushafi have paled into relative insignificance. Truly, Aatish is a very powerful poet. Listen to the power of his expression in this—

'There is no room for the abject, so unique is our pack,
We are all kings and queens here, not a single jack.'

POET. And Naasikh's response to it is equally powerful—

'The select few do not belong to common humanity,
Though sold with slaves, Joseph wasn't one, was he?'

COMPANION. Oh no! This is an uncalled for argument. The couplet is beautiful as such but full of artificiality and fake sentiment. It lacks the truth and fire of Aatish's poetry.

POET. Instead of looking at the beauty of Naasikh's response, you are searching for 'truth' and 'fire!'

BOOK-SELLER. O-oh! You gentlemen have started what our masters are doing in the courts of Delhi and Lucknow. Please stop this argument and let's listen to poetry. Yes, young man.

HAMID. What would you like to listen to?

TAZKIRANAWIS (*irritated*). Sing whatever you feel like.

KITE-SELLER. Sing Nazir's poem about the swimming fair. Do you know it?

HAMID. Yes sir.

'The poor, the lowly, and persons of high degree,
Everyone in Agra swims and swims wonderfully!
Some float with eyes closed, dozing all the way,
Others hold cages, or on their head a popinjay.'

Visibly annoyed, Tazkiranawis gets up and leaves. Everyone is surprised. Silence falls on the group. Several passersby have also stopped to listen to the poem. Seeing the crowd, Book-seller feels irritated. Hamid continues to sing.

HAMID. 'Many swim while flying kites, or stringing a bead,
Some smoke hookahs, and look happy indeed,
Such marvellous things they do, and do so easily,
Everyone in Agra swims, and swims wonderfully!'

BOOK-SELLER. Enough, stop now. (*Raising his voice*) And why have you all gathered here? Is this some kind of a roadside show? Or a public prayer meeting that everyone feels free to join?

The crowd pulls back a little. Complete silence prevails. Kakri-seller enters from the left.

KAKRI-SELLER (*in a lifeless voice*). Six for a pie! Six for a pie!

Book-seller stares at him angrily. Kakri-seller, hitherto unaware of the prevailing tension, notices Book-seller's angry looks and suddenly stops shouting. He runs to the right corner and sits down quietly. Kite-seller, who was in front of the crowd, advances towards the bookshop.

KITE-SELLER. Boy, come with me! (*Takes his hand and leads him towards his own shop.*)

BOOK-SELLER. I thought, the boy has a good voice and his rendering of poetry will please the Maulana. How was I to know that he would start singing this vulgar poetry! And now the Maulana is annoyed and has walked out in a huff!

COMPANION. But the poem was quite good, sir!

POET. Oh yes, indeed! Look at his diction! He uses the inelegant and illiterate speech of the common folk and you call it poetry?

COMPANION. But the vocabulary and constructions he employs are very much in usage. Great masters have used them too.

POET. Come on! Let's go now.

BOOK-SELLER. I'm truly sorry about this.

POET. It's not your fault, Maulana. All right, see you!

BOOK-SELLER. Goodbye.

Poet and Companion leave. The crowd has shifted to Kite-seller's shop.

BOOK-SELLER. Now the wretches have assembled there.

Book-seller busies himself with the account books. Kite-seller seats the singer at his shop.

KITE-SELLER: Listen, Mian Nazir writes—

'O Wine-giver, if it is destined that I drink this wine,
On its own, it'll find its way into this cup of mine.'

Young man, why didn't you tell me that you know Nazir's poetry by heart?

HAMID. I had come here to buy kites, sir. Giving recitals of poetry was not my purpose.

KITE-SELLER. But, my friend, you know that Mian Nazir and I have been friends for a long time. If you were going to recite his poetry, you should have done it at my shop. By singing there, you insulted him as well as me. Nazir has an apt couplet to describe this situation:

'This orphaned pearl of my heart was sold dirt cheap,
Well, it is the buyer's good fortune is all I can say!'

All right, now sing something for us.

HAMID. Which one would you like to hear?

KITE-SELLER. Sing the same poem—the one about the swimming fair—what
else!

HAMID. 'The poor, the lowly, and persons of high degree
Everyone in Agra swims, and swims wonderfully!

Some float with eyes closed, dozing all the way,
Others hold cages, or on their head a popinjay.
Many swim flying kites, or stringing a bead,
Some smoke hookahs, and look happy indeed

Such marvellous things they do, and do so easily,
Everyone in Agra swims and swims wonderfully!

Several swim standing, displaying a bare chest,
Their frames glistening, like gems on the river's crest,
Half their body wet with water, sweat moistens the rest,
Awesome sight of floating heads, eight or ten abreast.

Coloured sashes, gaudy turbans, so attractive and lovely,
Everyone in Agra swims, and swims so wonderfully.

At every stroke Syed Kabir they hail,
Then their mentors who they hail,
Remembering Krishna and his river as they sail,
And cheering members of their team without fail.

Spreading mirth and joy, thus shouting cheerfully,
Everyone in Agra swims, and swims so wonderfully.'

*A large number of people have gathered during the song. The crowd includes
the vendors.*

KITE-SELLER. Excellent! It is this kind of writing which appeals to the heart. But,
alas, the world did not appreciate this poet. He writes:

'Not the blossom, nor the thorn, nor the gardener
      can I call my own
Ah! Woe me, that in such a place
      I chose to build my home!'

ALL. Wonderful!

KITE-SELLER. All right, now how about singing something of your own choice.

Blind Beggar enters led by a companion.

BEGGAR (*sings*). Let's remember Lord Ganesh, bow to him our heads,
He brings success to every one and good luck he spreads,
Let's embrace the whole world, offer love to all,
Recount Mahadev's nuptials and hold you all in thrall.
As writ in all our ancient books and told by hoary saints,
As also every local priest in his daily discourse explains,
May all who listen be happy, may your luck increase!
May its readers thrive in health, comfort and peace!
He who wrote and sang about the glory of that wedding,
May he find name and fame in the path he is treading,
May his days be amply blessed, with life's elixir,
May Lord Shiva rain his bounty on the poet called Nazir.

One of the assembled listeners, a man dressed in a fakir's green cloak, is crying. Kite-seller notices him and runs towards him.

KITE-SELLER. Ah! Manzoor Hussain! (*The man turns away from him*) Why are you dressed like this? How are you? (*The man remains quiet.*)

A BYSTANDER. We have never heard him speak.

BENI PRASAD (*coming forward*). You didn't know? He has been in this condition for nearly a year now.

KITE-SELLER. What are you saying, Beni Prasad? Has he been in Agra for a year? He used to be a horse trader. About four years ago, he had gone to Hyderabad with his horses. This is the first time I've seen him since then. Isn't that so, Manzoor Hussain?

Manzoor Hussain leaves.

BENI PRASAD. It's strange you didn't notice him. Or maybe you saw him but failed to recognize him. He's been wandering around here for the several days now. He's deeply in love with a courtesan.

KITE-SELLER. And this vow of silence, this shroud-like cloak, this beard, this appearance of a mendicant—are these also the result of that infatuation? I couldn't bear to see him like this. That a fun-loving, good-natured and sociable man like Manzoor Hussain should change so radically! Do you know—he used to be very close to Nazir and was often found in his company? My own friendship with him goes back some twenty or twenty-five years.

BENI PRASAD. Yes. I know.

KITE-SELLER. But tell me, Beni, how did he come to such a pass? I'm totally perplexed.

BENI PRASAD. Brother, no one knows what actually happened to him. All I have heard is that during his journey from the Deccan, he was robbed of all his horses and other possessions near Jhansi. When he returned to Agra a year ago, he was already in a sorry state. But he had not yet assumed the garb of a fakir. Sometimes he even exchanged a word or two with people —but very rarely. He just sat in a tomb on the banks of the Jamuna, staring at the water. Then he disappeared suddenly. He was sometimes sighted in Mathura and sometimes in Meerut. He has only recently returned to Agra and in this condition.

KITE-SELLER. Is it the effect of paralysis or an attack of madness? There has to be some explanation!

BENI PRASAD. Different people say different things. Some say that he has turned religious. Some say he is still in a state of shock as a consequence of the robbery. Some even say that his condition is the outcome of pure love. In fact, cases of worldly love developing into divine love are not entirely unknown.

KITE-SELLER. 'Life's lease is no more than a dew drop,
Union with the beloved is but a rare pearl.'

He has always been a very sensitive person. I remember an old incident. Do you know how he first met Nazir? Nazir was on a pony, going from Tajgunj to Maithan to tutor Lala Bilasrai Khatri's son. At one point, when the pony became restive and refused to budge any further, Nazir lashed it with the whip. But the whip also brushed against Manzoor Hussain who happened to be walking by just at that moment. Nazir immediately jumped off and forced the whip into Manzoor Hussain's hand, urging him to strike him in return. Unable to persuade him to forget the incident, Manzoor Hussain touched him lightly with the whip, rushed to me, recounted the entire episode, went home and lay there without food or drink for two days. When Nazir heard about this, he was very upset. He immediately went to Manzoor Hussain, brought him to his house and showered him with hospitality. Offered him sweets, played Holi with him, read out his poetry to him. This made Manzoor Mian even more devoted to Nazir and their friendship grew. From that day on, they were always found in each other's company.

BENI PRASAD. Strange are the changes that time brings about!

KITE-SELLER. 'Stop worrying about things, man, just eat, drink and be merry.'

Enter Holi revellers, singing.

REVELLERS. Colour-drenched handsome lads with lissome lasses
All are drunk with music, and the heady bashful glance,
A glorious treat for eye and ear, brimming with romance,
Thrilling beats of the tabla drum, ecstatic pipes of trance,
Ankle bells weave their spell—such is the splendour of Holi.
Bowers of rosy damsels promise hours of fun,
On the clothes of every reveller rivers of colour run,
Faces dyed in pink and red, shining in the gentle sun,
The coloured jet makes blouses wet, blouses thinly spun
And bosoms glow as colours flow—such is the splendour of Holi.

KITE-SELLER (*to Beni Prasad*). Did you hear, Beni Prasad? Can there be a better verse on the subject of Holi? This poetic quality and inventiveness, these similes and metaphors, these images—this is what is called beauty of expression in poetry and literature. Let me tell you the secret of wisdom, listen to it and memorize it forever. A scholar took great pains to teach the art of expression to a disciple. When his education was complete, the scholar told the pupil: Now go and wander through streets and market-places and listen to how people talk and find out if there is any relation-ship between everyday speech and what I have taught you. The pupil wandered around for a long time but could not discover any connection between the two. He reported this to his teacher. The teacher taught him the whole thing again, from beginning to end, and sent him out again. Once again, the pupil wandered through the streets and markets. This time, he was able to discover some little connection. He reported to the teacher: 'Yes, there does seem to be a little connection between the two.' The teacher said: 'Your education is still not complete. You have to study everything all over again.' At the end of this third round the pupil realized that there is nothing in even the most ordinary, everyday conversation that is not related to the art of expression. Now, do you understand?

BENI PRASAD. Well, this is a really high level of poetry.

KITE-SELLER. So, young man, sing something else for us.

HAMID. What should I sing?

KITE-SELLER. Sing Nazir, what else. Every verse of his is unique.

HAMID. Nazir has sketched his own portrait in a poem. I could recite that, with your permission.

KITE-SELLER. Permission! Mister, you are not sitting with a person who merely trades in poetry and literature but with one who loves poetry more than his own life. Sing freely and boldly.

HAMID. I'll sing of Nazir the poet, please do listen to me,

'A man timid who tutored kids, and lived in poverty.
His height was low, his gait was slow, his skin was darkly brown,
A small, frail and well-bred man who lived in Agra town.
A wreath-like growth of thick long hair adorned a shiny pate,
Moustaches showed advancing years, by turning grey of late.
Melancholy or pensiveness pursued him everywhere,
Evident in his late years, in youth too it was there.
God to him was very kind, and though he had no luxury,
His basic needs were always met, and he lived with dignity.'

ALL. Remarkable! What humility!

Enter Nazir's granddaughter humming 'Krishna's childhood days'.

KITE-SELLER. Come here, child!

GRANDDAUGHTER. In a moment. (*Exits to the opposite side.*)

The cops who were among those listening to the poems and who were constantly turning to look at the brothel, approach the paan shop.

FIRST COP. Make two paans for us. (*To the other cop*) It's quite late in the day. But this fellow's still stuck there.

SECOND COP. Are you sure he's still there and hasn't already bolted?

FIRST COP. There's only one exit and I've had my eyes fixed on that door.

SECOND COP. What if he never went there? Will we keep waiting here for ever?

FIRST COP. How can that be? Constable-sahib himself has seen him there.

SECOND COP. He must've seen him last evening. Suppose he left in the night?

The madari enters with his bear, followed by a group of children. The bear performs.

MADARI. Wherever I go, I have in tow, this bear cub,
One day, along the way, I saw this lovely bear cub,
I looked around, until I found, this bear cub,
Cost money, and lived on honey, this bear cub,
He grew, and became a bear true, this bear cub,
Everywhere I go, I have in tow, this bear cub.

Wherever I walk, they only talk of one thing,
'What happened to the ape you used to bring?'
I laugh and say, this is the way I make a living,
I took that ape, by the nape, and untied its string,
The very day came home to stay, this bear cub.

I am wary and always carry this heavy whip,
With metal rings that crackle from top to tip,
A bowl in hand, and a bag from shoulder to hip,
I bring it to the market square to jump and skip,
I walk ahead and thus I lead this bear cub.

The cub is dressed in the best jewels of every hue,
Golden bangles on his wrists that shine like new,
Bells on his feet, in his ears rings like pearly dew,
The silken cord made up of red, green and blue,
That is the leash on which I lead this bear cub.

Called to grapple, he readies for the battle at hand,
Falls on me and soon you see us rolling in the sand,
Sometimes he, at others I, have the upper hand,
And so we strive, to give this performance grand.
I don't give in, nor accepts defeat, this bear cub.

The moves we devise are amazing in style
As this performance goes on for a while,
Money rains down and collects in a pile,
Everyone is happy and declares with a smile:
'Oh what show, what a marvellous show, by this bear cub!'

Madari exits. Nazir's granddaughter returns carrying a toy. Kite-seller brings her to the shop.

GIRL (*showing the toy*). Look what I bought!

KITE-SELLER. Wangled the money from grandpa, didn't you?

GIRL. Oh, no! Not really.

KITE-SELLER. Then, did you get it for free or what?

GIRLS. It was lying in the house.

KITE-SELLER. What was?

GIRL. You know my grandpa doesn't touch money. Just as my mother tells us not to touch anything dirty, grandpa too doesn't touch money. So he wrapped it in a kerchief and threw it into a corner.

KITE-SELLER. And you picked it up?

GIRL. But not all of it! (*Runs off. Kite-seller laughs.*)

KITE-SELLER (*to Beni Prasad*). 'If you are a lover true, even for the shroud don't save a soul.' Recently, Nawab Sa'adat Ali Khan sent a bagful of money to Nazir. The money lay there in the house and Nazir slept not a wink all night because of it. As soon as it was morning, he sent word to the Nawab saying that if a brief relationship could result in this, he shuddered to think what would happen if the relationship became a permanent one. He was invited repeatedly but he refused to leave Agra. His usual excuse was: 'I am but a small and insignificant pen-pusher, how can I dare think of anything else!' He saw the whole world sitting in Agra. He writes (*raising voice*):

'Nazir, all books revealed their meaning
When I read the book of the human heart.'

The reference is to Book-seller who cannot but be irritated by it.

KAKRI-SELLER. Where does Mian Nazir live?

KITE-SELLER. Why? What's the matter?

KAKRI-SELLER. You know I wanted to . . . No, it's nothing.

KITE-SELLER. Come on, tell me!

KAKRI-SELLER. I wanted him to write a verse or two on my kakri.

KITE-SELLER (*bursting into laughter*). What an excellent idea! Who better than Nazir for this assignment! A few days ago, a gentleman showed up at Nazir's door with a doleful tale of a broken heart. He was jilted by a beautiful woman. He told the poet his condition and wanted to know how he could console his heart which gave him no respite from the thought of his beloved. Nazir wrote a poem appropriate to his condition and gave it to him. This helped the gentleman find peace. Now he wanders about humming that poem and is perfectly happy and content.

KAKRI-SELLER. Where does he live, this poet?

KITE-SELLER. Have you seen Begum Banda's palace?

KAKRI-SELLER. No.

KITE-SELLER. Where are you from?

KAKRI-SELLER. From near Delhi.

KITE-SELLER. All right, do you know the Tajganj locality?

KAKRI-SELLER. Yes.

KITE-SELLER. Good. Go there and ask for Malikonwali Lane. Once you reach there, you'll find Begum Banda's palace. There is a small house next to it. That is where Nazir lives.

Excited, Kakri-seller runs towards the left where he bumps into a stranger.

STRANGER. Are you blind?

KAKRI-SELLER. Forgive me, sir, I am in somewhat of a hurry. (*Goes off.*)

The stranger wanders about the market.

KITE-SELLER (*ostensibly for the benefit of Hamid and others who are still gathered there*). Nazir makes no distinction between men, be it a kite-seller or bookseller. (*Raising his voice*) For him, they are both human beings.

Book-seller turns red with anger.

STRANGER (*to Book-seller*). Gentleman, do you have Naasikh's works?

BOOK-SELLER (*taking out his anger on the stranger*). Naasikh is a greenhorn. He's just started writing and you want his works! If you're so keen to read him, you should go to Lucknow and listen to him in person.

STRANGER. There were some people talking about him here. I heard one of his verses, so I thought . . .

BOOK-SELLER. That I have gathered people to advertise my books! What ignorance! God help me!

Stranger is cowed down for a moment, then turns and asserts himself.

STRANGER. Sir, why are so many persons gathered here?

BOOK-SELLER (*exploding*). Sir, they are all ignorant like you. They have assembled there to listen to the poetry of another ignoramus. (*Taken aback, the stranger goes off. A loud guffaw from those assembled.*) What strange people one has to deal with! I've been sitting here all morning and not a soul has come to buy a book. They just walk in with weird queries. Damn!

Munshi Ganga Prasad enters and approaches the bookshop.

BOOK-SELLER. Greetings, Munshiji! How are you, sir?

GANGA PRASAD. I am well, thank you. Who was this joker you sent to me? And why?

BOOK-SELLER. Why would I send him to you? Your name came up during the conversation. He was looking for somebody to finance the publication of his book. You know that I don't have any money. So he must have got it into his head to approach you.

GANGA PRASAD. Listen, I've had enough of Urdu–Persian books. I've decided to start a newspaper in English from Delhi. In fact, I came here to tell you that you too should give up selling books and get into the newspaper and journals business. Times are changing and you must adopt new ways.

BOOK-SELLER. This is exactly what I've been thinking. That I should leave Agra, move to Delhi and establish myself in the newspaper and journals business.

GANGA PRASAD. If you move to Delhi, who will send news reports from Agra? No, sir, you will stay right here.

BOOK-SELLER. But for an English language newspaper . . .

GANGA PRASAD. You send your dispatches in Urdu. I'll get them translated into English.

BOOK-SELLER. Why not bring out a newspaper in Urdu as well?

GANGA PRASAD. Come on, how many will read a newspaper in Urdu? No, sir, the newspaper will have to be in English. That is the language of the future. It will be the language of the whole country tomorrow. We will need to draw up an agreement. After discussing the conditions, we will sign a proper contract in order to avoid the kind of misunderstandings that had taken place in connection with the publication of *Diwaan-e-Haafiz*.

BOOK-SELLER. There is one thing that worries me. Before starting the newspaper business, I would have liked to lighten a burden that weighs on my mind.

GAGA PRASAD. Which burden?

BOOK-SELLER. There are a few small texts I want to publish.

GANGA PRASAD. For example?

BOOK-SELLER. Some madarasa textbooks—*Kareema, Ma-muqueema, Aamadnaama*, etc. I do not have even 10 rupees to invest in this project.

GANGA PRASAD. Why? You must have made some money from the 250 copies of *Diwaan-e-Haafiz*?

BOOK-SELLER. Sir, you are mistaken. I gave away all my copies to my friends and did not charge them anything.

GANGA PRASAD. And instead of giving me a share of the money, you just presented me with the rest of the 250 copies. I don't even have a single friend to whom I could gift the *Diwaan-e-Haafiz*.

BOOK-SELLER. As far as I remember that was what we had decided. I also incurred a loss in this venture. All my labour was wasted. However, if you still think that this was not the agreed arrangement, you could send those 250 copies to me and I will give you the money as and when they are sold.

GANGA PRASAD. Mister, there is hardly any chance of their being sold now. Who will buy them? Let's forget about it. Why don't you just start the newspaper business? That work will itself bring you the necessary capital to publish *Kareema, Ma-Muqueema,* and other such useless stuff. Though, in my view, publishing these texts will be a futile exercise and you are again likely to incur a loss. How many in the new schools will read *Aamadnaama*? I must take your leave now. I'll see you again in a day or two. Goodbye.

Ganga Prasad leaves. Rake comes down from Benazir's brothel. The cops hide in a corner and as soon as Rake appears, they pounce on him and hold him down.

RAKE. Let me go, you bastards! Why are you attacking me, you sons of bitches? Since when has it become a crime in this crazy town to visit a tart?

KITE-SELLER. What is the matter, friends? Why are you arresting this man?

FIRST COP. He instigated a riot here yesterday.

RAKE. Hey! Who instigated a riot? And when? Do you have any witnesses?

SECOND COP. Come to the police station. You can meet your witness there.

POTTER. Brother, you've caught the wrong man. The quarrel was between some other people. I didn't see him here at the time.

SECOND COP. We don't know all that. We have to follow our orders.

FIRST COP. Come on, let's do our work. Don't pay any attention to him.

RAKE. Your constable turns out to be quite a sissy. I had thought I was dealing with a Ravana, that he and I would fight over Sita's abduction in a face-to-face battle. I didn't realize your town is full of the fairies of paradise!

FIRST COP. This is not a court. Whatever you have to say, you should say there. Enough, now come on! (*Exits with Rake.*)

KITE-SELLER. What was that all about?

POTTER. I was here. I never saw that man during the quarrel yesterday.

LADDOO-SELLER. How can one be sure in all that confusion? He could have been here, who knows?

BENI PRASAD. So many people were there. How could you notice everyone? Can you identify all of them, Ramu?

POTTER. I can't say that, brother. However, if I see them, I'll perhaps be able to identify some of them. But, friends, had this man been among the rioters, I could not have failed to notice him. I would definitely have known.

LADDOO-SELLER. On what basis can you say that? What is so special about this man—does he have wings?

POTTER. His clothes, his face, the flowers around his wrist. No one of his description came into the market yesterday. This man seems to have come from some other place. I saw him pursuing a prostitute in the evening.

LADDOO-SELLER. It is also possible that he was the one who instigated the riot. He does not have to appear in public to do that.

POTTER. That I don't know. But just think. If he is a stranger in this town, how can he instigate a riot here?

MELLON-SELLER. Why can't he?

POTTER. You should look to your own safety and not talk so big.

Kakri-seller enters briskly. His face blooming, a song on his lips, he is followed by a row of noisy children. He sits on the bench in front of the paan shop and starts singing while selling kakris. Every stanza brings him a customer or two.

KAKRI-SELLER. O how wondrous are the kakris of Agra,
    The best of course are those from Iskandara,
    How slender and delicate, how lovely to behold,
    Like strips of sugarcane, or threads of silk and gold,
    Like Farhaad's liquid eyes or Shirin's slender mould,
    Like Laila's shapely fingers, or Majnu's tears cold,
    O how wondrous are the kakris of Agra.

    Some are pale yellow and some lush green,
    Topaz and emeralds in their lustre and sheen,
    Those that are round are Heer's bangles green,
    Straight ones like Ranjha's flute ever so keen,
    O how wondrous are the kakris of Agra.

    Crunchy and crisp, though tender to touch,
    In beating the heat the kakri helps much,
    Cools the eyes, soothes the heart, I can vouch,
    Call it not kakri, it's a miracle as such,
    O how wondrous are the kakris of Agra.

Kakri-seller goes out singing and dancing. Enter Melon-seller, singing.

MELON-SELLER. Melons these days are the town's talk,
    You will find this fruit wherever you walk,
    Irrigates the heart when it's dry as chalk,
    In quenching the thirst it's right on the mark,
    Come buy my melon don't stand there, don't balk.

Exits. Laddoo-seller enters, singing.

LADDOO-SELLER. I sent for molasses and rolled sesame laddoos,
   In one street after another, I sold sesame laddoos,
   Promising pleasures untold, sesame laddoos,
   For everyone, young or old, sesame laddoos,
   I sent for molasses and rolled sesame laddoos.

Constable enters and goes straight to Benazir's brothel.

CONSTABLE. Is madam alone?

DRUMMER. Please have a seat. I will go and tell her. (*Goes out.*)

SARANGI PLAYER. You are early today, sir?

CONSTABLE. Why, it's already time for the evening prayers.

SARANGI PLAYER. That's right, sir.

Benazir enters.

BENAZIR. Greetings. It seems your heart could not find peace at home or at work today.

CONSTABLE. When has my heart ever found comfort at home or at work? Besides, yesterday I discovered that you have introduced a new rule of 'first come first served.' So you might say that I set out yesterday and have at last arrived at the beloved's doorstep. You have not promised this evening to any one else, have you?

BENAZIR. I have promised it to you too.

CONSTABLE. Well, you trade in promises. It is remarkable that you remember. Anyway, today I am armed.

BENAZIR. Did you come here yesterday without your weapon?

CONSTABLE. Yes madam, I had forgotten my weapon yesterday. But today the bow and arrows are all intact.

BENAZIR. What kind of archer are you to carry all your other equipment except the crucial bow and arrow? Well, where should I begin? (*Opening the paan-daan*) How careless of them! There is not a single paan in here and no one has had the sense to go down and buy a few.

Drummer comes forward to take the money to buy the paans. But he is pre-empted by Manzoor Hussain, who had come in earlier and who now hurries off to buy paans.

CONSTABLE. Is he one of your lovers?

BENAZIR. A very old one.

CONSTABLE. Never saw him before.

BENAZIR. Do you keep a list? He has been known to me for the last 8 or 10 years. He has only recently adopted this mendicancy, humility and silence. He used to be a rich man. He would express his love through words and deeds—in other words, in the practice of love he employed his tongue, his limbs, every part of his body. Now he has wrapped me up entirely in the blanket of his heart and soul.

CONSTABLE. You must be very cosy in there. He does not feel jealous, does he?

BENAZIR. He is long past that stage.

CONSTABLE. Is he mad? Is he able to comprehend when one talks to him?

BENAZIR. His name is Manzoor Hussain, but he turns away if anyone calls him by that name.

CONSTABLE. Why?

BENAZIR. Who knows! Maybe he has started hating his own name. He seems all right mentally. People say he will start speaking again one day when conditions improve.

Manzoor Hussain returns with the paans.

CONSTABLE. Manzoor Hussain!

Manzoor Hussain gets up hurriedly and leaves. Constable guffaws. Fakirs enter singing 'Aadminaama'. The actors enter and join in the chorus.

CHORUS. Man is the king who rules over the rest,
Man's the one who is wretched and oppressed,
Man the one clad in rags or richly dressed,
He also is man who dines on the best,
And the one who lives on crumbs too is man.

They are men who build temples and mosques,
Men are also those who perform religious tasks,
Men also those who pray and recite holy texts,
Men steal devotees' shoes and indulge in other thefts,
And the one who catches the thief too is man.

Here, a man is willing to give his life for another,
He too is man who kills and commits murder,
It's man who betrays and humiliates his brother,
It's man who calls for help and succour to another,
The one who rushes out to help too is man.

It's man who has shops and trades in things,
One man buys what another man brings,
Man makes and sells a variety of things,
To hawk his wares he shouts or sings,
And the one who offers to buy too is man.

Man earns greatness by scaling great heights,
Another on man's fair name is a blight,
He too is man who is dark as the night,

Another like the moon is fair and light,
The one who is brutish and ugly too is man.

Men wash the dead and stitch the shroud,
Collect round the body, their sad heads bowed,
Friends lift the coffin, followed by a crowd,
Some chant the *kalma* and some weep aloud,
And the one who lies there dead too is man.

The noble, ignoble, the king and his slave,
Respectable wise man to contemptible knave,
He who sought knowledge and he who knowledge gave
Man is the best of the best that we have
And the worst and the meanest too is man.

The singing and the music reach a crescendo and the curtain comes down briskly.

THE END

1 Interpretation of the Prophet's words; analysis and criticism; and the art of *tazkira* writing, respectively.

2 'The Tale of the Four Wanderers'.

3 Akbar II (1760–1837), also known as Akbar Shah II, the penultimate Mughal emperor of India.

4 The Greatest Fort, a reference to the Red Fort in Delhi.

5 Used during the British Rule as a title for anyone who had an English education.

6 In the original couplet, which is in Persian, the wit is in the use of the words 'idol' and 'Ram'. The former traditionally refers to the hard-hearted beloved and the latter, as a verb, means 'to conquer'.

7 Fughan (Ashraf Ali Khan) was an eighteenth-century Urdu poet. Dard refers to Syed Khwaja Mir, also an Urdu poet of the eighteenth century. Mir Hassan was a stylist who wrote the famous *mathnavi* 'Sahar-ul-Bayaan'.

8 An obscene song traditionally sung at weddings.

9 The Rake is here playing with Benazir's name which, literally, means 'matchless'.

10 Benazir asks this question in Punjabi and the guest's response is in the same language.

11 *The Kareema* is a book of poems in Persian by the famous Sufi poet Sheikh Sa'adi. *Ma-Muqueema* is a similar book by another author. Both works formed part of the Persian syllabus in the madarasas. *Aamadnaama* is the first book of Persian grammar.

12 A traditional form of address for fakirs.

GLOSSARY

Aflatoon	the Arabic name for Plato
baksheesh	tip
besan roti	bread made of gram flour
chana	chickpea
chhadam, damri	small denomination of the prevalent currency
dholak	traditional drum
fakir	mendicants who sing or chant and receive alms; often associated with the *sufi* (mystical) tradition
ghazal	poetic form specific to Urdu and Persian
kafni	traditional shroud-like robe (usually green) worn by fakirs
kakri	variety of cucumber, peculiar to north India
Kalma	basic text of the Muslim creed
kauri	cowry shell, used as small currency in the past
laddoo	round sweets made of sesame seed and molasses or sugar
Madari	one who trains animals and makes them perform
mathnavi	poetic form in Urdu and Persian poetry
Maulana, Maulvi	title or form of address for a learned person
mridang	traditional drum
mushaira	poetry-reading session

nazm	poetic form in Urdu and Persian poetry
paan	betel leaf prepared as a popular digestive
paan-daan	traditional partitioned container to hold all the ingredients necessary to prepare paan
quasida	poetic form of eulogy
rewri	small sesame-seed candies
Shahar Ashob	traditional poetic form which laments or describes the hardships faced by the denizens of a town
Tazkiranawis	one who compiles and chronicles biographical as well as literary information about known poets and writers; the closest English term perhaps is 'biographer'.

CHARANDAS CHOR

Translated by Anjum Katyal

INTRODUCTION

JAVED MALICK

'Folk' became the buzz word in cultural parlance somewhere during the 1960s. It wasn't so when Habib Tanvir began his career in the theatre at least a whole decade before that. In fact, he can be regarded as one of the pioneers of the interest in folk forms and traditions in modern Indian theatre.

Tanvir's interest in the folk dates back to his IPTA (Indian People's Theatre Association) days in Bombay during the late 1940s. The Bombay IPTA was divided into various linguistic groups—Hindi, Gujarati, Marathi, Konkani and so on. All these groups, Tanvir recalls, had strong music squads and 'some of the great names in the world of music—among them, Annabhau Sathe and Amar Sheikh—were associated with them.' They drew upon traditional forms like the burrakatha and pawara in their work. Exposure to their work had the effect of making Tanvir interested in his own (Chhattisgarh) background. As a child, he had often visited villages and listened to the music and songs of the local folk. He was so fascinated by their catchy melodies that he memorized quite a few of them. His association with IPTA rekindled this early interest and he returned to that music and began to collect Chhattisgarhi folk songs in earnest.

In 1954, Tanvir moved to Delhi where he wrote and produced Agra Bazar, his first major stage production. The play is based on the works and times of a very unusual eighteenth-century Urdu poet, Nazir Akbarabadi, who not only wrote about ordinary people and their everyday concerns, but wrote in a style and idiom which disregarded the orthodox, elitist norms of decorum in poetic expression and subject matter. Using a mix of educated, middle-class urban actors and more or less illiterate folk and street artists from the village of Okhla, what Tanvir, in a highly interesting (and, for its time, revolutionary) artistic strategy, put on the stage was not the socially and architecturally walled-in space of a private dwelling, but a bazar—a marketplace with all its noise and bustle, its instances of solidarity and antagonism, and, above all, with all its sharp social, economic, and cultural polarities.

Agra Bazar is neither strictly biographical in theme nor simply commem-orative in impulse and form. Its overall flavour is simultaneously contestatory and celebratory. It deals with and valorizes a poetry that takes the ordinary people, their lives, and their everyday struggles as both its inspiration and its addressee. It offers a joyful celebration of what Mikhail Bakhtin calls 'the cul-ture of the marketplace.'[1] At the same time, it also uses the example of Nazir's poetry and his plebeian appeal to challenge orthodox, elitist aesthetics.

Tanvir produced Agra Bazar at a time when the urban stage scene in Delhi, as in many other places, was dominated by amateur and collegiate drama groups which offered English plays in English or in vernacular translation to a socially restricted section of the city's anglophone elite. These groups, as also the National School of Drama (NSD) a decade later, derived their concept of theatre, their standards of acting, staging and direction from the European mod-els of the late nineteenth and early twentieth centuries. There was little effort to link theatre work to the indigenous traditions of performance, or even to say anything of immediate value and interest to an Indian audience. In contrast to this, Tanvir offered an experience radically different, both in form and content, from anything that the fashionable westernized theatre could offer.

Agra Bazar also marked the beginning of that artistic and ideological predilection for the plebeian, popular culture which continues to inform Tanvir's approach to theatre to this day. Soon after this production, he went to England for training in theatre. He spent more than three years studying theatre at the Royal Academy of Dramatic Arts and Bristol Old Vic Theatre School, as well as travelling extensively through Europe and watching a lot of theatre.[2] On returning to India, he quickly unlearned much of what he was taught at RADA—thus following a trajectory of development diametrically opposite to that followed by other British-trained theatre persons. However, he did feel greatly inspired by the experience of watching theatres of different European peoples.[3] And he returned doubly convinced that no truly worthwhile theatre—that is, no socially meaningful and artistically interesting theatre—was possible unless one worked within one's own cultural traditions and context.

Disregarding the colonial mind-set that dominated the contemporary theatre scene at the time, Tanvir began his long quest for an indigenous performance idiom. This period marks the beginning of his involvement with the folk artists of Chhattisgarh. His first production, mounted soon after returning from Europe, was *Mitti ki Gadi*, a translation of Shudraka's Mrichchhakatikam. The cast included six folk actors from Chhattisgarh and the production derived its conventions and techniques from the folk stage, thus giving it a distinctly Indian form and style. The production, which is still revived from time to time (although it is now performed entirely by village actors), is considered by many as one of the best modern renderings of the ancient classic.

Mitti ki Gadi was based on, and illustrated, Tanvir's conviction that the style and techniques of the folk theatre are akin to the ones implied in the dramaturgy of the Sanskrit playwrights. He believes that the theatrical style of the latter can be accessed through folk traditions. The imaginative flexibility and simplicity with which the classical playwrights establish and shift the time and place of action in a play, Tanvir argues, is found in abundance in our folk performances.[4] *Mitti ki Gadi* is a practical demonstration of this belief. For example, changes in time and locale in the production are suggested through dialogues and movements without formally interrupting the performance. When a character orders his subordinate to go to the garden and see if there is the body of a woman there, the subordinate simply runs around the stage once and returns with the answer, 'I went to the garden and found that there is a woman's body there.'

In 1959, Tanvir and his wife Moneeka Misra formed their own company, Naya Theatre, and continued to produce a variety of plays, including modern and ancient classics of Indian and European traditions. Although most of these plays were produced with urban actors (mostly college students, teachers, and other types of drama enthusiasts), Tanvir's interest in the folk traditions and performers had come to stay and continued to grow. However, it was not until the early 1970s that this involvement reached a new and more sustained phase.

Tanvir was not entirely satisfied with his work with folk actors. He recognized two difficulties or faults (as he calls them) in his approach to them. One, the way he fixed the performance rather rigidly in advance by blocking movements and arranging lighting on paper. This, he felt, did not work with the rural artists who could not read or write and could not even remember which way and on what line they should move. The second difficulty was that he was doing plays in Hindi or Hindustani. Making these actors speak standard Hindi, a language they were not accustomed to, was to make them work with a severe handicap. It impeded the full and free expression of their creativity. As a result, their confidence and impact as actors was undermined.

Tanvir began to rid his style of work of these flaws. He started using the method of improvisations. He also allowed the folk actors to speak in their native Chhattisgarhi dialect. From 1970 to 1973, which he regards as an exploratory phase, he worked intensively with rural performers in their native language and style of performance. He allowed them to do their own traditional pieces mostly in their own way, merely editing and touching them up here and there to make them more stageworthy. During this period he tried many things, from temple rituals to stock skits and pandavani.

The breakthrough came in 1973, during a month-long nacha workshop that Tanvir conducted in Raipur. More than a hundred folk artists of the region participated, along with several observers including university students and professors from Raipur and folklorists and anthropologists from Delhi and Calcutta. During the workshop, three different traditional comedies from the stock nacha repertoire were selected and more or less dovetailed into one another to make one compact, full-length play. A few short scenes were inserted to link them up into one story. A number of songs, which had never before been brought on the stage—such as the songs that the villagers sing while working in the fields, marriage songs, or temple songs—were also included after appropriate editing. The production which was thus created was called *Gaon ka Naam Sasural, Mor Naam Damaad*, an almost wholly improvised stage play.

Tanvir felt that he had broken new ground. After several performances in Chhattisgarh and Bhopal, the play was brought to Delhi and found an appreciative audience filling the hall evening after evening. This was something which had never happened to his productions before. 'The audiences not only came in large number but enjoyed the play from beginning to end, laughing at the jokes, relishing the music and so on. Despite the chaste Chhattisgarhi dialect, the abhinaya of the folk actors was so clear and their performance so remarkable and energetic that nobody had any problem in following or enjoying the play. And I felt that my theatre had now transcended the language barrier.'

This was a turning point in Tanvir's development. Ever since his arrival on the urban theatre scene as a director in the 1950s, he had been searching for a form of theatre which would draw upon and reflect India's cultural traditions. After the 1973 workshop, Tanvir felt that he had found such a form. It now became easier for him to go on with the construction and casting of a play through improvisations—a method that he continues to use to this day.

Tanvir's theatre derives its inspiration, its actors, techniques, stage conventions, and often, even its plots from the folk tradition. This invests it with an unmistakable folk flavour. Nonetheless, it cannot be described as folk theatre.

Tanvir is a conscious artist with a modern outlook, sensibility, and a strong sense of history and politics. His interest in folk culture and his decision to work with and in terms of traditional styles of performance was an ideological choice as much as an aesthetic one, whether Tanvir himself was fully conscious of it as such or not. There is a close connection between his predilection for popular traditions and his left-wing disposition. I have mentioned that his approach to theatre is rooted in his IPTA and PWA (Progressive Writers' Association) background during the politically surcharged atmosphere of the 1940s. This involvement with the left-wing cultural movement, an association which he has maintained (no matter how loosely) to this day, already meant a commitment to the common people and their causes. His work in the theatre, in style as well as in content, reflects this commitment and can be seen as part of a larger (socialist) project of empowerment of the people.

In the half century of his association with the stage, Tanvir has written and staged many original plays, offered improvisations from the traditional folk repertoire, produced Sanskrit classics as well as translations and adaptations of Shakespeare, Molière and Brecht. An overview of his oeuvre—particularly from Agra Bazar to his recent adaptation of Shakespeare's *A Midsummer Night's Dream*—reveals a sustained endeavour on his part to develop and perfect a style of theatre which is both 'traditional,' in the sense of being oriented towards folk and popular forms, and 'modern,' in the sense of being alert to the major issues and concerns of contemporary existence and experience. These concerns may be cultural (as in *Agra Bazar* which focuses on the conflict between the elitist mores and a robustly plebeian concept of poetry and language), psychological (as in *Bahadur the Wine-Seller*, a powerful folktale dealing with a son's incestuous disposition towards his mother), philosophical (as in *Dekh Rahey Hain Nain*, which is based on a short story by Stefan Zweig and explores the questions of action and its consequence in terms of human suffering), or expressly political (as in *Hirma ki Amar Kahani* which foregrounds and critically interrogates the issues of development and centralization of political power). But no matter what the issue or theme and how traditional the basic plot, Tanvir has a way of imbuing his work with a socio-political dimension. He weaves into any material that he works with certain elements (such as choric comments and sequences of action) which unmistakably point to the play's political import and emphasize the harsh reality of the everyday life of the people. For example, when Tanvir took up *Mrichchhakatikam* for staging, he not only sharpened the political theme already present in the original but also gave it a subtle plebeian bias by foregrounding, as a prominent cognitive concern, the vision of a just, happy and liberatory social arrangement.

Tanvir's approach to the folk distinguishes itself from that of many others in contemporary theatre in two significant ways—both of which, I feel, are aspects of his political consciousness and are reflected in his attitude to traditional forms and traditional performers. First, Tanvir's fascination with the folk is not motivated by a revivalist or an antiquarian impulse. It is based, instead, on an awareness of the tremendous creative possibilities and artistic energies inherent in these traditions, and, equally, on a recognition of their continuing social vitality in rural India despite a serious erosion and debasement in the wake of ruthless urbanization and homogenization through cinema and TV. He does not hesitate to borrow themes, techniques, and music from them, but he also desists from the impossible task of trying to resurrect old traditions in their original form and also from presenting them as stuffed museum pieces.

Although Tanvir's theatre is based on folk and tribal traditions, it does not, a popular misconception notwithstanding, really belong within any one form or tradition in its entirety or purity. In fact, as he is quick to point out, he has not been 'running after folk forms' as such at all but only after folk performers who brought their own forms and styles with them.[5] The performance style of his actors is, no doubt, rooted in their traditional nacha background, but his plays are not authentic nacha productions.

For one thing, while the number of actual actors in nacha play is usually restricted to two or three, the rest being stop-gap singers and dancers, Tanvir's productions involve a full cast of actors, some of whom also sing and dance. More significantly, his plays have a structural coherence and complexity which one does not usually associate with the authentic nacha plays. Songs and dances in his plays are neither purely ornamental in function nor are they formally autonomous units (musical interludes) inserted into a loose collection of separate skits, as they are in the nacha. They are integrated into the action and form an important part of the total thematic and artistic structure of the play.

Secondly, Tanvir does not romanticize the 'folk' uncritically or ahistorically. He is aware of their historical and cognitive limitations and does not hesitate to intervene in them and allow his own modern consciousness and political understanding to interact with the traditional energies and skills of his performers.

His project, from the beginning of his career, has been to harness elements of the folk traditions as a vehicle and make them yield new, contemporary meanings and to produce a theatre which has a touch of the soil about it. 'This,' he declares, 'has been the driving force of all my work since *Agra Bazar*.'

However, Tanvir also recognizes and respects the immense creativity of the folk imagination. His approach is not exploitative in the sense of merely using the folk for one's own ends. In fact, he is quite careful not to create a hierarchy by privileging, in any absolute and extrinsic way, his own educated consciousness as poet-cum-playwright-cum-director over the unschooled creativity of his actors. In his work, the two usually meet and interpenetrate, as it were, as equal partners in a collective, collaborative endeavour in which each gives and takes from, and thus enriches, the other. An excellent example of this non-exploitative approach is the way Tanvir fits and blends his poetry with the traditional folk and tribal music, allowing the former to retain its own imaginative and rhetorical power and socio-political import, but without in any way devaluing or destroying the latter.

Thus, in contrast to the fashionable, folksy kind of drama on the one hand and the revivalist kind of 'traditional' theatre on the other, Tanvir's theatre offers a rich and incisive blend of tradition and modernity, folk creativity and skills and modern critical consciousness. He works consciously and painstakingly (sometimes retiring to the interiors of Chhattisgarh for weeks) in order to achieve this strong sense of socio-political immediacy and artistic sophistication without losing any of the energy, beauty, and simplicity of a folk performance.

Of all his productions, Tanvir's *Charandas Chor* is the most popular. It is also his most frequently performed and most widely travelled production. In the 20 years since its creation, the play has had hundreds of performances in scores of places in India and Europe. It has come to be regarded as a masterpiece, indeed, a classic of contemporary Indian theatre. It is also an excellent example of the kind of theatre Tanvir has been practising and which I have tried to describe above.

Charandas Chor had a long and interesting genesis, involving a protracted process (about two years) of experimentation and improvisation before it reached its final shape in 1975. Briefly, Tanvir first heard the story in 1973 from the writer-folklorist Vijaydan Detha, who had, in turn, recorded it from the oral cultural tradition of Rajasthan. Later that year, Tanvir tried to use the story during a *khayal* workshop in Rajasthan. But it did not work. Some time later, he held a month-long workshop with several nacha groups in Bhilai, towards the end of which he made his actors do an improvisation on this Rajasthani folktale about a thief. A rough shape emerged from this exercise. Tanvir presented this far-from-finished attempt at an all-night function of the Satnamis (a religious sect) in the open-air Bhilai maidan, incorporating into it a number of *panthi* songs and instantaneously improvising some others.[6] This became the first, embryonic form of the play. It was about fifty minutes in duration and Tanvir called it *Chor, Chor*.

Encouraged by the enthusiastic response that the play received (mainly because of its theme, according to Tanvir) from that huge gathering of Satnamis, Tanvir went on to work on it and rehearse it more seriously. He wrote new scenes to flesh out the basic plot of the story. He slightly modified the original ending. In Detha's version, the thief is killed for his vows and the queen's offer is accepted by the guru who becomes the king. Tanvir's play departs from this. While he ends the story itself with the dramatic highpoint of the thief's execution (leaving out the guru's opportunism), he prolongs the play itself by adding a sequence which, accompanied by a chorus in praise of truth, shows the thief's posthumous deification by the people. Through this and the last chorus, he brings the performance to an anti-climactic conclusion.[7]

The production also broke new ground in terms of staging. Its simple, bare stage design was arrived at after a number of experiments, during which several things (including a long, painted curtain for the backdrop) were tried out. The design is austere in its simplicity but highly effective in functional terms. All that it requires is a stage and, mounted on that stage, a rectangular platform which is 9 inches high, 6 feet wide and 12 feet long, with just foliage or a leafy branch of a tree behind it. The spaces created by this austere architectural design are used in different ways throughout the production. For the opening scene between the policeman and the thief, only the forestage is used. But in the 'guru dakshina' scene, the entire stage comes into use, with the guru and some of his followers sitting on the platform and the rest scattered all over the stage. It is the same in the next scene where the landlord and his storage of foodgrains are on the platform, but the peasants, Charandas and, finally, the Rawat dancers use the forestage.

In an innovative and visually pleasing strategy, the platform on the stage is approached sometimes in a rectilinear fashion (as, for example, in the 'guru dakshina' scene where the guru sits facing the audience), and sometimes diagonally (as in the temple scene where the idol is placed downstage left and congregation stands facing it). This creates an interesting variation in the spectator's perception of the stage, which appears physically altered.

Stage props are kept to the minimum—only objects which are actually used in the action, such as the treasure chest or the idol or the sacks of rice—and no elaborate lighting is required. Change in the locale is suggested almost entirely through changing the grouping and not by any physical rearrangement of the stage. During the early scenes, the stage is quite flexible and informal. But after the first half of the play, it suddenly takes on a formal and sharply defined quality in order to present the royal treasury, the queen's court and her bedchamber. The grouping is also significantly more formal in these last scenes.

The spartan stage design also allows the actors and their performances to be foregrounded. This is important since a great deal of the play's appeal in performance depends on the remarkable quality of Tanvir's folk actors. The uncluttered performance space brings the amazing dexterity and skill of the actors and their various antics into sharper focus. Further, this minimalist stage design reinforces the sense of openness that lies at the heart of the play's story. Unhampered by any physical changes in the scene, the action unfolds briskly and grippingly from one scene to another, like a tale of adventure or a fairytale (which is what this story about an honest thief really is, on one level), until the last episode when its serious import suddenly bursts into focus.

Songs are a major element in *Charandas Chor*, as they indeed are in every production of Tanvir's. Tanvir worked closely with some Chhattisgarhi folk poets to get these songs composed. They possess a certain simplicity of style and expression which comes from the folk tradition. They are set to delightful folk tunes and contribute immensely towards enhancing the play's pleasurability in performance.[8] However, in a style reminiscent of Brecht, Tanvir also uses them to comment on an action and to elucidate and underline its larger moral and social significance. In some cases, they reflect a certain complexity of articulation and consciousness which is obviously Tanvir's contribution. For example, the refrain in the *panthi* song in the second act, 'Oh, Charandas, don't try to rob Death of his due,' was deliberately added because Tanvir wanted it to work on the audience's mind subliminally, preparing them for the death that comes at the end of the play. Similarly, the last chorus, 'An ordinary thief is now a famous man', which comments on Charandas's fate and articulates its significance, was almost half written by him using 'the simplicity of Nazir Akbarabadi's poetry'.

I feel that in Tanvir's major productions the real protagonist, almost invariably, is the ordinary people. This protagonist is sometimes latent, operating on the deeper, subtextual level (or, if you like, in the interstices of the episodic structure), and sometimes not so latent. In either case, it is almost always there somewhere. This collective subject of the dramatic action is implicated in a tendency towards what may be described as a Utopian horizon—akin to what the German Marxist philosopher, Ernst Bloch, refers to as 'the hope principle.' It signifies a desired, but empirically unavailable, state of happiness, the idea of an egalitarian rearrangement of society which critically reflects on and offers a radical alternative to the prevailing social order.

This Utopian dimension is particularly strong in *Charandas Chor*. It is explicit in the scene where the hoarded rice is cunningly liberated from the clutches of a cruel and avaricious landlord and redistributed amongst the starving peasants. But it also underlies the rest of the play. The central character, Charandas, himself implies it. He is a figure of the common man who is capable of virtues rare in an unjust, class-based society. He rises from the status of a petty, village thief to that of a popular hero. Significantly, the exact moment of this transformation of his image coincides in the play with his redistribution of the hoarded food amongst the poor. The moment is sharply focused by the Chorus announcing that 'Charandas is not a thief, not a thief, no way!' This chorus also underlines the contrast between Charandas's moral uprightness and benevolence and the injustices of a corrupt, anti-people system. It sings:

> There are so many rogues about, who do not look like thieves,
> Impressive turbans on their heads, softly shod their feet.
> But open up their safes and you will surely see
> Stolen goods, ill-gotten wealth, riches got for free.

Charandas, thus, can be said to stand for the ordinary toiling masses. He is conceived in terms of paradoxes and contradictions. He is a thief. Like any ordinary thief, he lives by duping and robbing people and dodging the law. But he is also an extraordinary man of principles. He is kindhearted and cannot bear to see a woman in distress. He has a strong sense of social justice and aids the poor against the rich. Above all, he is truthful and a man of his word. Caught in a critical situation, he had jokingly taken certain vows before a priest. Amazingly, he lives up to and in the end, dies for them.

Charandas Chor is constructed on the principle of carnivalesque reversal, the principle of a world turned upside down. There is a reversal of hierarchy, particularly on moral and ethical levels. Truthfulness, honesty, integrity, ethical values, and even professional efficiency are shown to belong exclusively to a thief, leaving the upper echelons of society devoid precisely of these values and virtues. Through his acts and deeds Charandas debunks religion, the state, and class economy. He shows up in the existing social order as a disorder. His integrity, uprightness, and professional efficiency are in direct contrast to the lack of these qualities in the policeman, the priest, the government official (the *munim*), the wealthy landlord and, finally, the queen. Interestingly a carnivalesque reversal of roles is also suggested when Charandas assumes the identity of the new minister to rob the royal treasury. His unshod feet, although, technically, a means through which his real identity is later recognized by the *munim*, seem symbolic of his earthiness and his link with the common (unshod) masses as against the exclusiveness and distance of the khadi-clad politician.

Furthermore, Tanvir's play does not allow the audience any monocular, cosy point of reference. Instead, it employs what is called, in the context of Shakespeare, the principle of 'multiple consciousness' and which Brecht describes as 'complex seeing.' This principle designates a complex and dialectical process of presenting a thing in such a way that its underside also becomes visible. It has the effect of destabilizing smug responses based on received, orthodox values and norms.

This can be exemplified in the way religiosity, in its orthodox sense, is constantly undercut in the play through a subversive comedy and juxtaposed with a secular, social viewpoint. There are three representations of religious ritual and practice in the play and in all of them this process of undercutting is evident.

First, there is the 'guru dakshina' scene. Although ostensibly a religious congregation, the song significantly deals not with religion or spirituality but with the impossibility of salvation without first paying the guru in material terms. Also, the guru ashram virtually becomes a hideout for drunkards, drug-addicts, gamblers, and thieves; and Charandas refers to the guru as one who robs people in broad daylight. In visual terms, too, the 'spirituality' of the scene is seriously undermined, on the one hand, by the constant in and out movements of the thief and the policeman, and, on the other hand, by the gambling and drinking that goes on merrily in a corner downstage.

The second instance occurs in the temple scene. The main action in this scene is the *arti*, a traditional religious ritual before a deity. The song that is sung at length is also devotional in tone and content. But then this religiosity is again comically undercut by the actions of the thief and the policeman who, although pretending to be part of the congregation of worshippers, actually form a comic pair of chaser and chased. They constantly weave in and out of the crowd throughout the arti with Charandas stealing the idol itself!

In the third instance, which comes at the end of the play, Charandas is posthumously deified as a saint and people pay homage to him by worshipfully filing past his *samadhi* and placing flowers on it. There is no comedy there. The entire action—beginning from the ritual of lighting a lamp and breaking a coconut to the action of filing past—is performed with great reverence. Yet there is something which distances and differentiates it from the usual kind of religious experience. No doubt we see, and are perhaps moved by, the people's worshipful attitude towards their saint. But if we are alert to the context of the play as a whole, we also see that this saint did not come out of the blue yonder. The play shows us the actual process through which a very ordinary man attains sainthood in the eyes of the common people and we recognize that the process is entirely this-worldly. In other words, we see the secular and historical stuff that saints are made of.

It is tempting to read this ritual of homage to a thief as an ironical comment. In some ways, the play is steeped in comic irony. The way in which Charandas is confronted with the choices that oblige him to live up to the pledges that he had jokingly taken; the very coexistence of honesty and integrity in a thief; the guru's acceptance of stolen goods as 'guru dakshina'— these are some of the elements which contribute towards this irony. Nonetheless, in its totality, in terms of the overall mood and flavour, the play is unmistakably celebratory rather than ironical. In this context, the last popular homage scene, too, becomes a celebration of a popular hero, and, by that token, a celebration of the people and their desire for truth and justice.

NOTES

1 See Mikhail Bakhtin, *Rabelais and His World* (Hélène Iswolsky trans.) (Cambridge, MA: MIT Press, 1968).

2 There were no drama schools in the modern sense of the term in India in those days. Anybody who desired formal and sustained training in acting and stagecraft and had the necessary financial wherewithal, went abroad, mainly to England. However, Tanvir's response to the kind of training that Royal Academy of Dramatic Arts offers was radically different from that of other Indians who went there. He found their teaching irrelevant and useless in the Indian context and objected to its alien content and orientation. He was enrolled in a two-year programme but he left it after one year and went to Bristol Old Vic Theatre to learn production.

3 For example, Tanvir spent about eight months in Berlin in 1956 and saw several recent productions by Bertolt Brecht (who had died earlier that year). He was profoundly influenced by Brecht's work.

4 Tanvir maintains that the fact that the Sanskrit drama does not conform to the Aristotelian unities of space, time and action is not a sign of structural naivety or deficiency. He finds it 'infuriating' that the Western Orientalists and their Indian followers should apologize for 'our ancient playwrights' by saying that, although they were excellent poets and had great imagination, they did not know how to construct a play, did not possess a sense of dramatic time and space. 'These scholars of Sanskrit drama did not even try to investigate as to how such imaginative and creative people as Shudraka, Bhasa, Kalidasa, and Bhavabhuti, could fail to have this organic sense of dramaturgy. In our folk tradition, it is common for a character to say, for example, "I must go to Lanka" and then run clockwise in a circle and arrive in Lanka. Then he would perhaps run anti-clockwise and return to his original place. I see a direct link between the classical and the folk as far as this

kind of disregard for the Aristotelian unities is concerned. With that kind of living tradition, I feel that there is a continuity of a certain attitude to drama, that flows from the basic tenets of Bharata Muni's *Natyashastra*.' (This and all subsequent quotes, unless differently referenced, come from a conversation I had with Tanvir in August 1955).

5 Tanvir says: 'I was not running after folk forms, I was running after folk actors. There is a big difference here because when I used the folk actors, they brought the folk forms with them. I did not have to academically impose upon them. And I did not really think a lot about the forms as such, I was freely using my imagination to interpret a play and these actors had the form. So to that extent, in that subtle and indirect manner, their forms came. But, in another sense, none of these forms are represented in my productions.'

6 To continue the story in Tanvir's own words: 'There were some 18,000 people sitting there all night and they all seemed so receptive. The crowd was full of Satnamis. Listening to them and looking at them, I thought that this play about a thief who does not abandon truth as he clings also to his profession of thievery, was very much up their street. I was inspired by these people, the central article of whose faith is "god is Truth". (Incidentally, the reason why this Rajasthani folktale took root in Chhattisgarh was precisely because of a strong Satnami tradition in that region.) So, at about 6 a.m., I announced that we had a little greenroom show—not at all stageworthy at the moment but, considering that there were so many Satnamis present and the fact that the play's theme was truth, I felt inspired to present it no matter how raw it was. They welcomed it. I also told them that they should not mind if I intervened in the middle to correct something or to sing something or to improvise something. I had a book of *panthi* songs. We improvised the melodies from that. I also sang together with the others and they caught on. We even managed some songs sitting there. In the killing scene I had to intervene to correct the soldiers, because I knew that they would go wrong.'

7 Detha, Tanvir recalls, was not very happy with this modification. 'But, being a very cultivated and open-minded man, accepted it as *my* version without any argument. He merely said: Your end is the end of evil, mine is a continuation of evil. And, of course, he had a point there. The reviewer of a Hindi

journal from Bhopal also agreed with Detha's ending, suggesting that my end does not bring out the significance. I remain unconvinced to this day.'

8   'We had a great time composing these songs,' Tanvir recalls, 'I, our folk poets, Swaran Kumar Sahu and Ganga Ram Sakhet, and a Calcutta musician, Ranu Bardhan, would sit up until two or three in the morning, listening to all kinds of tunes, playing them and improvising upon them. They would give us a tune, I would give them a tune. And we all blended tunes and imaginations together to produce the music for the play.'

Charandas Chor was first performed in the original Chhattisgarhi by Naya Theatre at Kamani Auditorium, Delhi, on 3 May 1975, with the following cast (in order of appearance):

WOMEN DANCERS	Mahila Panthi Nritya Party of Durg, led by Toran Bai
CHARANDAS	Madan Lal
HAVALDAR	Babu Das
WAYFARER	Ravi Shankar
BEJEWELLED WOMAN	Mala Bai
GURU	Thakur Ram
DRUNKARD	Majid Khan
DRUG ADDICT	Govind Ram
GAMBLER	Ravi Shankar
LANDLORD	Devi Lal
TETKU	Udai Ram
RAWAT DANCE LEADER	Jhadu Ram
RAWAT DANCERS	Prem Lal, Bishal, Krishna,
PUJARI	Lalu Ram
MUNIM	Govind Ram
SAINIKS	Brij Lal, Budharu Ram Gendre, Prem Lal, Agarahij
DIWAN	Udai Ram
RANI	Fida Bai
DASI	Mala Bai
PUROHIT	Lalu Ram
TOWN CRIERS	Mala Bai, Nageen Tanvir, Habib Tanvir
PANTHI DANCE LEADER	Deodas Banjare
PANTHI DRUMMER	Budharu Ram Jangde

PANTHI DANCERS	Lala Ram, Jaipal, Ghanshyam, Sampat Agarahij, Bala Ram, Bhaiya Ram, Phiranta Ram, Budharu Ram Gendre, Puranik Lal Chelak
CHORUS	Brij Lal, Bhulwa Ram, Mala Bai, Fida Bai
HARMONIUM	Devi Lal
TABLA	Amar Das
CLARINET	Narain Rao
CHANDRA SARANG	Gian Sharma
VIOLIN	K. C. Mehra
FLUTE	Ashok Bhattacharya
DRUMS	Gaurang Chowdhary
DOTARA	Hemen Das Gupta
DIRECTION	Habib Tanvir
COSTUMES, SETS, PROPS	Moneeka Misra Tanvir
EXECUTION OF PROPS	Inder Razdan (Naika)
LYRICS	Swaran Kumar, Ganga Ram
ORCHESTRATION	Hemen Das Gupta, Ranu Bardhan

A NOTE ON THE CHOR

The film *Charandas Chor* featured Lalu Ram as the protagonist. The first actor to play the chor in the play was Madan Lal. Subsequently, he has been played by Dwarka Prashad, Govind Ram and Deepak Tiwari.

At the very first trial or green room performance of the play, then a shorter version entitled *Chor, Chor* and performed at the Bhilai Maidan in December 1974, the chor was played by Ram Lal.

ACT ONE

SCENE ONE

A rectangular platform centre stage. About 6 feet deep, 12 feet wide and 9 inches high. At the back of this platform, slightly off-centre to the left, a tree. A group of panthi dancers[1] singing and dancing vigorously.

Satyanam! Satyanam! Satyanam!
Praise the truth, nothing better,
Praise the guru, no one greater,
Who alone brings down to us
The divine nectar of Truth.
This nectar will redeeem us,
Brought down from on high—
Where pure Truth resides—
By our holy guru.
Our guru does teach us
That Truth is so precious,
Only a handful can
Uphold the truth;
And those few are gurus

Who lead by example,
They raise the world high
On the scales of truth.
Satyanam! Satyanam! Satyanam!

As they exit, still dancing and singing energetically, Charandas enters from the other side, a heavy bundle of clothes on his back. He comes in singing:

The cat is out, the cat's about
The cat is on the prowl
All in a trice she brings down mice
And then she has a fall.

The mice they gather round about her
And tickle her whiskered chin
They giggle and wiggle, her ears they twiggle
'How come you're all done in?'

Rumble, tumble, take a ride
Off with the lid, and what's inside?
The cat is up, she wants to sup
The mice had better beware
She'll hobble, she'll wobble, she'll gobble them up
She's searching everywhere.

Rumble, tumble, take a ride,
Off with the lid, and what's inside?

As he ends his song, the havaldar comes running in and grabs hold of Charandas.

HAVALDAR. Got you! Thought you could get away, did you? What've you got there? Better confess right away! Don't you know who I am—Mister Babu Das, havaldar of the old cadre. (*Lifts Charandas up and down thrice, then throws him down. Charandas cowers, holding his bundle.*) I'll stuff you with sawdust, you bastard! Put down that bundle, you bloody thief—or I'll chop off your goddam head and suspend it in midair, you fool! Put it down!

CHARANDAS. Oh my god! He'll chop off my head and suspend it in mid air! Oh, oh, oh! And what else will you do, maharaj?

HAVALDAR. I'll cut off your hands and feet and scatter them to the winds, you swine!

CHARANDAS. My god! He'll cut off my limbs and scatter them all over! Ah, ah, ah! And what will you do next, maharaj?

HAVALDAR. I'll grind your skin and bones into a fine paste, and serve it to the dogs, you scoundrel!

CHARANDAS. Oh god, I'll be turned into mincemeat and fed to the dogs! Ai, ai, ai! And when will you do all this, maharaj?

HAVALDAR. If I had my way, I'd do it straight away, you rogue. But what to do, I'm on government duty right now. (*Shouts*) Put down that bundle! (*Menacingly*) Put it down! (*Charandas lets go of his bundle. He unties it and examines the contents.*) So many clothes—do they belong to your father, you bastard?

CHARANDAS. They're not mine.

HAVALDAR. Of course they aren't. Whose are they, then?

CHARANDAS. My customer's.

HAVALDAR. Your customer's? Ha, ha, ha. Are you a dhobi, then?

CHARANDAS. Yes, maharaj. Original dhobi.

HAVALDAR. Why didn't you say so earlier, you ass?

CHARANDAS. You didn't give me a chance, maharaj!

HAVALDAR. All right, listen, beta. There's been a theft in this village. A golden platter has been stolen. Have you done it? If you have, just tell me and I won't report it. We'll share the booty.

CHARANDAS. I don't steal, maharaj.

HAVALDAR. Good, good, you shouldn't steal, my son. Listen, you go from house to house and you know everybody. If you happen to know the thief, just tell me and I'll give you a reward.

CHARANDAS. A reward?!

HAVALDAR. Yes.

CHARANDAS. I won't tell you here.

HAVALDAR. Why not?

CHARANDAS. Can't you see all the people gathered here?

HAVALDAR. Where?

CHARANDAS. Look in front of you.

HAVALDAR. What to do, then?

CHARANDAS. Let's go over there. (*They go to a corner of the stage.*)

HAVALDAR. Come on now, tell me.

CHARANDAS. Give me the reward.

HAVALDAR. Tell me first!

CHARANDAS. First the reward.

HAVALDAR. You don't trust even a high-ranking officer like me, do you, you suspicious lowborn bastard? Here, take two rupees. I'll give you more later. Come now, out with it.

CHARANDAS. Achcha, maharaj, listen. He who's done the stealing is—thief.

HAVALDAR. That I know!

CHARANDAS. You know that?

HAVALDAR. Of course!

CHARANDAS. Then what're you waiting for? Go catch him!

HAVALDAR. Who?

CHARANDAS. Thief!

HAVALDAR. I'll thrash you, you idiot! Do I look like a thief to you! Son, I'm asking you his name.

CHARANDAS. His name?

HAVALDAR. Yes.

CHARANDAS. He who steals, maharaj, is only called—thief. He has no other name.

HAVALDAR. Arrey, bhai, he who steals is a thief, who doesn't know that! But his name . . .

While the havaldar is pondering this, Charandas slips out. Turning around, the havaldar can't believe his eyes. He stares at the ground. A passerby, noticing him, stops and does the same. The havaldar looks up at the sky. The passerby does the same. Suddenly the havaldar sees him and they both freeze. The next moment the passerby suddenly takes to his heels. The havaldar chases him. Charandas enters from the other side, undoes his cloth bundle and takes out the golden platter.

CHARANDAS. So that's how I saved the golden platter. He didn't see it. (*Sings*)
All the mice are on the run,
A fat one lags behind,
He stumbles, fumbles, down he tumbles
The cat pounces on her find.

Rumble, tumble, take a ride,
Off with the lid, and what's inside?
Lo, it's little pussy!
The mice all squeal and run!

Rumble, tumble, what a ride,
Lift the lid off, what's inside?
A juicy, dark-skinned aubergine
A puffing, panting engine
A doll just like an engine
A doll as soft as butter
A dancing, prancing little doll
To set our hearts aflutter
The cat licks up the butter
The cat becomes the cover

Oh, rumble, tumble, take a ride
Lift the lid, there's lots inside!

A poor peasant enters, carrying some sattu tied in a piece of cloth slung over his shoulder.

CHARANDAS. Hey you—what's that you've got there? Hand it over, quick. Or I'll gobble you up raw!

PEASANT. Oh ho! Gobble me up raw, will you? I'll gobble you up, you damned hijra!

CHARANDAS. Come here, yaar. (*Affecting an effeminate manner*) May I ask you something, my friend?

PEASANT. Ask away.

CHARANDAS. Tell me, how did you guess? (*The Peasant laughs*) Shut up! Do I look like a hijra, you son of a bitch? (*The Peasant freezes*) What've you got

there in that bundle, you fool? Go on, put it down. Give it here, you bastard! Now get lost! Scram! (*The Peasant runs off, scared. Charandas undoes
the bundle.*) Arrey, sattu, only sattu! Oh sattuwala! Come here! Come on
back, don't be scared. Sit down, let's share this like brothers. Come, sit.
(*Shoving him down*) Arrey, sit, you ass! (*As the Peasant falls, Charandas
catches the clink of coins tucked into the waistband of his loincloth.*) What've
you got hidden there? (*Snatching the purse*) Come on, hand it over. Now
get lost! Go on now! Beat it!

He makes a threatening gesture. The peasant runs off in fear. Charandas sings.

The cat is out, the cat's about,
The cat is on the prowl,
She's after prey, day after day,
In weather fair or foul.

Rumble, tumble, take a ride,
Lift the lid and what's inside?
The cat's become the cover,
The mice all run and hide.
Lift the lid and what's inside?
The cat's the cover, so we find,
Everyday you see less mice
They're gobbled up, this isn't nice,
The cat she preens, she is the queen,
She wears a royal crown
And one by one she sights the mice
And then she brings them down.

Rumble, tumble, take a ride,
Lift the lid off, what's inside?

A wealthy merchant's wife enters, covered in ornaments from head to toe.

CHARANDAS. Arrey baap re! What a load of jewellery! (*Thinks briefly, then abruptly starts bawling gustily.*)

WOMAN. What's the matter, bhaiya? Why're you crying? Don't cry.

CHARANDAS (*crying*). I have bad news for you.

WOMAN. Bad news? For me? Are you from my village?

CHARANDAS. Yes. I'm from Bhatgaon.

WOMAN. Bhatgaon? But I come from Nandgaon.

CHARANDAS (*hitting himself*). What a fool! Nandgaon, bai, Nandgaon. I'm also from Nandgaon.

WOMAN. All's well with Chhotey Babu, I hope.

CHARANDAS. Keeps calling for his didi all the time.

WOMAN. His didi? But he doesn't have an older sister! I'm his bhabhi.

CHARANDAS. Oh, yes, of course. He keeps calling for his bhabhi. He's very ill, you know. Insists that he'll only drink his medicine from your tender hands. Better come along at once.

WOMAN. All right, I'll just let them know at home . . .

CHARANDAS. No time for that. Hurry up, or he'll pop off.

WOMAN. Oh my god! All right, all right, let's go!

CHARANDAS (*after walking a few paces*). Arrey baap re!

WOMAN. What's the matter now, bhaiya?

CHARANDAS. Bai, this is a very dangerous place. A man was attacked right here just the other day and left to die a slow, painful death. (*Points at his own bundle*) Look, his things are still lying there.

WOMAN. Oh my god!

CHARANDAS. I think you'd better take off all your jewellery and wrap it in this gamchha. (*He hesitates*) And after all, you're a helpless lady.

WOMAN. Yes . . .

CHARANDAS. What if someone should attack you?

WOMAN. Oh my god!

CHARANDAS. It is best to put your jewellery here. (*Spreads the gamchha on the ground.*)

WOMAN. All right, bhaiya, I'll do as you say.

As she removes her ornaments one by one and places them in the gamchha, he interrogates her.

CHARANDAS. Where did you get these ornaments made, bai?

WOMAN. At Raigarh.

CHARANDAS. Raigarh! That's the best place, of course, for jewellery. What's the jeweller's name, bai?

WOMAN. Ramlal.

CHARANDAS. Ramlal! Who doesn't know Ramlal? He's the very best jeweller in all Chhattisgarh! They're made of pure gold, of course, aren't they?

WOMAN. Yes, bhaiya. Hundred per cent gold. (*She ties the gamchha into a bundle.*)

CHARANDAS. Come, give it to me.

WOMAN. No, I'll carry it.

CHARANDAS. You might lose them, bai. I'll look after them carefully.

WOMAN. No, I'll look after them.

CHARANDAS. Bai, you're a woman. What'll you do if a thief attacks you? I'm a man! I'll tackle him bravely. Give them to me.

WOMAN. No.

CHARANDAS (*snatching the bundle from her*). Give it here!

WOMAN (*crying*). You rogue! You tricked me! You told me lies, you scoundrel, and now you've stolen my jewels! You thief!

CHARANDAS. Why are you crying, bai? What to do, god made me a thief.

WOMAN. You bastard! You've brought me all the way here, and now you're thugging me! May your corpse be laid out!

CHARANDAS. No, don't curse me, bai. That won't suit me—too much enforced rest.

WOMAN. May you die!

CHARANDAS. Don't say that, bai! Then we won't see each other again. (*As she continues to cry, he also begins weeping.*) Oh, my god! It breaks my heart to see a woman weep. Oh no, I shouldn't rob a woman. No, no, I won't do it. (*He hands her the ornaments.*) Here, take this, bai. Take good care of it.

WOMAN (*taking the bundle and giving him a sound beating*). You chandal! Cheat! Leper!

She goes off. He falls down. The havaldar comes on. Charandas starts polishing the havaldar's shoes with his gamchha. As the havaldar looks down to examine his shoes, Charandas escapes. The havaldar, realizing that he's been fooled again, chases him.

HAVALDAR. Arrey, I'll get you yet, you bastard! Arrey, bachhu, where can you run to?

SCENE TWO

Village square. The guru enters singing.

> The baba roams the forest alone
> The sadhu roams the forest alone
> The koel's lonely song
> Resounds through the groves
> As the baba sings all on his own
> The householder is snug in his home
> The tramp on the road prefers to roam
> While the baba roams the forest alone

GURU. Rise! Open your eyes! Look at the world!

The guru sits down on the platform, spreading his mat. His followers begin to gather around. A few of them come up and touch his feet, then join the others, who start to sing a hymn.

DISCIPLE 1. Gurudev, I touch your feet! Gurudev!

GURU. Glory to lord Shiva Shambhu!

DISCIPLE 2. I touch your feet, maharaj!

GURU. Jai ho, jai ho, jai ho!

DISCIPLE 3. I touch your feet, Guru-ji!

GURU. Bless you, my son. Bless you.

> (*They join the others in singing the hymn*)

> All you have to do is just
> Give the guru his due
> That's all you have to do, just
> Give the guru his due.
> Is it salvation you want? Just

Give the guru his due
All learning is a sham, till you
Give the guru his due
Nothing will work for you, till you
Give the guru his due
Watch good things happen to you, once you
Give the guru his due
So why don't you just follow the rules, and
Give the guru,
And in return he'll be quick to bless you if you—
Cash down!—give the guru his due.

A gambler and a drunkard enter quarrelling over money.

DRUNKARD. Come on, pay up!

GAMBLER. I don't have the money.

DRUNKARD. Honour your losses! You've lost a rupee. Give it to me!

GAMBLER. I'll pay up the next time we gamble.

DRUNKARD. Don't cheat! At least be honest when you're gambling! (*Snatches the money from the gambler's pocket.*)

GAMBLER. That's the last bit of money I had!

DRUNKARD. You can win it back next time.

GURU. Oh, Uday Ram!

The drunkard moves forward, in reponse to the guru's call. The gambler joins the marijuana smoker sitting in a corner.

GAMBLER. Arrey, Ramcharan! Well met, yaar.

SMOKER. Chait Ram, is it?

GAMBLER. Come, let's have a round.

They start to gamble. Meanwhile, the drunkard has gone up to the guru.

DRUNKARD. I touch your feet, gurudev!

GURU. Bless you my son. May you live a thousand years. May you be successful. Ah ha ha ha, my son, I see you here every day. Every day you come, pay your respects—but you vowed to give up drinking. Have you done so?

DRUNKARD. Why did you mention drinking, gurudev? You've pierced me to the quick.

GURU. Arrey, arrey!

DRUNKARD. Listen, gurudev, d'you know what happened to me the other day? I walk into the house and what should I see but a bottle standing right there. A thought flashed through my mind . . .

GURU. Ah ha ha . . .

DRUNKARD. Don't worry, gurudev. Having drunk deep of the nectar of your holy words, what use do I have for liquor? I told the bottle sternly, 'Let alone drinking from you, it's a sin even to set eyes on you!'

GURU. Well done, well done, beta!

DRUNKARD. From that day, guru-ji, my body aches kut-kut, kut-kut . . .

GURU. Kut-kut, kut-kut . . .

DRUNKARD. Aches . . .

GURU. Let it ache.

DRUNKARD. It hurts, gurudev!

GURU. Arrey, let it hurt, my son! Think of your guru's words as medicine. Like nectar, as you said. If you have drunk up my teachings like nectar and renounced the bottle, why then you've begun a new life. Live like a man, my son!

DRUNKARD. Gurudev, I have a friend who has a very bad habit. He can't stop gambling. Can you help him, gurudev?

GURU. Why not, my son? It's my job to make people renounce bad habits. What else is a guru for?

DRUNKARD (*shouts*). Hey, Chait Ram! Come here!

GAMBLER. Coming! (*Comes up to the guru on his platform, shuffling a deck of cards*) I've been waiting a long time, gurudev! What a lot of stuff you've managed to gather! Come on, let's have a round. Here, you deal.

GURU (*threatening him with his iron tongs*). I'll give you such a hiding I'll break your head! You rascal, d'you take this for a den of gamblers?

GAMBLER. Gurudev! You're everyone's guru! Show me a way of winning at cards. I've lost very heavily, guru-ji.

GURU. Babu, this is the seat of a sadhu. If you want to learn card tricks go to a card sharp. Look at this poor drunkard—he's been coming here for three days now. The first day he was sloshed he couldn't talk straight, couldn't walk straight. He said, 'Guru-ji, make me your disciple.' I said, get lost, I'm not going to take on a drunk like you as a disciple! He took a vow right away that he'd give up drinking, and hasn't touched a drop since. If you want to be my disciple then you must give up gambling just like he's given up drinking.

GAMBLER. Gurudev, the only kind of gambling I indulge in is cards. Nothing else.

GURU. Arrey, give up all forms of gambling.

GAMBLER. It's the only way I can afford my omelette and bread, guru-ji.

GURU. Don't you dare mention omelettes! If you're so concerned with omelettes, go ask a canteenwala to be your guru! If you want me as your guru, you'll have to stop gambling.

GAMBLER. All right, guru-ji, I'll give up. Now will you take me on as a disciple?

GURU. Arrey, I only take human beings as disciples, not cats and dogs!

GAMBLER. Gurudev, I won't gamble any more. Here (*lays down the cards*). Now, make me your disciple, please.

GURU. Come.

The marijuana smoker steps forward.

SMOKER. Gurudev, can I also be your disciple?

GURU. Wait, my son. One at a time. (*To the gambler*) Now my son, you have to give guru dakshina.

GAMBLER. Guru dakshina?

GURU. It's not much, only one rupee twenty-five paise.

GAMBLER. My god, one rupee twenty-five paise!

GURU. What's the problem? Is it such a lot?

GAMBLER. I only have twenty-five paise, guru-ji (*takes it from his pocket*).

GURU. That's the minimum, beta.

GAMBLER. Hey, Uday Ram! Give me back my rupee!

DRUNKARD. Oh, so you've found a way to get it back, after all! You damned cheat!

He hands it over to the guru, who whispers the mantra in the Gambler's ear.

GURU (*turning to the smoker*). Now, my son, what's your vice?

SMOKER. I have no vices, gurudev (*puffing at his bidi*).

GURU. Then you're a readymade saint, my son. Why come to me? (*Coughs*) Where's this smoke coming from?

SMOKER. It must be from that factory over there, guru-ji.

GURU. Factory? Funny, it's never bothered me before.

SMOKER. It depends on the way the wind blows, guru-ji.

GURU (*noticing the bidi*). You rascal! Have you ever entered a sadhu's akhara before, you rogue?

SMOKER. It's my first time, gurudev.

GURU. Without so much as a by-your-leave you start puffing away like a steam engine! And you give the factory a bad name! I was wondering where all the smoke was coming from. A regular power house you've got going here!

SMOKER. Forgive me, guru-ji.

GURU. My son, this is a sadhu's akhara. If you want to be my disciple then you'll have to give up smoking just as this drunkard gave up drinking and this gambler gambling.

SMOKER. All right, gurudev. Here, I give it up!

GURU. Well done, beta. There's just one more thing.

SMOKER. What's that?

GURU. You'll have to give guru dakshina.

SMOKER. No problem! I'll just give it to you. Here! (*Hands over his gamchha with something knotted in the corner.*)

GURU. Excellent! Here's a true disciple! How much is there, beta?

SMOKER. A full bundle of twenty-five, guru-ji.

GURU (*undoing the knot*). Arrey, what's this? I thought it was twenty-five rupees, but you've given me bidis!

SMOKER. You just made me give them up, gurudev, so I'm giving them to you!

GURU. Arrey, beta, I don't smoke either! Nor should you. Throw them away.

SMOKER. There you are (*puts them away*).

GURU. Well done, son! Now give me something towards my expenses.

SMOKER. Money?

GURU. Yes, money. Just one rupee twenty-five paise.

SMOKER. That's all I had, guru-ji. I spent it on bidis.

GURU. Look, beta, nothing happens without guru dakshina. It's a must.

SMOKER. But I don't have any money, gurudev.

GURU (*begs*). Beta, if nothing else, at least fork out a few coins for a cup of tea.

SMOKER. Not a coin, guru-ji. Take it tomorrow.

GURU. Credit! All of you want credit! You tell me—how do I manage?

SMOKER. You tell me, guru-ji, how do I manage, without any money?

GURU (*threatening him with his chimta*). And you say you have no vices! (*As the smoker ducks, the guru notices a chillum tucked into his turban.*) What's this— a chillum! God is great! What disciples he blesses me with—a gambler, a drunkard, and a ganja addict! Praise he to god! Beta, since you don't have any money, let this chillum be your guru dakshina.

SMOKER. Gurudev, I gave up bidis because you asked me to, but I can't give up my ganja smoking (*tries to snatch it back*).

GURU. Arrey, arrey, arrey, beta, this belongs to the guru now! You can't just take back your dakshina, it's not done. Jai bholenath! Come, I'll give you the mantra (*breathes the mantra in his ear*).

The group resumes the song. Meanwhile, the three new disciples sneak out of sight of the guru, to one side of the stage. Making sure that they can't be seen by him, they surreptitiously begin to indulge in all the vices they are meant to have renounced. The drunkard takes a swig from a bottle tucked into his waist, the gambler deals out from the deck of cards he had placed before the guru and has since slyly retrieved, and the smoker lights up and starts puffing away. The song continues.

All you've got to do is just
Give the guru his due
Whatever you want to do, first
Give the guru his due
Make your offering quick, just
Give the guru his due
So just follow the rules
Give the guru
And in turn he will bless you!

Charandas comes darting in and flings himself at the guru's feet, head down. The havaldar runs in after him, jumps over his prostrate body, and looking in the other directions, says:

HAVALDAR. Sadhu maharaj! Did you see a thief run past?

GURU. Arrey, beta, would a thief come here? And even if one did, would he remain a thief for long? Just as ditch water gets purified when it mingles with the Ganga, in a sadhu's akhara, thieves, loafers, drunkards, gamblers, rogues, ruffians, all get purified. There's no thief here, my son. Go look somewhere else.

The havaldar turns to leave, but stops short when he overhears the gambling trio squabbling.

HAVALDAR. Just look at these bastards, gambling openly in the middle of the road! Such a waste of money! You'd ruin your homes for the sake of gambling, would you? You'd starve your children, would you? Sons of bitches! You ought to be ashamed of yourselves! (*He quickly pockets the money lying on the ground.*) Hey, who is this fellow sitting up there?

GAMBLER. Are you asking about him, sarkar? He's sadhu maharaj.

HAVALDAR. When did he arrive?

SMOKER. A week ago. He's our guru.

HAVALDAR. Your guru! Looks like the king of thieves to me.

DRUNKARD. Who said that? Did you call me the king of thieves, you bastard? Did you say that?

SMOKER. Arrey, no one called you anything! Calm down.

DRUNKARD. You dare to, you son of a bitch!

GAMBLER. Hey, keep quiet. It's the havaldar you're talking to.

DRUNKARD. I'll beat him to pulp!

SMOKER. This idiot will get us all into trouble.

HAVALDAR. Abbe! I'll show you what's what! I'll give you something to remember, you swine!

The havaldar starts beating up the drunkard, whose friends, under the pretext of separating the two, bring down the havaldar. All four fall in a heap, with the havaldar at the bottom. Terrified, he crawls to the guru and throws himself at his feet, prostrate in a pose which echoes Charandas, who is still stretched out before the guru. Charandas enacts a charade of first checking to see where the other three are—they have meanwhile slipped into the crowd of followers— then tapping the havaldar on the shoulder and gesturing to indicate that his tormentors have gone. The havaldar picks himself up, retrieves his cap, salutes Charandas and slinks away.

CHARANDAS. Gurudev!

GURU. Bless you, my son!

CHARANDAS. Wah, gurudev! You saved my skin.

GURU. Not me, my son. It was the lord above who saved you. Who are you, beta? Where do you come from? What's your name?

CHARANDAS. I'm Charandas, maharaj.

GURU. What do you do?

CHARANDAS. Don't ask me that, guru-ji.

GURU. What's the matter?

CHARANDAS. I'm ashamed to say it, gurudev.

GURU. Ashamed to tell me what you do? Ah, I understand, beta. Lying to your guru is like hiding a pregnancy from the midwife. The havaldar is after you, isn't he? And you're here to save your skin.

CHARANDAS. You've got it, guru-ji. What can I say?

GURU. If you want to be my disciple you'll have to give up stealing, my son.

CHARANDAS. Then how will I survive—what will I eat?

GURU. Arrey, do you mean to say everyone in this world lives by thievery? Get a job. Live honestly. Earn some respect. Is robbery the only way to make a living? Come on, speak up. You want me to be your guru, don't you? Then make a vow. Not a thousand vows—just one. Just give up one thing.

CHARANDAS. Why just one, gurudev. I'll renounce four things!

GURU. What four things?

CHARANDAS. My first vow, guru-ji!

GURU. Go on, I'm listening.

CHARANDAS. I'll never eat off a golden plate.

GURU. Well said!

CHARANDAS. My second vow, guru-ji!

GURU. I'm listening, I'm listening, carry on.

CHARANDAS. I'll never mount an elephant and lead a procession.

GURU. Very good, very good.

CHARANDAS. My third vow, guru-ji!

GURU. Yes, yes, go ahead.

CHARANDAS. If a queen says, 'Marry me, marry me!' I'll refuse to oblige her. No matter how young, how pretty. I won't ever marry a queen, guru-ji.

GURU. Excellent, excellent!

CHARANDAS. My fourth vow, guru-ji!

GURU. This'll be the big one. I'm all ears.

CHARANDAS. If all the people of a country get together and beg, 'Charandas! Be our king, take the throne,' I'll refuse. I'll say, 'No, I won't be your king.'

GURU (*laughs*). Beta, I've heard all your vows. You won't eat off a golden plate. It seems you're sick of golden plates, having eaten off them since you were a child. And today you've taken a vow before your guru to renounce eating off golden plates. Great! Secondly—you'll never ride an elephant in procession. Because you're such a great leader, and you've done it so often, that you've grown tired of it. So you vow to your guru to renounce this honour. All right. The queen of the land is panting for your manly good looks, isn't she? After today, you forswear marriage with a queen, even if she should beg you. You saintly, unwordly man! And as for your fourth vow, you'll never accept the kingship of a country. The entire population is clamouring for you, right? Take the throne, Charandas! Only you can rule us well! But you refuse to oblige. There's no greed in you, beta. You're content with your lot. Good for you! Charandas—

CHARANDAS. Gurudev.

GURU. I had heard that when a man sleeps, he dreams. But you're dreaming with your eyes wide open, beta! You're nothing but a thief—none of these unlikely things is going to happen to you. Why insist on dreaming such dreams?

CHARANDAS. Guru-ji, it's just a matter of chance—just in case, some day . . . one never knows.

GURU. And a thief is always on the lookout for the perfect chance, isn't he? Look, beta, you've forsworn four things of your own choice, now take a vow that I ask of you.

CHARANDAS. What's that, guru-ji?

GURU. Give up telling lies.

CHARANDAS. Now you've fixed me good and proper, guru-ji! You know very well I can't steal without telling lies.

GURU. Yes, that's why I'm insisting, my son. The cure for all ills—stop telling lies. And the crime of theft will stop automatically.

CHARANDAS. Gurudev! You can't separate sunshine from the sun, can you? You can't separate a nail from the flesh, can you? Then how can you separate thieving and lying—they go together, guru-ji.

GURU. Then get out of here, find another place to hide. I've no time for you.

CHARANDAS. I fall at your feet, gurudev!

GURU. Sorry—I can't help you.

CHARANDAS. Guru-ji! (*Sees the havaldar approaching and hides behind the guru. The havaldar looks around, doesn't see him, and departs.*) All right, guru-ji, I swear—I'll give up lying from today. That's a vow.

GURU. Is that a firm vow? Or did it firm up because you saw the havaldar?

CHARANDAS. Guru-ji, I swear in front of everyone gathered here from now on I'll never tell a lie. That's a solemn vow. I stand by it.

GURU. Well done! Bless you, my son. May you live long. (*Gives him the mantra.*) Now, beta, let's come to brass tacks. What're you thinking of for your guru?

CHARANDAS. I'm thinking, guru-ji, to each his own. You're flourishing in your own way—

GURU. What d'you mean?

CHARANDAS. Well, I steal at night, in the dark, stealthily, entering homes through holes in the wall—while you sit here in broad daylight, openly, with a crowd of people around you. And you make much more than I do.

GURU. Shut up!

CHARANDAS. You're the one who told me not to lie, guru-ji.

GURU. Well, congratulations, oh truthful one! Arrey, beta, I was asking about something else. I want to know what you've thought of by way of guru dakshina.

CHARANDAS. Oh, that. (*Placing his cloth bundle before the guru*) Here, take it all, guru-ji.

GURU. Such a fat bundle! Baap re! You're very generous, my son! What have we here . . . yah ha ha! A sari for guru-ji, a skirt for guru-ji! Even a pair of pants and a necktie! Arrey, beta, what use is all this to, me? All your guru needs is a loincloth.

CHARANDAS. Guru-ji, all you see is the clothes. Reach inside and see what you find—here, a golden thali.

GURU. Ah, now I get it! This is the golden thali you've been eating off which you've sworn today to renounce! So now you're giving it to my as dakshina—but wait a minute, does this platter belong to you?

CHARANDAS. Guru-ji, what can l say? You know it all. Just put it away before the havaldar catches sight of it.

GURU. Ah, I understand you—I put the platter away so when the havaldar comes he can put me away!

CHARANDAS. No problem. Plenty to eat and drink where you'll be going.

GURU. Ah, you're doing me a favour, are you?

CHARANDAS. Guru-ji, everyone who goes to jail comes out strong and healthy.

GURU. Oh, I see, you think I need fattening up! Forget it son—just give me cash.

CHARANDAS. All right, guru-ji. I have two rupees seventy-five paise on me. Two rupees from the havaldar, and seventy-five paise from the sattuwala. Here, take it.

GURU. Arrey—only seventy-five paise! You just said you had two rupees seventy-five paise.

CHARANDAS. That was after putting the two together, guru-ji.

GURU. So give me the two together, beta.

CHARANDAS. No, guru-ji, things are so expensive nowadays, two rupees won't even buy a meal.

GURU. Are things expensive for you alone?

CHARANDAS. You have so many followers, guru-ji. If each of them forks out seventy-five paise you'll collect a fortune.

GURU. But they'll be buying their own salvation, not yours.

CHARANDAS. Guru-ji, the havaldar's coming! Give me your blessings before he lands up.

Noticing his approach, Charandas hides behind the guru, on his hands and knees. The guru sits astride his back. The havaldar looks around, and, appearing not to find Charandas, perches on the platform right in front of the guru. After keeping a silent vigil for a few seconds, he speaks.

HAVALDAR. So, from now on you'll never eat off a golden thali, right?

CHARANDAS (*lifting the front of the guru's dhoti and looking out through his legs*). Never!

HAVALDAR. And from now on you'll never ride on elephant back, right?

CHARANDAS. Never!

HAVALDAR. And you'll never ever marry a queen, right?

CHARANDAS. Never!

HAVALDAR. And from now on you'll always tell the truth, right?

CHARANDAS. Always.

HAVALDAR. Son of a whore! (*He grabs at Charandas, misses and catches the guru's leg instead. Charandas escapes. Looking at the guru*) Swine! (*Exits.*)

The guru quickly collects his things and gets up. The crowd begins to move out after him, singing the refrain 'The Baba Roams the Forest Alone'. Charandas runs back on stage, followed by the havaldar. Charandas hides and the havaldar begins to search the faces of the crowd as they file out. Charandas slips behind him, and mimics his movements. Finally the havaldar turns and comes face to face with Charandas who salutes him. The havaldar salutes him back and turns away, then realizes that this is the very man he is looking for and whips around, sees no one and runs off stage in search of Charandas. Charandas, meanwhile, had slipped behind him; he now looks after the havaldar and saunters off casually.

SCENE THREE

The Landlord's verandah. On one corner of the platform the Landlord is seated on his gaddi, with his cash box, his account register and his gun. Tetku, his servant, carries four sacks of rice and places them on the other side of the platform. In front, Sattuwala, the peasant, enters lamenting.

PEASANT. Hey bhagwan! What shall I do, where can I go, how will I feed my family, how will I earn a living, *parmatma*?

Charandas enters.

CHARANDAS. What's happened? Why're you crying?

PEASANT. You? Come to rob me again? Go ahead—take it all. All I have left is this loincloth, take that as well. Strangle me if you will.

CHARANDAS. Arrey, what're you blubbering about? I'm asking you what's happened? Say something!

PEASANT. There's terrible famine in the village. Many of us have starved to death. My own children haven't eaten a thing for three days. Not a crumb.

CHARANDAS. Arrey, Ram, Ram!

PEASANT. There is a big landowner in our village. He has fields in ten villages, a tubewell, a water pump, electricity—his crop is flourishing. But he won't share even a kilo with those of us who have nothing. If anyone goes near his godown, his hirelings beat them off with their lathis.

CHARANDAS. What a tyrant!

PEASANT. He's a bloody miser.

CHARANDAS. Where is he?

PEASANT. Look, there he is. Can you see? Sitting there, counting his ill-gotten gains—all money from usury. That's him.

CHARANDAS. So that's him. Ask him for some rice, let's see what he says.

PEASANT. I'm too scared, bhaiya.

CHARANDAS. Why're you scared?

PEASANT. His loaded gun's right beside him, don't you see?

CHARANDAS. Arrey baap re!

PEASANT. Shocked?

CHARANDAS. Why don't you go ahead and ask? Let's see what happens—if chance favours you the gun might not work!

PEASANT. You won't run off?

CHARANDAS. Look, friend—I may be a thief but I'm not a coward.

PEASANT. And I'm not a gullible fool, either. You're bound to be lying.

CHARANDAS. Call me a liar, and I'll thrash you black and blue. Idiot! You dare call me a liar! I'm no longer the same Charandas. I've sworn to my guru that I won't ever lie. Go ahead and ask.

PEASANT. Promise you'll wait here?

CHARANDAS. Promise.

PEASANT. All right, then, I'll try.

CHARANDAS. Go on.

The Peasant hesitantly and humbly approaches the Landlord and sits by his side.

PEASANT. Ram, Ram, malik!

LANDLORD. Ram, Ram. Come, sit closer, sit on my head! Bloody fool! Sit down there on the floor, can't you? My gaddi's all ruined!

PEASANT. Forgive me, malik, I made a mistake.

LANDLORD. Mistake? Nonsense! You don't know your place.

PEASANT. I came to see you, malik.

LANDLORD. What for?

PEASANT. My children haven't eaten for three days, malik. They're half-dead of star-vation. If you could spare a kilo or so of rice, it would save them, malik . . .

LANDLORD. Am I under the obligation to save everyone's sons and daughters?

PEASANT. By the grace of god, you have so much, malik! I'll repay every bit as soon as I can. Save my children!

LANDLORD. Just because I have plenty, doesn't mean I start giving it all away to the likes of you!

PEASANT (*pleading*). Please, malik, help me!

LANDLORD (*notices Charandas striding up and down*). Hey you, what're you strutting about for? Be careful, your limbs might stiffen up. (*To the Peasant*) Is he with you?

PEASANT. Yes, malik. He's with me.

LANDLORD. Oh, so you've brought your strongman along!

PEASANT. No malik, I can't feed myself, how can I afford to keep a strongman!

LANDLORD (*to Charandas*). Who're you?

CHARANDAS. A man.

LANDLORD. I can see that. I'm asking your name and what you do.

CHARANDAS. Don't ask. You won't like it.

LANDLORD. Oh, so I won't like it! Impudent oaf! Spill the beans!

CHARANDAS. My name is Charandas and my profession thieving. Taken together, that makes me Charandas the thief!

LANDLORD. Ooh my, a thief! You'll steal the roof over my head, will you?

CHARANDAS. Yes. Given the opportunity.

PEASANT. Malik, he has a reputation for doing as he says, and for never telling a lie.

LANDLORD. Great, oh Dharmraj, you guardian of Truth! I say get him out of here! At once!

CHARANDAS. I'm telling you to give this poor man some food. You have more than enough.

LANDLORD. You only have to ask, and I'll comply—is that what you think?

CHARANDAS. I'm warning you—you'd better listen to me or I'll rob you of all your rice.

LANDLORD. You dare to threaten me?

PEASANT. Do as he says, malik, or he'll turn things upside down.

LANDLORD. You think the two of you can turn things upside down? Get out!

CHARANDAS. Come on, let's go. I'll sort him out. (*They leave.*)

LANDLORD (*examining his ledgers*). Bloody loafers! Wastrels! Idlers! Just land up and beg—gimme, gimme, gimme, all the time. (*Calls out*) Arrey, Tetku re!

TETKU (*enters running*). Yes, master?

LANDLORD. Those two who were here—bloody rogues, idle wastrels! Spoke a load of rubbish. They looked like real thieves to me.

TETKU. Thieves? Arrey, malik, I'm here, aren't I? Why should you worry? Forget it. Such thieves are a dime a dozen. The alleys are full of them.

LANDLORD. One of them was very insistent that once he said he'd do something, he'd keep his word.

TETKU. It's all nonsense, malik. Pay no attention. I'll mount a guard on the godown right away. Don't worry (*leaves*).

LANDLORD (*looking at his ledgers again*). Gimme, gimme, gimme, all the time. Tetku re! (*Tetku runs in again*) Oh yes, do one more thing. Just in case they do try something, just warn the villagers—if they hear my call, they should come running with their lathis!

TETKU. They'll come, master. They'll all come running with their lathis as soon as they hear your voice (*leaves*).

LANDLORD. Gimme, gimme, gimme, all the time! Arrey, Tetku re! (*Tetku runs in again.*)

TETKU. What's happened now, malik?

LANDLORD. Have you counted the sacks of rice?

TETKU. Not yet. Shall I do it now, master?

LANDLORD. Yes, count them and let me know how many there are. (*Looking at his ledgers again*) Gimme, gimme, gimme, all the time.

TETKU (*counting sacks*). There are 380 sacks, malik.

LANDLORD. Did you count them properly?

TETKU. Yes, malik.

LANDLORD. Gimme, gimme, gimme all the time.

TETKU. Gimme—(*gestures, asking for a bidi*).

LANDLORD. What?

TETKU. A bidi, please, malik. Give one . . .

LANDLORD. Has my horse been fed?

TETKU. Not yet, malik.

LANDLORD. Go, then, feed him first, you can smoke your bidi later.

(*A group of Rawat dancers comes on. Charandas and the peasant disguised as members of the troupe, are among them. As they twirl and whirl, these two stealthily drag out the sacks of rice one by one from the godown and carry them off unnoticed by the Landlord and Tetku who are engrossed in the dance. The Rawat leader finally comes up and touches the Landlord's feet and receives some money by way of a donation. The group exits.*)

That was great fun, Tetku.

TETKU. Great fun, master.

LANDLORD. What a show they put up!

TETKU. They really danced well, malik.

LANDLORD (*suddenly noticing*). Hey, where've all the sacks gone?

TETKU. They were right here, malik!

LANDLORD. So where are they now?

TETKU. Who knows, malik.

LANDLORD. Arrey, I told you to be careful, and you got as involved in the dance as I did!

TETKU. I just joined in for a few steps, malik. Just a few steps!

LANDLORD. Arrey, your few steps have cost me a fortune! You idiot!

TETKU. I'll just go and feed your horse . . .

LANDLORD. With what, you fool? No, no, bring your lathi! Call all the villagers! Shout for them.

TETKU. Come! Run! Our rice has been stolen!

VOICES. Come on! Come on! Come on!

The Landlord exits. Tetku runs off, yelling. A group of villagers, armed with stout lathis, crosses the stage.

SCENE FOUR

The village square. Sattuwala brings in a sack of rice, sits on the platform, accompanied by Charandas, and they both start busily doling out rice from the sacks lying beside them. A long line of villagers—young, old, male, female—enters from one end. They receive a share, and leave from the other side. The chorus sings.

Oh listen, brothers and sisters, to what we have to say.
Charandas is not a thief, not a thief, no way!

Palaces and mansions, he'll break into and steal,
The poor man's hut is safe from him, he gives us a good deal.

There are so many rogues about, who do not look like thieves,
Impressive turbans on their heads, softly shod their feet,
But open up their safes and you will surely see,
Stolen goods, ill-gotten wealth, riches got for free.

So listen, brothers and sisters, to what we have to say,
Charandas is not a thief, not a thief, no way!

Don't take liberties with the Truth, truth has its own power,
Even cops and zamindars regard it with due awe,
The Truth is greater than this world,
  the Truth can set you free,
The Truth can even put you on par with divinity.

Oh, listen, brothers and sisters, to what we have to say
Charandas is not a thief, not a thief, no way!

The Landlord joins the queue, and comes up to Charandas unnoticed. He is offered a share. He grabs Charandas by the throat.

LANDLORD. Hey you—So you call yourself Charandas the thief!

CHARANDAS. You're the thief, not I!

LANDLORD. You dare call me a thief!

CHARANDAS. Yes—thief! Thief!

LANDLORD. Police! Police!

CHARANDAS. Thief, thief! (*The havaldar runs in*) Catch him!

The havaldar catches the Landlord. Charandas and the peasant stroll out unobserved.

HAVALDAR. Just begging for a thrashing, aren't you? I'll break your hands and feet! Got you at last, you bastard!

LANDLORD. Arrey, can't you see who I am? I'm the landlord! The thief's gone!

HAVALDAR. Oh god, did I make a mistake again? Forgive me, master! (*Turns to look for Charandas*) You just wait and see, malik, what I do to him when I catch him—I'll fix him! He's always running away. Doesn't slow down for a moment, does he?

LANDLORD. Then go after him, don't just stand there!

The havaldar notices the same passerby he had seen earlier. The man freezes, then runs out. The havaldar runs after him.

SCENE FIVE

A temple. There is a puja is going on. Noticing the havaldar, Charandas slips into the temple and joins the congregation. The havaldar comes on, looks about and then finally he, too, enters the temple. As he begins to study each worshipper, Charandas keeps on moving and changing his position till the havaldar bypasses him. As the havaldar from his position right behind the priest turns around suddenly for a final look at the gathering, Charandas, who is standing right beside him, drops to his knees. The havaldar folds his hands and joins in the hymn which is a traditional devotional song based on the Ramayana.

Son of Kaushalya, all-merciful,
He who wins the minds of munis
He whose appearance is fulfilment
To the mother,
He who pleases the eye, cloud-dark, four-armed,
With the conch, chakra, lotus, divine bow,

Bejewelled, bedecked with flowers,
He of the enormous eyes—this is how
The ocean of grace, the destroyer of rakshasas,
Manifested himself.

Palms folded, the mother asks—oh, infinite one
How do I welcome you?
The vedas and puranas show you as distanced
From maya, graces, knowledge, and beyond consequences.
Holy verses and holy men all sing your praises,
Call you the storehouse of all virtues, he who loves
His believers and followers,
Oh, the husband of Lakshmi appears for my salvation.

Jai, jai ram lala ho jai jai janak lali
Jai jai Lakhan lal bajrang bali
Sri ram jai ram jai jai ram
Treasurehouse of incomparable strength, mountain of gold,
He of awesome, fiery visage, wisest of the wise,
Virtue personified, monkey king, Raghunath's
Favourite disciple, Son of the wind,
Sri Hanumanji, I offer my obeisance to you.

The puja over, the priest takes around a platter/ thali to distribute prasad and collect offerings. Men and women place a few paise on the plate, get blessed by the priest and depart. The last to leave is the havaldar. Charandas hides right behind him. The havaldar takes the prasad and suddenly lifts the priest's face by the chin to examine him closely. After a close scrutiny, he says 'Sorry!' and finally steps out of the temple and crouches in a corner outside, waiting and smoking a bidi. Charandas puts a basketful of jewellery and gems on the plate.

PRIEST. Arrey, baap re! That's a fortune! Are you giving it all?

CHARANDAS. Yes, maharaj.

PRIEST. Glory be to god! What a large-hearted soul! What's your name, beta?

CHARANDAS. Charandas.

PRIEST. What do you do?

CHARANDAS. I steal. I'm a thief.

PRIEST. You've made such a generous donation, how can you be a thief? I don't believe you. You're kidding! You shouldn't fool around with sadhus and holy men. How come you're here today, my son?

CHARANDAS. I've come to ask for more wealth, maharaj.

PRIEST. Ask for wealth, did you say?

CHARANDAS. Yes.

PRIEST. You've just given so much to God—he'll give you twice as much. How long do you plan to stay, beta?

CHARANDAS. I'll leave once god fulfils my request, maharaj.

PRIEST. My son, god won't let down a generous soul like you. Stay here tonight, get some rest, refresh yourself, and leave tomorrow after you've eaten some prasad.

CHARANDAS. Don't hold me back, maharaj.

PRIEST. Why not?

CHARANDAS. It'll be your loss.

PRIEST. Arrey beta, this is the house of god. Think of what benefits you, and leave god's losses alone. He'll make up for them. Here—take some prasad, and go to sleep.

CHARANDAS. As you say, maharaj.

PRIEST. Good, good, sleep peacefully.

(*Charandas lies down. The priest tidies up, lies down beside him while chanting his mantra and falls asleep. Once the priest begins to snore, Charandas tries to get up. Just then the sleeping priest turns and throws a leg over Charandas. Charandas begins to massage his leg.*)

That feels good, beta. God bless you, my son. What a kindhearted soul!

Charandas massages his legs till he falls asleep again. Then he gets up slowly and stealthily, and begins to move towards the idol. He stops, startled, as the priest slaps a mosquito on his thigh. There's a pause. Finally, Charandas approaches the idol and clears the temple of everything valuable, including the jewellery he had donated. As he is leaving, he stops, turns, notices a precious jewel embedded in a niche and plucks it out. He turns again, then looks back, goes up to the idol, bows in obeisance before the throne of the deity almost as if begging pardon, then surprisingly lifts up the golden idol and takes it away.

CHARANDAS (*touching the sleeping priest's feet in reverence*). Sleep well, maharaj. I'm off, all right? (*He leaves.*)

PRIEST. I'm sleeping well, beta. Go to sleep.

(*As Charandas leaves the temple, the havaldar, sleeping, stretches and yawns hugely. Charandas delicately jumps over his prostrate body and exits. Groping for Charandas, the Priest mumbles.*)

Beta, where are you? (*Half-rouses*) Probably gone for a pee . . . (*yawns and falls back asleep. Wakes up again and sees that Charandas is still not there*) Still not back? (*Suddenly notices the theft*) Arrey, everything's gone! Everything! (*Notices that the idol is missing*) Even you, my lord, have left me! Thief! Thief! Thief!

He runs out, shouting. A crowd enters. The havaldar, by now wide awake, discovers the theft.

HAVALDAR. But I was right here! (*Runs out.*)

The chorus sings. Throughout the song, Charandas keeps coming in with stolen goods. Each time the havaldar chases him but Charandas gives him the slip. The first time, he assumes a Hanuman pose, fooling the havaldar into mistaking him for an idol. The second time, he chucks his bundle at the havaldar who involuntarily chucks it back—and then Charandas runs off with it. The third time the havaldar makes a grab for him, but he ducks; then the havaldar grabs at him again and he jumps. Each time the havaldar misses. The fourth time he pretends to be a crippled beggar and fools the havaldar yet again. With this, the song ends, and there is an intermission.

Tari nnari nahan mor naha nnari nahaannare suva mor
Taricha nari naha naari na!
Nare suva mor taricha nari naha naari na.

Oh, what can we say, friends, he is everywhere,
In nooks and in crannies, he's here and he's there.
So, friends and neighbours—quick, look over there,
Here comes the thief, out of thin air!

Tari naari nahan mor naha naari nahaanaare suva mor!
Taricha nari naha naari na!
Nare suva mor taricha nari naha naari na.

He robs and he steals in broad daylight,
Make sure your belongings are stowed out of sight,
In the village we'll shout as loud as we dare,
Here comes the thief, out of thin air!

Tari naari nahan mor naha naari nahaanaare suva mor!
Taricha nari naha naari na!
Nare suva mor taricha nari naha naari na.

It's fun to deceive, to cheat and to lie,
The cheats and the liars are doing just fine,
Oh friends, your belongings aren't safe, best beware
For here comes the thief, out of thin air!

Tari nnari nahan mor naha nnari nahannnare suva mor!
Taricha nari naha naari na!
Nare suva mor taricha nari naha naari na

The thief is a king, the king is a thief,
The gods and the thieves, they dance cheek to cheek,
The doctors themselves are too sick to take care,
Oh, here comes the thief, out of thin air!

Tari naari nahan mor naha naari nahannaare suva mor!
Taricha nari naha nnari na!
Nare suva mor taricha nari naha naari na

ACT TWO

SCENE ONE

The royal treasury. Music plays as four soldiers briskly enter carrying a treasure chest, preceded by the munim, the custodian of the treasury. The soldiers place the chest on stage left and take positions—two on the left, and two on the right. The munim sits on the platform in the centre and begins to go through his books. The guru enters and the chorus sings in accompaniment.

> The baba roams the forest alone,
> The sadhu roams the forest alone,
> Offer the sadhu a tiger skin,
> Offer a clerk some dough,
> Offer a peon a cup of tea,
> Need we say any more?
> With money it's done in a jiffy,
> That we know for sure.

CHARANDAS. I fall at your feet, guru-ji.

GURU. Jai ho! Jai ho!

CHARANDAS. I hope you haven't forgotten me, maharaj.

GURU. Arrey, beta, who can forget you? Your name echoes in people's hearts! Of all my disciples, you alone, Charandas, have brought glory to my name.

CHARANDAS. Yes, gurudev, I've stuck to my vow never to tell a lie.

GURU. As you have stuck to stealing! Only you could manage such a miracle.

CHARANDAS. Actually, guru-ji, I don't really steal any more either. Thanks to you I've gathered such a lot of wealth! There's only one bit of thievery left for me to do. Once that's done, I'll give up stealing altogether.

GURU. What's that one last bit of thievery, beta, that you have to do?

CHARANDAS. Look over there, guru-ji.

GURU. Arrey, baap re! You plan to rob the royal coffers! Arrey beta, you'll never get away with it. Her royal highness the queen won't rest till you're caught and punished. Arrey, you say you've collected a lot of wealth—why don't you just devote your days to looking after my welfare? It's much safer.

CHARANDAS. Guru-ji, from this day on you can relax. Now that we've found each other again, you have nothing to worry about. I'll never leave you. You stay with me and I'll look after you day and night. I'll just quickly rob the royal treasure and be back right away.

GURU. Beta, don't do it, or you'll never be back. There's a new minister due.

CHARANDAS. Let him come, maharaj. I have just one desire left—to rob the royal treasury. If I can't do that, then I'm not Charandas Chor, I'll change my name. What's that you said, guru-ji? There's a new minister expected?

GURU. Yes. There's strict security all over town.

CHARANDAS. What's the purpose of his visit?

GURU. He's here to do a stock taking of the royal treasury. The whole town knows about it.

CHARANDAS. Ah ha! I've just had an idea.

GURU. What?

CHARANDAS. I'll be back in a moment (*turns to leave*).

GURU (*following him*). Arrey, listen to me, Charandas—

CHARANDAS. Don't worry, guru-ji. Just go to my house. Ask anyone. Everyone knows my place, they'll direct you.

GURU. Listen—

CHARANDAS. You just stay there, I'll be along in a jiffy.

GURU. Just look there—see who's coming.

CHARANDAS. Is that the new minister?

GURU. It looks like it, Charandas.

CHARANDAS. Guru-ji, you stop the minister—

GURU. Why?

CHARANDAS. And then keep him chatting.

GURU. Good gracious! Chat to a minister? How can I do that?

CHARANDAS. You can do that, guru-ji, and meanwhile I'll do the job and be back.

GURU. I can't do it.

CHARANDAS. Guru-ji, this is the only request I've ever made of you. I beg you!

GURU. No, no, absolutely not. Out of the question.

CHARANDAS. Guru-ji, this is my very last robbery. Just help me out this once. I touch your feet, guru-ji.

GURU. Arrey, Charandas, you'll put me behind bars along with yourself!

CHARANDAS. If that happens, guru-ji, I'll get you out!

GURU. But you'll get me in first!

CHARANDAS. Look, he's come. Now it's in your hands, guru-ji!

GURU. Arrey, Ram, Ram! You'll be my ruination! Why did I even meet you, you rogue! Charandas, do one thing before you go—get me a heap of garlands.

CHARANDAS. Oof! I've got things to do, guru-ji! Why don't you get them yourself? (*Noticing the havaldar who has entered and is standing in a corner*) Hang on, let me send the havaldar.

GURU. Why d'you want to send the havaldar?

CHARANDAS. Why so scared, guru-ji?

GURU. He's a government servant, isn't he? Shouldn't I be scared of him?

CHARANDAS. But he's a pal, guru-ji.

GURU. A pal?

CHARANDAS. Yes, a real buddy of mine. I'll send the garlands through him.

Charandas steps forward till he can be seen by the havaldar. They look at each other. The havaldar who was about to light a bidi, pockets it and shrugs sadly, holding open his arms. Charandas comes into his arms. They embrace. Charandas whispers into his ear. The havaldar perks up and smiles. Charandas hands over a wad of notes. The havaldar walks out jauntily with the money. The minister enters upstage left. Charandas freezes. The minister passes him by. The guru accosts him, and Charandas makes his escape.

GURU. Huzoor, sarkar, may god bless you! May you live for ever!

MINISTER. This is no place to beg for alms, maharaj. Come to the house and you'll get something.

GURU. Begging, sarkar? Not at all! I've been waiting for you!

MINISTER. Waiting for me?

GURU. Yes, to ask you to an inauguration.

MINISTER. Inauguration? What inauguration?

GURU. There are so many concerns and organizations, all waiting for your arrival. When will the new minister come? When will he inaugurate our venture? They've all sent you garlands.

MINISTER. Garlands? Where? Where're the garlands?

GURU. You got here earlier than expected, maharaj. They're on their way, they'll be here any moment. Just wait a bit, I'll check—there, see, they've arrived! Bring them here, havaldar, bring them here!

(*The havaldar comes on upstage left, with flower garlands on his baton. The guru keeps garlanding the minister.*)

This is from Chhattisgarh, Delhi, India, London, the whole world.

By now the minister is covered with so many garlands that he can't see.

MINISTER. But I can't see a thing! My eyes are totally covered!

GURU. Don't worry, maharaj, I'll be your eyes.

(*Then the guru takes him by the hand and begins to guide him as if he was a blind man. The havaldar hands the minister a pair of scissors. One by one the guru announces a long series of inaugurations. The havaldar holds up the ribbon, and the minister cuts it.*)

Here you are, maharaj, a cycle shop. Please inaugurate it. (*They go through the charade*) This is a ration shop. (*Repeat*) And this is a shoe shop. A cloth shop. A paan shop.

MINISTER. And this? What's this?

GURU. The government has made the first public latrine in the city. Please inaugurate it. And this is . . . this is . . . I don't know what it is, but please inaugurate it all the same.

MINISTER. Is it over? Have we finished?

GURU. Not yet, minister-ji. We still have a few market places left to visit. People are waiting eagerly for you. Come, come with me. There's a lot to inaugurate yet.

He leads the minister off. The havaldar follows. Charandas comes on from the other side, posing as a minister of the Treasury. He freezes till they pass. Then he confronts the sentry authoritatively.

CHARANDAS. Why haven't you shaved today?

MUNIM. Minister-ji, minister-ji (*keeps bowing, ushers Charandas in*).

CHARANDAS. Where's the key?

MUNIM. Here it is, maharaj.

CHARANDAS. Where's the treasure chest?

MUNIM. There it is, maharaj.

CHARANDAS. Get back to your work. (*The munim returns to his place. Charandas goes up to the chest. He unlocks the chest.*) Ah ha! Diamonds! Precious stones! Silver! Gold bricks! But I don't want any of it. Wait—I'll take these gold coins, though. They have the queen's insignia on them. One, two, three, four, five—that's enough. What's the point of more? Five mohurs are more than enough for her to know that she was robbed.

He throws the keys back to the munim and departs. He finds himself face to face with the real minister at the gate. He salutes the minister by folding his hands silently. The minister reciprocates. Charandas begins to walk out. The minister, who has been struck by his clothes, turns around for another look. Charandas salutes him again and runs out. The minister tries to enter but finds his way barred by the sentries who cross spears to prevent his entry.

MINISTER. What impudence! How dare you!

SENTRY. Where d'you think you're going?

MINISTER. Don't you know who I am?

MUNIM. Stop him, stop him! Don't let him go!

MINISTER. What's happened to all of you? Can't you see who I am? I'm the new minister. I'm here to check the royal coffers.

MUNIM. Like hell you're the minister! Scoundrel, loafer, con man! Keep turning up in new disguises! Minister-ji has come, checked everything, and left. Get lost. Try making a fool of someone else.

MINISTER. The minister's come and gone?! Idiot! That must have been some thief! I'm the real minister.

MUNIM. That must have been a thief! You are the real minister! Arrey, please forgive me, minister-ji. Please forgive me! I didn't recognize you. And now that I think of it, that man wasn't wearing any shoes! A terrible blunder, please pardon me!

MINISTER. Go check the coffers. There's bound to have been a robbery. (*He sits in the munim's place while the munim goes to check.*)

MUNIM (*checking the contents*). This is intact . . . this is fine . . . And these gold bricks—are they genuine or has he changed them—no, they're okay. These gold mohurs—one, two, three, four, five, six, seven, eight—five mohurs are missing. One, two, three, four, only five mohurs missing! Now who's going to believe that someone stole only five gold coins? That's no theft at all! I think I'd do well to keep five myself and claim that ten were stolen. (*Pockets five coins and shouts*) Minister-sahib! Minister-sahib! Ten gold coins have been stolen!

MINISTER. Ten gold coins stolen! In your presence! How will I explain this to the queen? It's all your fault.

MUNIM. I didn't know, minister-sahib. (*To the sentries*) Come on, let's go.

They start to walk off, with the minister leading, followed by the cowering munim and the sentries.

MINISTER. Can't you tell the difference between a thief and a minister?

MUNIM. He was dressed just like you, minister sahib—kurta, dhoti, cap and all.

MINISTER. Does anyone who dresses like a minister become a minister?

MUNIM. He didn't have any shoes, though . . .

MINISTER. Well, you'll rot in jail for this. The queen's really going to give us hell—and you're coming with me to court, to get your share!

They exit.

SCENE TWO

The royal court. The queen enters in a rage, accompanied by two bodyguards, followed by the minister, the munim and the raj purohit. The queen is on the platform, with the guards who take position on the platform. The others are on the stage.

QUEEN. What? Theft in the royal treasury?

MINISTER. Yes, rani-sahib.

QUEEN. When?

MINISTER. Just now.

QUEEN. In broad daylight?

MINISTER. Yes, rani-sahib.

QUEEN. A dacoity?

MINISTER. I guess you could call it that.

MUNIM. It's not my fault, rani-sahib. I thought it was the new minister.

QUEEN. How much was stolen?

MUNIM. Ten mohurs.

QUEEN. That's all?

MINISTER. The thief is called Charandas, rani-sahib.

QUEEN. If you know who the thief is, why don't you catch him?

MINISTER. He's run off, rani-sahib.

QUEEN. So what did you expect? That he would hang around waiting for you to catch him? Or perhaps he's here, inside the palace?

PUROHIT. Rani-sahib, Charandas is a renowned thief. It's not easy to catch him.

QUEEN. Easy or not, purohit-ji, catch him we must. How can we let him go scot-free?

PUROHIT. There is a way of getting him to give himself up.

QUEEN. What's that?

PUROHIT. Charandas has sworn to his guru that he'll never tell a lie, and he takes great pride in keeping his word. My suggestion is that you make a public proclamation announcing that if Charandas is truly as truthful as he claims, he should present himself at your durbar and confess his crime. He's sure to respond.

QUEEN (*descending from the platform*). That's a good idea. Purohit-ji is right. (*To the minister*) Send out the messengers and tell them to spread the news that the queen has summoned Charandas to her durbar.

MINISTER. As you command, rani-sahib.

The queen exits, followed by the purohit. The minister, munim and soldiers exit in the other direction. Two messengers circle the stage, singing to the beat of drums, followed by two soldiers.

The rani-sahib wants it known,
Known both far and wide,
A thief broke into her treasury and stole,
Ten mohurs from inside.
Charandas, you truthful thief,
Don't you try and hide,
Since you are a truthful man,
Remember your pride.
Confess your crime in the durbar,
At the rani's side.
There's nothing greater than the truth,
The truth, tested and tried,
An honest man, even though he fails,
Can never be decried.
The rani-sahib wants this known,
Known both far and wide.

SCENE THREE

The palace. Charandas enters the court with his guru, preceded by the purohit who conducts them in. The queen, the minister and the munim come in from the other side.

QUEEN (*to the guru*). I touch your feet, maharaj.

GURU. Bless you! May you live long.

QUEEN (*calls to her maid*). Dasi! (*The maid enters.*)

MAID. Yes, rani-dai?

QUEEN. Bring alms for maharaj.

MAID. Yes, rani-dai.

PUROHIT (*noticing that Charandas is looking away*). Pay your respects. What are you gaping at?

CHARANDAS (*to the queen*). I touch your feet.

QUEEN. So your name's Charandas.

PUROHIT. Charandas the Thief, right?

CHARANDAS. Right, maharaj. Charandas the Thief.

QUEEN. A thief, and so proud!

CHARANDAS. I do a good job. Why shouldn't I be proud?

QUEEN. So stealing is a good job, is it?

CHARANDAS. Good or bad, everyone steals, rani-sahib.

QUEEN. What do you mean?

CHARANDAS. Others steal on the sly, while I do it in broad daylight, with great fanfare. That's the only difference.

QUEEN. And you never tell a lie?

CHARANDAS. If I manage to do my job without lying, why should I lie, rani-sahib?

QUEEN. Thieving and truthfulness—what an unheard-of combination! But tell me—you broke into the royal coffers, which were brimming over with riches, but you took only ten gold coins. What made you stop at that?

CHARANDAS. Not ten, rani-sahib, I took only five gold mohurs.

MUNIM. Arrey wah! (*The purohit glances at him sharply.*)

CHARANDAS. I did it because I wanted to bring myself to your notice. Everyone knows of me—I wanted you to hear of me too. So I stole only five mohurs, just enough to get noticed.

QUEEN. Mantri, how many mohurs were stolen?

MUNIM. Ten gold coins were stolen, rani-sahib. How can a thief ever be trusted to tell the truth?

QUEEN. Well, mantri-ji?

MINISTER. The munim counted them, rani-sahib.

GURU. Rani-sahib, Charandas is my disciple. He vowed to me that he'd never tell a lie. He's a thief, to be sure, but he's not a liar.

QUEEN. Mantri-ji, I demand to know who the liar is—Charandas or the munim!

MUNIM. I'm telling you, rani-sahib, ten mohurs are missing from the coffers!

CHARANDAS. He's probably telling the truth as well.

QUEEN. Meaning?

CHARANDAS. Ten mohurs may be missing from the coffers, but I took five, that's all I know. Munim knows best about the remaining coins.

QUEEN. Mantri!

MINISTER. Rani-sahib!

QUEEN. Who stole the other five mohurs?

MUNIM. I just told you, rani-sahib.

The queen looks at the purohit who is deep in thought.

PUROHIT (*after a moment's thought*). Mantri, search the munim.

The munim wails, runs to the queen and falls at her feet.

MUNIM (*pleading*). Rani-sahib!

QUEEN. Well?

MUNIM. Please have mercy on me, I made a grave mistake. Forgive me!

QUEEN. Where are those five gold coins?

MUNIM (*removing them from his pocket*). Here they are. Pardon me, rani-sahib! One, two, three, four, five (*handing them over*).

QUEEN. Get out of my sight! Don't let me set eyes on you again. Liar!

CHARANDAS (*to the munim*). Thief! (*The munim leaves.*)

QUEEN. Tell me this, Charandas—you vowed to give up lying but not to give up stealing. Why not?

CHARANDAS. But it's my dharma! How can I give up my dharma?

QUEEN. And it must be fun, too.

CHARANDAS. Great fun!

QUEEN. Okay, go, I pardon you. And you can keep these five mohurs as well, as a reward.

CHARANDAS. But I didn't earn them. The coins I earned are in my pocket. I live off my own hard-earned wealth. I have no need for the extra five coins. By the grace of god I have more than enough.

QUEEN. Charandas, you may be honest but you're far too rude.

CHARANDAS. I can't tell the difference between being honest and being rude, rani-sahib.

QUEEN. Yes, yes, I can see there's a lot you don't know.

CHARANDAS. That's right. (*The purohit gestures to him to keep quiet*)

QUEEN. All right, then I give these five coins to the maharaj for teaching Charandas never to lie (*hands them to the guru*).

GURU (*taking the coins*). Bless you, rani-sahib!

QUEEN. And I bequeath the five mohurs stolen by Charandas to him as a gift.

CHARANDAS. But that's my hard-earned money, rani-sahib. You can't gift them to me, I've already taken them. They're mine. Simple. Jai Siya Ram! (*He leaves.*)

GURU. God bless the queen! God bless the queen! (*He follows Charandas out.*)

MINISTER. Just say the word, your highness, and I'll have him arrested. (*The queen laughs.*)

PUROHIT. No, let him go. We should honour an honest man like him, send a procession to honour him, carry him in state through the town.

QUEEN. Quite right! Purohit-ji is right. Take a procession of horses and elephants and request Charandas to lead it on elephant-back. Parade him through the town, then bring him back here to the durbar. I wish to award him state honours for his honesty. Why are you standing there? Get moving!

MINISTER. As you command, rani-sahib.

He leaves. The queen moves onto the platform and exits followed by the purohit and two soldiers.

SCENE FOUR

A procession enters, with a group of panthi singers and dancers in front, who are singing and dancing.

Oh, Charandas, don't try to rob Death of his due,
Your name and your fame will be taken from you.

The liar, try as he might, can never give up lying,
Nor the gambler gambling though he may be trying,
Oh, Charandas, don't try to cheat Death of his due.

The drunkard, try as he will, can never give up drinking,
The thief may attempt it but can't give up stealing,
Oh, Charandas, don't try to rob Death of his due.

Truth is an addiction just like all the rest,
You might find your honesty put to the test,
Oh, Charandas, don't try to cheat Death of his due.

The minister enters, goes off and returns with Charandas.

CHARANDAS. Wah! What a grand procession! So many people, soldiers, horses. Arrey baap re! Even an elephant! Just look at it, all covered with gold!

MINISTER. Yes, Charandas, and all this is just for you. The queen has ordered it.

CHARANDAS. You mean the queen's sent this elephant specially for me?

MINISTER. Yes, she has ordered that we invite you to lead this procession on elephant-back all the way to her durbar, where she wishes to award you state honours.

CHARANDAS. Great! My guru and I will both ride in state! (*Suddenly he recalls his vow*) Oh—but I can't, mantri-ji. I can't ride elephant back. Please take this procession away.

MINISTER. Why? What's the matter now?

CHARANDAS. I've just remembered something.

MINISTER. What?

CHARANDAS. I vowed to my guru that I'd never lead a procession on elephant-back.

MINISTER. Look here, Charandas, a moment ago you were more than willing! What is this nonsensical vow! Think of how upset the queen will be. How will I explain it to her?

CHARANDAS. That's upto you, mantri-ji. I can't come.

MINISTER. The queen won't like this one bit, Charandas. Come along. Please.

CHARANDAS. No, I can't.

MINISTER (*shouts*). You must.

CHARANDAS (*shouts*). I won't. (*He leaves.*)

MINISTER (*thinks for a moment, then announces*). All you people may go home! Soldiers, come with me. Did you hear me? Come with me.

The procession breaks up. The minister and the soldiers follow Charandas off.

SCENE FIVE

The palace bedroom. The maid enters, prepares the bed, places a fan beside it and leaves. The queen enters, lies down, fans herself.

MAID (*re-enters*). Rani-sahib, mantri-ji is here.

QUEEN. Is the food ready?

MAID. Yes, rani-sahib.

QUEEN. Is Charandas with him?

MAID. I don't know, rani-ma.

QUEEN. Send him in!

MAID. Here, rani-ma?

QUEEN. That's what I said! (*The maid bows and exits.*)

MINISTER (*enters, bows with folded hands*). Rani-ma.

QUEEN. Well?

MINISTER. Charandas refused to come, rani-sahib. He refused to lead the procession.

QUEEN. Refused?

MINISTER. Yes, rani-sahib

QUEEN. But why?

MINISTER. He said he had vowed to his guru never to lead a procession or elephant-back.

QUEEN. The audacity! To spurn the royal command!

MINISTER. So I just brought him along by force, rani-sahib.

QUEEN. You've brought him? Where is he?

MINISTER. Bring him in!

Soldiers lead in Charandas tied with ropes. His guru is with him.

QUEEN. What have you done, mantri-ji? By whose orders have you done this? I said I wished to honour him for his honesty and you've dragged him here like an animal!

MINISTER. Your highness, I thought—a common thief flouts the queen's orders, if I don't take action against him, how will I explain things to the queen? So I ordered him bound and brought here by force.

QUEEN. Whose orders prevail here? Mine? Or the minister's?

MINISTER. I didn't know, your highness. I'm a new minister.

QUEEN. Listen carefully, then, and don't you ever forget it! Not a leaf stirs in this kingdom without my orders. Untie him at once!

MINISTER. Untie him. (*The soldiers set Charandas free.*)

QUEEN. Dasi, serve the food! I ask your pardon, Charandas. Here, have something to eat. (*The maid and two soldiers bring in dishes of food. The main dish is placed on the platform.*) Come, this feast is in your honour, you must eat.

Charandas comes up to the platform, glances at the minister who turns away, then reaches greedily for food. He sees the guru staring at him just as he is about to put the first morsel into his mouth. He drops it.

QUEEN. What's the matter, Charandas? Help yourself! Why have you stopped?

CHARANDAS. It's nothing, rani-sahib.

QUEEN. Do you suspect something? Shall I eat first, to reassure you?

CHARANDAS. No, no.

QUEEN. Then what is it?

CHARANDAS. I won't eat this, rani-sahib.

QUEEN. Don't you like the food?

CHARANDAS. It's not that.

QUEEN. Is it against your principles to dine at the queen's table? Answer me!

GURU. Rani, he's vowed never to eat off a golden platter.

QUEEN. Yet another vow! Look, forget your vow, and obey my command instead. (*Pause*) Eat something! Charandas. (*Pauses, then shouts*) I order you to eat. What? You won't? Tell me straight, will you eat or not? (*Charandas pushes away the plate in anger*) Mantri-ji, Charandas has insulted the state. Put him behind bars.

MINISTER. Arrest him!

The soldiers catch hold of him and carry him off. Charandas calls out.

CHARANDAS. Gurudev!

GURU. Bless you, my son! Bless you.

The guru and the minister leave. The queen paces up and down, talking to herself.

QUEEN. How could I? What have I done? (*Calls out to her maid*) Dasi!

MAID. Rani-ma.

QUEEN. Call him back.

MAID. Whom, rani-ma?

QUEEN. Charandas. Here, take the keys. (*She hands over the keys.*)

MAID. Yes, rani-ma.

QUEEN. Be careful. Don't let anyone see you. Use the back door.

MAID. Yes, rani-ma.

> *She exits. The queen continues to pace up and down. The maid returns and bows.*

QUEEN. Well?

MAID. He's here, rani-dai, in the outside room.

QUEEN. Did anyone see you?

MAID. Not a soul. We came through the back door. Here are the keys, rani-ma (*hands them over*).

QUEEN. Good. Listen—

MAID. Yes, rani-sahib?

QUEEN. Will he agree?

MAID. What a thing to say, your highness! Of course he'll agree! Why shouldn't he? All you have to do is ask. He's sure to agree.

QUEEN. He hasn't agreed to a single thing I've asked of him so far.

MAID. He only refused you before because you asked in front of other people. Alone he would have agreed to anything you asked. Is there a man alive who can refuse such a request? If you ask him in private, he'll never say no, I'm sure of it.

QUEEN. My heart is pounding.

MAID. Go on, call him in. Shall I go?

QUEEN. What will you say?

MAID. I'll say—rani-ma has called you . . .

QUEEN. When you brought him out of jail, what did you say?

MAID. I said rani-ma had summoned him.

QUEEN. And what did he say?

MAID. The poor chap said nothing.

QUEEN. He said nothing?

MAID. He kept asking, is the queen going to kill me?

QUEEN. Then what did you say?

MAID. I said, kill you? On the contrary, it's you who's killed the queen—she's dying for you! You've stolen her heart.

QUEEN. Then what did he say?

MAID. Nothing.

QUEEN. Nothing?

MAID. He said, I'm a thief, after all. It's my job to steal things, but the one thing I've never stolen before is a heart. Now it seems I've done that too! And he began to laugh (*maid laughs*).

QUEEN (*joins in, then stops abruptly*). What? So you've been making merry with him, have you?

MAID. Rani-ma, you asked, so I told you. But the poor fellow didn't say much.

QUEEN. Poor fellow indeed! Then why do you exaggerate?

MAID. I was only repeating what happened, rani-ma.

QUEEN. Go, bring him in. But, listen, do it nicely. Don't scare him.

MAID. Yes, your highness.

QUEEN. And listen—you wait outside. Go, now. (*She exits. The queen moves about restlessly. In a moment Charandas enters, rubbing up a wad of tobacco*) Come in, Charandas. What's that in your hand?

CHARANDAS. A little tobacco, that's all.

QUEEN. Let me have a little . . . is it good?

CHARANDAS. Gives you a bit of a kick. (*The queen tries some and starts coughing. Charandas laughs.*)

QUEEN. Charandas, please forgive me.

CHARANDAS. Don't talk like this, rani-ma.

QUEEN. Don't call me ma! My name is Kalavati . . .

CHARANDAS. I touch your feet and beg forgiveness. Please forgive me!

QUEEN. No, no, don't touch my feet!

CHARANDAS. What to do? I'm nothing but a thief, used to rough and abusive talk all my life. I have no idea how to talk to a queen. Excuse my poor manners, rani-ma!

QUEEN. Charandas, there isn't another man like you in the entire kingdom. I have a great respect for you, but it's hard for me to talk of it openly . . . Now you tell me—if I hadn't had you locked up, how would I have managed a moment alone with you? You would have gone away. It was the only way I could think of to stop you from leaving!

CHARANDAS. Rani-ma!

QUEEN. Don't call me that, please . . .

CHARANDAS. I'm not feeling well . . .

QUEEN. Why, what's the matter? Why don't you sit down? Relax . . . (*takes him by the hand, makes him lie down, massages his legs*).

CHARANDAS. I feel as if you're about to test me.

QUEEN (*checking that no one's about*). My life is empty without you, Charandas! I want to marry you. (*Charandas pulls away*) Look, don't say no. You've refused me everything I've asked of you so far. Please agree to this one request. The kingdom needs a king like you. (*Charandas moves away*) What do you say? Think well before you answer. Don't refuse me, Charandas.

CHARANDAS. Rani-ma . . .

QUEEN. Haven't I already told you not to call me that!

CHARANDAS. Rani-sahib, I can't agree to this. Please excuse me.

QUEEN. Why? Don't you like me?

CHARANDAS. Don't say such things, rani-sahib! You're so beautiful, and I'm a man after all, not a saint!

QUEEN. To me you're a god. I'll worship you, adore you, serve you. No other man has ever touched my mind and heart the way you have. Ever since I set eyes on you, I can't sleep, I can't eat or drink a thing! Charandas, take pity on me! Don't refuse me.

CHARANDAS. I can't forget the vow I made to my guru, rani.

QUEEN. What? Yet another vow? Don't tell me that you took a vow never to marry a queen, never to sit on a throne or rule a kingdom!

CHARANDAS. Yes. What can I say? I was playing the fool. It was just a joke. I vowed never to do four things—and such is fate that one by one each of those things has been offered to me! How was I to know that a queen like you would really want to marry me? Now you tell me, what can I do?

QUEEN. Since you took these vows as a joke, forget about them. Ask your guru to pardon you. Do penance, if necessary. We can hold an atonement ceremony and gather all the ascetics and holy men and fulfil all the rituals necessary to absolve you. We'll shower your guru with alms and ask his forgiveness. Then we'll get married. All right?

CHARANDAS. Now I've had it! Sorry, rani-sahib, I can't break my vow. I just can't.

QUEEN (*quivering with anger*). Vow! Vow! Vow! Damn your vows! Charandas, I'm warning you for the last time! Think it over carefully. Will you change your mind? (*Charandas turns away. The queen moves about restlessly, then suddenly falls at his feet.*) All right, Charandas, I accept your four vows, but you must listen to me. I'll never bring up the subject of marriage again, but you must agree to one request. Will you say yes?

CHARANDAS. What's the request?

QUEEN. Never reveal what has passed between us to anyone, otherwise I will be ruined! Promise me this.

CHARANDAS. Rani!

QUEEN. What is it?

CHARANDAS. You're forgetting something.

QUEEN. What?

CHARANDAS. I've taken a vow always to tell the truth.

QUEEN. Vowed to tell the truth! Vowed to tell the truth! You can do that only if you live to tell the truth!

CHARANDAS. Rani-ma!

QUEEN (*rushes to the platform*). Dead men tell no tales! Have you lost your desire to live, Charandas?

CHARANDAS. Whether I live or die, I won't go back on my word to my guru. I can't break my vow. I beg you, rani-sahib, forgive me! Don't have me killed! Don't commit the sin of murder!

QUEEN (*shrieks*). Thief! Chandal! Impertinent rogue!

CHARANDAS. Rani! Rani-sahib!

QUEEN (*shouts*). Guards! (*Attendants and guards come running in, followed by the purohit, minister and maid, all from different directions.*) Who allowed this thief to escape? Who set him free? How did he get into my room? Where were all of you? The cheek of this lout! Charandas was actually suggesting that I marry him!

CHARANDAS. Rani-sahib!

QUEEN. The gall of the man! And a common thief at that!

CHARANDAS. Rani-sahib!

QUEEN. What are you all gaping at? Such a rogue should be slaughtered, sliced into pieces, hung, drawn and quartered!

To slow drumbeats, the sentries advance towards Charandas with stylized move-ments, with their weapons drawn. They close in on him. They attack and fell him. The drumbeats cease. The queen crouches in distress. The purohit, telling his beads, looks on appalled. The queen slowly rises, starts to walk off, turns for a last look, then breaks down and rushes out in tears. One soldier turns the body over with his spear. Everyone leaves. Two servants enter with a clay lamp, roll back the carpet, and lift the body. The lamp is placed where Charandas's head lay. As they leave, the Satnamis, barebodied with white loincloths, carrying their white flags, enter. On the spot where his head lay, they plant the flag on a pedestal, place the lamp on the pedestal, break a coconut, shower the spot with flowers, circling the pedestal and singing their song.

The truth is divine,
Divine is the truth,
Nothing compares,
So saith our guru,
With the sacred, the

Holy, the power of
Truth.

We worship our guru,
We offer our prayers,
We chant him this hymn,
We sing him this air.

They go off stage. The chorus comes on and sings the closing song.

An ordinary thief is now a famous man,
And how did he do it?
By telling the truth.

His heroic exploits, dear friends, are now immortalized,
And how did he achieve this?
By telling the truth.
Thieving was his destiny, he was both rich and poor,
He lived a strange, unusual life
By telling the truth.

Jokingly he made a vow never to tell a lie,
Even though he had to die
For telling the truth.

Charandas the Thief he was, he was an honest thief,
Charandas the honest thief,
Who always told the truth.

An ordinary thief, dear friends, who's now a famous man,
And how did he achieve this?
By telling the truth!

On the last refrain, the entire cast comes on stage. When the song ends, the stage is full. Curtain call.

THE END

BAHADUR THE WINE-SELLER

Translated by Anjum Katyal

TRANSLATOR'S NOTE

ANJUM KATYAL

The translation of *Bahadur Kalarin* was set in motion by Habib Sa'ab in 2004; he sent me a handwritten script, along with an English translation of the songs done by his wife and partner in theatre, Moneeka Misra Tanvir. Although the script was in Devanagari, the language was Chhattisgarhi. My previous translations of Habib Sa'ab's plays—*Charandas Chor* and *Hirma ki Amar Kahani*— had benefited from the close involvement of Habib Sa'ab himself. But by the time I took up *Bahadur Kalarin*, he had left us.

The biggest challenge was the Chhattisgarhi dialect, at once blunt and colourful, economical and expressive. Social relations are efficiently conveyed through speech, mode of address, and relative formality or informality of tone. Retaining the same nuances in English was a struggle. Some words have been deliberately left in the original, as an English equivalent would sound inappropriate and out of place. In such instances, a footnote supplies the approximate meaning. This also serves as a marker and reminder of the process of translation, rendering it transparent, which to my mind is preferable to opacity and the erasure of the original text.

With the songs I have taken the same approach as in my previous two translations of Habib Sa'ab's plays: to convey the spirit and message while ensuring that thanks to rhythm and rhyme they can in fact be performed as songs if so desired. In the interest of consistency, I chose to translate the songs straight from the Chhattisgarhi, despite my access to the English translation.

I am grateful to the inputs and help provided by Prabha Katyal and Nageen Tanvir, without whom this translation would have taken much, much longer.

Calcutta, August 2017

THE LEGEND OF KALARIN

And the Challenges of Preparing a Stage Presentation

HABIB TANVIR

In Durg District of Chhatisgarh, in Balode Tehsil, there are three villages—Navagaon, Sorargarh and Chirchari. These three villages lie close to one another; in fact, Sorar and Chirchari are almost adjoining. A woman named Bahadur lived here. She belonged to the Kalar or wine-brewing caste. Bahadur would sit on her golden macholi, or stool, and dispense her liquor. Not just neighbouring villagers, people would come from far and wide to her wine shop.

The land hereabouts is rocky. There are deep ruts and grooves, like drains, in the rocks, and scattered all over are round hollows that look man-made rather than natural. People say that customers would come in their bullock carts from miles around to drink at Bahadur's shop; the ruts have been worn by the wheels of these innumerable vehicles. As for the row upon row of round hollows, they say these are mortars. Bahadur would hand pestles to her many daughters-in-law and order them to go and pound grain. Bahadur had only one son—Chhachhaan Chadu. He had married 'six agar six kori' times. The unlettered inhabitants of Chhatisgarh count in 'koris'. One kori equals the number twenty. This is similar to the way calculation is done in France, in units of twenty. 'Agar' means 'ahead' or 'more than'. Adding up to a total of

126. So Bahadur had 126 daughters-in-law. Those holes were pounded by them.

In 1975–76, I visited this area for the first time. At the time there were still some local villagers who knew the story of Bahadur and her son. I had managed to lay my hands on a slim volume titled *Durg Parichay* (An Introduction to Durg) written by Baldev Prasad Misra, a Hindi writer from Rajnandgaon, which contained a brief history of Durg. It also contained the geography of the region, including maps, as well as information about some minerals found locally. This book devoted a couple of pages to the legend of Bahadur Kalarin. Bahadur was a beautiful woman, renowned as much for her beauty as for her wine. So people travelled to Sorar and Chirchari village with the dual intention of seeing her legendary beauty and partaking of her excellent wine.

Chhachhaan Chadu took 126 wives but remained unfulfilled and dissatisfied. Finally, when he cast lustful eyes on his mother, Bahadur was stunned. She decided that it was best to end the boy's life. So she prepared a range of hot and spicy dishes and fed them to him lovingly with her own hands. She told her daughters-in-law that they need not fill water from the well that day. She had influence in the village. She was a wealthy woman. She commanded the respect of the village folk. She informed them that if Chhachhaan should ask for water, no one was to give him even a drop to drink. Chhachhaan was disliked by them anyway. At this chance to take their revenge, they all agreed to obey Bahadur. As a result, he returned home maddened by thirst and begged his mother for water to drink. She replied: 'Today there's no water in the house. Go and draw water for yourself.' When he went to the well to draw water, she pushed him in and killed him. She then plunged a dagger into her own breast. Later people saw that a bush had sprouted in the well, bearing multi-coloured flowers, with each petal of a different hue. People came from far and wide to see this extraordinary flower, including some tourists from Germany. One of them, a scientist, plucked a sample to take back to his laboratory. However, his experiments came to nought. He was unable to discover how such a miraculous flower could bloom, nor if any such flower was to be found elsewhere on the globe. The only strange and wonderful outcome was that this strange and wonderful flower withered and died, and despite a hundred attempts was never to flower again. All the colours of the flower were those of the jewels Bahadur had been wearing when she died.

This tale was in the book. The villagers also knew the story. When I visited Sorar-Chirchari I saw that all over the place, in the fields, the open areas, the lanes, were strewn little stone figurines. The people said that whenever they dug the ground for any reason, they uncovered these little statuettes. Sometimes they unearthed bits of gold as well. I saw that in a nearby field there was a large rock, bearing inscriptions in Pali script. Even this ancient rock, according to them, was linked to the legend of Bahadur. Some also said that this was the very rock on which Bhimsen had slain Keechak. Close by was a temple-like structure in ruins. I heard that this marked the spot from which Bahadur sold her wine, sitting on her golden stool. A large statue was lying close by. It was about four and a half feet long and about three and a half feet wide. It was of a heavily bejeweled woman and a young man with a sword at his waist. I was told that it was a statue of Bahadur and her son Chhachhaan Chadu.

At the time, Nurul Hasan was the Education Minister in Delhi. I told him the whole story and said, why not remove one or two of the larger artefacts for safe keeping in the museum? What harm can that cause? They could be easily shifted to the nearby Raipur museum if nothing else. Nurul Hasan told me, 'Habib, how many things can we shift, and from how many places? The whole country is full of such things; the very soil is marked with myriad such historic signs. Museums will not have space enough for it all.'

Three or four years later I once again got the opportunity to visit the Sorar-Chirchari area. I saw that the large statue of Bahadur and Chhachhaan had been shifted by the village zamindar into his own compound. It was now his personal property. Before I drew attention to it, no one had paid any heed to this remarkable statue, or thought it of any value. When I first narrated the tale of Bahadur only a few village elders knew about it. This young zamindar certainly had never heard it before. I asserted that such treasures belonged in a museum. At the time I was a member of the Rajya Sabha [the upper house of the Indian parliament]. No doubt my words had an impact on him, and he quickly appropriated it for himself without knowing its real worth. I still regret that I did not myself pick up that statue at the time!

Later I saw that when the dam came up at Gangrel, with the aim of creating new channels of irrigation from the river Mahanadi, the villages of Sorar-Chirchari and Navagaon came under the scheme. I noticed while passing by that the digging up of the land for canals had begun. Bits of gold and ancient statuettes and relics were still being unearthed. Why not inform the Archaeological Survey to conduct their own digs to explore what comes out of this earth, before the canal digging takes over? Once again my suggestion was ignored. After all, irrigation was also important. Without water for the fields how can progress take place? Why delay such urgent work?

Meanwhile, I made up my mind to write a play based on this story. But I faced a few problems which it took me about two years to resolve. First I narrated the story to the Chhattisgarhi artistes in my group. Then I asked them, from time to time, to take up portions of the story for improvisation, to create some scenes. We kept busy with other plays, but in between whenever we had some time we'd turn to this story of Bahadur and do some interpretation, some exploration. I'd say, 'Thakur Ram, you play the Raja and let Fida Bai be Bahadur. You know the story, now improvise a scene. Let's see.' Both Fida Bai and Thakur

Ram had a great facility for inventing dialogue, but despite their great imaginative and language skills, I was left dissatisfied. Something was missing.

I was facing three main problems with this play. First, how should a delicate and sensitive subject like that of the incestuous desire of a son for his mother be dealt with and shown; second, in which way was I to depict 126 marriages on stage? Third, Bahadur apparently never looked at another man after the king, her first lover, deserted her. She was a beautiful woman, and she made a huge success of her wine business, growing wealthy and powerful in the process. Considering the feudal times she lived in, why highlight her faults and contradictions?

Finally, I decided to sit and down and talk fully and frankly to the actors, so that certain issues could be brought into the open and made clear. I said, 'Bhai, you are depicting the lovers as badmash, rascals. But why? Think of your own lives, the lives of those around you, your friends and relatives. Isn't it possible that you can fall in love, then part from your sweetheart with the genuine intention of returning, but get so caught up in your life and its problems that you fail to keep your promise? Is it always a deliberate plot to fool the girl?'

Actually, the folk legend is only about mother and son. The lover, who is the medium via which she acquires a son, plays no real role in the tale, nor is anything mentioned about his background or personality. This is a creation of my imagination. I had the myth of Oedipus Rex in mind. Our scriptures do occasionally hint at incestuous tendencies between siblings but I was astonished at the psychological depth of the Oedipus Complex revealed in this folk myth—and I felt a kind of pride, too. Western countries have a high regard for Greek literature. Indeed, it is seen as the source of their civilization. Our own civilization, so much older than theirs, with its many cultures and various philosophies, is not just held to be of no account, but on the contrary, we are told that the origin of all art, culture and science in the world can be traced back to Greece and Rome.

I said all this to my actors. I thought to myself, what would such simple village folk know of matters like this? I said, 'Perhaps you all don't know about incest.' I had barely said this, and they began to relate such stories! One better than the other. One said, 'Just recently in Khairagarh a man was killed. He used to live with his daughter.' Another spoke of a relationship between an uncle and niece. A third about a father-in-law and his daughter-in-law, a fourth about something else. It was like a chorus of voices. I was amazed. They knew more about this than I did! One even said, 'In Dhamtary, there's a rumour of an unnatural relationship between a mother and son. Who knows if it is true. That's what everyone says. But it's certainly true that mother and son both live in the same house.' I told him, it need not necessarily be true. What matters to me is not whether the rumour is true or false, but that if such a possibility exists in the minds of ordinary folk, then they are familiar with such matters. That's all we need for our play.

Then I said to them, Incest can be a sickness. I spoke about Freud and asked: 'Why do you put all the blame on Chhachhaan? Isn't it is possible that some responsibility rests with Bahadur? Imagine this—after all, he was the only male in the house. Suppose she allowed him to sleep in her bed till he was quite grown, perhaps twelve or thirteen? Perhaps he even wet the bed occasionally, and she would bathe him, clean him, massage him with oil, comb his hair. The outcome of this may have been the growth of a sickness within the boy. Think of it as an umbilical cord that remained uncut. The result—he undertook marriage after marriage but each time felt as if his body was inert. Yet if his mother touched his head or stroked his hair his body sprang to life. He felt his virility return. When, after 126 brides he realised this fully, he blurted out to his mother, 'I've seen many women but I've never seen a woman like you.' From that day on, there was a difference in the rehearsals. Fida Bai was a very thoughtful and sensitive actor. She changed her whole approach and the effect could be felt on Chhachhaan Chhadu's acting as well.

In order to complete the complex Oedipal aspect, I added another link to the story. As I have said, there was next to no mention of Bahadur's lover in the original tale, which centres on mother and son. I increased the importance of the father's role. When, after a long absence of many years, the father comes into the area in the course of buying land, and encounters Chhachhaan Chhadu, the two men get into a confrontation and the son kills the father. The only difference is that in Sophocles' *Oedipus Rex*, the son kills the father without knowing who he is; while in Bahadur Kalarin the son kills the father knowingly. In the course of their confrontation, when Chhachhaan realizes that the Raja of Gangrel is his father, he is enraged. He accuses him of deserting them, and then tells him to come home with him. When the king prevaricates, he challenges him to fight. The king holds back, refuses to lift his lathi, tries to calm him down, but the boy will not back off. Finally the king is forced to pick up his lathi; the two fight; and the king dies.

In today's narrow minded and intolerant times, if Bahadur Kalarin was to be made into a film, it would immediately be censored or banned. People are bound to protest, take out processions, petition the cinema hall and demand the film be shut down, and even, given what one sees all around us nowadays, destroy the hall and perhaps tear down the screen—who knows. I was even worried that, quite apart from political goons, perhaps even the local village people would object to this play being staged; but when we presented it in the open air at Korba, to a massive audience consisting of factory labourers, middle-class office workers, along with thousands of others, I was astounded at the pin drop silence in which they watched the entire tragedy. And when this play was performed in Jamshedpur to a Chhattisgarhi audience, there too the reaction was the same. But after this, when it was discussed in a workshop, two men objected. They were members of the Chhattisgarh Assembly. When I replied that this was a local folk story, and that I took pride in the fact that a story like that of Bahadur Kalarin could form part of the oral literature, they said, even if it is one of the Chhattisgarh stories, why should this one be flaunted to the whole world? What could I say to that? I couldn't even reply that not just in the towns, even in the rural areas people had not just accepted, but praised the play. In fact, in Kolkata, where the organizers did not promote it well, there was just one show scheduled, and the audience was very sparse. However, amidst them was the leading Bengali playwright and writer Jyotirmoy Dutta. He wrote in the influential publication *Desh* the very next day, not only showering praise on the production, but also castigating the organizers for the poor publicity which had deprived theatre goers from seeing this excellent play.

As for the challenge of depicting 126 marriages—I solved it as follows.[1] After showing the first two marriages, I introduced a chorus song in the course of which the multiple marriages were shown. I stopped short of the final wedding. In the first wedding, while the wedding song is being sung, both mothers-in-law are shown praising their own offspring to the skies. Suddenly there is the sound of a quarrel between the bride and groom and Chhachhaan storms in. The bride's mother leaves, singing her daughter's praises and badmouthing the groom. Bahadur slaps her son and tries to reason with him but he is adamant and insists that he wants to remarry. The failure of the second marriage is shown thus—Bahadur is sleeping on her mat, when Chhachhaan comes out of his room and lies down next to her. She is startled awake and questions him. He refuses to return to his bride, and she asks him, 'How long can you carry on lying in your mother's lap?' In this way, the play hints at incest. For the third marriage, we use a Baiga (shaman) who conducts rituals and goes into a trance, speaking in the devta's voice and advocating a third marriage. This takes care of the third marriage. After that I had to find a way of showing the remaining marriages in a dramatic and interesting way. What I did was, I devoted an entire scene to the final marriage. The Gond dancers of Mandala perform a sequence in which six boys and six girls sing and dance. Chhachhaan and his mother are standing at the threshold of their house. The girls come dancing one by one and stand before Chhachhaan. The ritual arti is done, each girl is handed a pestle by Bahadur, and she rejoins the line of dancers. So the song and dance continues while the marriages are dramatized.

A professor at some performing arts university wrote a strange comment on the 'pestle dance' in *Bahadur Kalarin*. The subject of the book was Indian dance. He airs his little knowledge on the spectrum of dance across India even though his information is restricted to the Mandala Adivasi Gond dances—in other words, those dances in which he himself participated. When he lists the other traditional Chhattisgarhi dances, he mentions the 'pestle dance' which had grown extinct but received a fresh lease of life by being included in Habib Tanvir's *Bahadur Kalarin*. In fact, the so-called pestle dance is not a traditional dance at all. It was created especially to help the plot of the play. Indeed, who can presume to teach the Mandala Gond dancers how to dance—they have rhythm and dance running in their veins. All we needed to do was weave in the pestle movement, and they pounded and swung around as if they had done it for generations. This dance was what the learned professor titled the 'pestle dance'. He thus increased the pages of his book, expanded the list of traditional Gond dances, and got it prescribed as a college text for students, thereby earning himself some additional income. Not just that, he also endowed the Bahadur tale with a fake history, as a result of which Surargarh village is in Ratanpur zila; he even added a paragraph on the ancient history of Ratanpur. There is no connection between this play, the dance and the history of Ratanpur, nor does any village by the name of Surargarh exist anywhere in Ratanpur. The wonder of it all is that Professor Sahib has actually worked as a dancer with me in *Bahadur Kalarin*. He has heard the whole history of this play from me, along with the entire cast. I have no idea whether he is genuinely mistaken or whether he has deliberately invented all this to suit his purpose.

Through the dialogue of the final marriage scene one gets to know that 125 marriages have already been held, and it is now time for the 126th one. I wanted to present the solution of my third problem in this scene. The villagers are up in arms, and band together to prevent this marriage. Their daughters are all suffering in Bahadur's home. They converge on the house of the bride-to-be's father, and threaten to attack. One man prevents this, and says, 'You should be attacking Bahadur's home.' They start to move towards her place. Bahadur comes out to face them, and they freeze as if they've seen a poisonous snake. She scolds them and proudly claims: 'It's no problem for me to find a bride for my son. If not this village, another village will provide a girl.' At this point Chhachhaan says, 'No, ma, If I marry I will only marry her.' The father of the bride protests, 'You've all married off your own girls, and now that my daughter has a chance you're trying to stop it!' Bahadur tells him, 'Why are you standing there? You go prepare for the ceremony, and I'll take care of this end.' Saying which, she leaves. One by one the villagers, liked cowed dogs, file out with their tails between their legs. In this way, the change in Bahadur's and Chhachhaan's mentality and behaviour is clearly shown. There is a clear stamp of feudalism on the encounter.

Apart from this, any loose ends left to complete the story were tied up through the medium of song. Some are traditional, such as the wedding song. Some were written with the purpose of communicating to the audience what couldn't be relayed just through dialogue. Or you could say that these songs helped move the storyline forward, or threw light on aspects of the narrative, or helped uncover deeper nuances and layers. Gangaram Saket was invited to be part of our rehearsals in Delhi. He was attending rehearsals, listening to me talk, watching me direct, and writing the songs. Gangaram was a leading folk poet of Raipur. He had worked with me previously. He had written some songs for *Charandas Chor* along with Swarna Kumar Sahu. So we were comfortable working with each other. Both have passed on. Their work, their songs, live on.

Bhopal, 3 July 2004

NOTE

1 This description differs from the sequence followed in both the printed and handwritten script on which this translation is based. As Naya Theatre's working process involved continuous improvisation, it is possible that it belongs to a slightly different version of the play. [Trans.]

The first production of *Bahadur Kalarin* was staged at AIFACS Auditorium, Delhi in 1978. The credits reproduced below appear in the Hindi volume published by Vani Prakashan, New Delhi, 2004.

BAHADUR KALARIN	Fidabai Markam
BAHADUR'S UNCLE	Babudas Baghel
KING/RAJA	Habib Tanvir
WASHERMAN/DHOBI	Ravi Sen
WASHERWOMAN/DHOBIN	Rikadbai Markam
LANDOWNER OF MOHARA	Govindram Nirmalkar
LANDOWNER OF NAVAPARA	Devilal Nag
CHHACHHAN	Amarsingh Lahrey
FRIEND OF CHHACHHAN	Murli Markam
KING'S TWO SONS	Ravilal Sanghrey, Dwarka Prasad
RAVI (FATHER-IN-LAW)	Brijlal Lenjvar
VILLAGE HEAD	Ramcharan Nirmalkar
CUSTOMER	Hridayram Nishad
SIX DAUGHTERS-IN-LAW	Shyama Tekam
	Kalavati
	Sonia
	Janaki
	Narbadiya
	Tulsiya
OTHERS	Repertory

COSTUMES, PROPS	Monika Misra Tanvir
SCRIPT, DIRECTION, SET DESIGN	Habib Tanvir
	The songs are by Gangaram Saket

OPENING SONG

Oh come hear us tell of a lovely maid
A Kalarin of wine-brewer caste
Famed in Chirchari and Sorar village
Her story we must broadcast
Bahadur Kalarin and her tale—
Long may her memory last!

Our village of Sorar-Chirchari indeed
Is a popular pilgrimage site
With her as the grand presiding deity
Her shop a temple bright
A stream of pilgrims have left their mark
Believe us, it's quite a sight.

Deep the grooves of bullock cart wheels
Hollows by pestles pounded
The rocks around still bear these signs
Of when visitors abounded
From as far afield as Kashi Mathura
They came and their gaiety sounded
These rocks still yielding relics untold
Show the legend is not unfounded

We'll spread her story far and wide
Long may her name resound
She was a legendary lass indeed
She does Chhattisgarh proud!

SCENE ONE

KING. So this is where you're hiding!

BAHADUR. Why are you following me around?

KING. What were you doing in that jungle?

BAHADUR. Collecting mahua.[1] And you? What were you doing there?

KING. I was out hunting. Why did you run when you saw me? Scared?

BAHADUR. Sitting high up on your horse staring at me like that! So I came home.

KING. So this is your home?

BAHADUR. Yes it is.

KING. Who all live here?

BAHADUR. My uncle and I.

KING. Where is he?

BAHADUR. He's gone to buy vegetables

KING. Okay then give me some water to drink . . .

BAHADUR. That will be two rupees for a double.

KING. Two rupees for a double?

BAHADUR. Yes, we serve wine here, not water.

KING. Oh, so you're a Kalarin, are you?

BAHADUR. Yes.

KING. What's your name?

BAHADUR. Bahadur[2]

KING. Liar! Come, give me some water.

BAHADUR. Go drink from the well.

KING. How can I drink straight from the well?

BAHADUR. Like the animals do, put your mouth to it!

KING. Okay, tell me where the bucket is.

BAHADUR. There, up on the roof thatch.

KING. Where?

BAHADUR. There.

KING. Oh the bucket is kept up there?

BAHADUR. Yes.

KING. Where is the ladder?

BAHADUR. We don't have a ladder.

KING. Then how do I get to the bucket?!

BAHADUR. Jump.

KING. Jump? Tell me how . . .

BAHADUR. Shall I show you?

KING. Show me?

BAHADUR. Here, get down on your hands and knees.

She gets on his back, falls, the King bends down, she climbs onto his back.

KING. Did you sprain your foot?

BAHADUR. No, I didn't sprain it, a thorn pricked me.

KING. You got pricked by a thorn?

BAHADUR. Yes, you have a thorny back.

KING (*laughs*). Let me see . . . Yes, I actually do have thorns caught in my clothes. Must be from roaming the forest while hunting. Look, such a big thorn.

BAHADUR. What a liar! Where is it?

KING. What, can't you see it? There, I've thrown it away.

He looks at her and laughs, then picks up a macholi.[3]

BAHADUR. Arrey, arrey, don't go into the shop, there's no water-shawter there! Where are you taking my stool? That's what I sit on! Don't dirty it!

KING. I'll wipe it clean and put it back. Let me get the bucket down.

He falls while reaching for the bucket.

KING. Your macholi is as wayward as you are.

BAHADUR. Hey, don't abuse me!

KING. And what kind of strange bucket is this? It has no rope! How am I to draw water? I'm sure that if I ask for a rope you'll say there isn't one!

BAHADUR. We really don't have one.

KING. Didn't I say so?

BAHADUR. Here, tie this dhoti to the bucket.

King ties the Washerman's laundry to the pail. Both the bucket and the clothes fall into the well.

KING. Looks like I'll die of thirst here in front of your house!

BAHADUR (*looking into the well*). Oh look, you've thrown the clothes into the well! When my uncle gets back he'll really let you have it!

KING. Well if you fetch a hook I'll fish it out for you. Now you'll say there's no hook!

BAHADUR. Are we ironsmiths to keep hooks lying around?

KING. Then how do I get the clothes out?

BAHADUR. Jump in! Don't you know how to swim?

KING. I don't know how to swim in a well.

BAHADUR. Didn't your parents teach you anything? In our village, little boys can jump right in, and if you throw in some coins, they find them, and bring them back to you clenched between their teeth!

KING. Great, I'll throw in some coins, bring all the village lads!

BAHADUR. Just get those clothes out or my uncle will be furious!

WASHERWOMAN. Bahadur, what's happened?

BAHADUR. A cow has eaten up your clothes.

WASHERWOMAN. Oh, oh! Really? I can't see the clothes . . . Where is it?

BAHADUR. Where is what?

WASHERWOMAN. The cow?

BAHADUR. It's standing right there.

WASHERWOMAN. What? Why did you take my clothes? Are you fooling around with this child? Where are my clothes!?

KING. Arrey bhai, your clothes were coming in the way of our fun and games, so I picked them up and put them aside, that's all.

WASHERWOMAN. Where are they?

KING. That side.

WASHERWOMAN. I can't see them.

KING. (*turning her around*) Look there!

WASHERWOMAN. Oh! Oh, how dare you touch me! Just see, Seema's father!

WASHERMAN. What's the matter?

WASHERWOMAN. He has defiled me!

WASHERMAN. Defiled you? How dare you?

KING. Like this.

WASHERMAN. Look, my dear, all the clothes are lying in the well.

WASHERWOMAN. What? Bahadur!

BAHADUR. He threw them in.

KING. I'm telling you, she knows witchcraft! Under her spell all the clothes ended up in the well. I must say I've been to many places but I've never seen a village like yours.

BAHADUR. How could you have? It wasn't in your destiny.

KING. And I've never set eyes on a girl like you.

BAHADUR. Really? Here, take a good look!

UNCLE. Now what's the problem? What's the matter, bhaiya? What new ruckus has she kicked up?

WASHERMAN. The clothes have fallen into the well. If I had a hook I could have taken them out.

UNCLE. Bahadur, why did you throw their clothes into the well? Bahadur!

KING. He's right. I'm seeing her for the first time. So her name is Bahadur. Is she your daughter?

UNCLE. Like my daughter, Maharaj. She's my brother's daughter. She lost her parents when she was a child. I brought her up, but she's a real handful. I can't control her. What brought you here? Which village are you from?

KING. I am the Raja of Gangrel. I was out hunting. My falcon led me here. I was looking for it and ended up here.

UNCLE. Falcon!

KING. Yes, it's a bird I reared and trained myself. Helps me in bird hunting.

BAHADUR. Oh we call it a chhachhaan. Where is your chhachhaan?

KING. Must be around here somewhere, it'll show up.

UNCLE. How can I be of service, Maharaj? Would you care for some milk?

KING. No, I don't want milk but I'm very thirsty. I'd like some water.

UNCLE. Bahadur my child, fetch some water for him, will you.

BAHADUR. I offered him some but he didn't want any.

KING. Do you have no children of your own?

UNCLE. No, Maharaj.

KING. How many are you?

UNCLE. Me and my niece. Just the two of us, Maharaj. (*Bahadur brings water*) Give it to him, my child.

BAHADUR. I'll pour it for him.

UNCLE. All right. Come, Hriday bhai, bring a hook and get the bucket.

The Washerman, Washerwoman and Uncle exit. Bahadur pours water for the King to drink[4] *and dumps some on his head.*

KING. Enough, my dear. It seems I won't be able to quench my thirst.

BAHADUR. Drink up, go on, drink!

UNCLE. You still haven't given him water?

KING. No, no, the thing is, I was so thirsty I asked for a second round.

BAHADUR. Dadda, he is really thirsty. Shall I fetch him a full gundi?[5]

UNCLE. Go sit in the shop.

KING. May I have a measure of wine, please?

UNCLE. Bahadur? My child, fetch a helping of wine, will you?

BAHADUR. I've been telling him to have wine right from the start, but he wouldn't listen to me.

KING. Here's the money.

UNCLE. No, My lord, let it be. After all, how often do we get visited by a king like you.

KING. No, no, it's a matter of business.

BAHADUR. Why shouldn't we take the money? Take it!

KING. Here you are.

BAHADUR. Don't you know the going rate?

KING. Why, what's wrong?

BAHADUR. You've given me two rupees.

KING. So? You yourself told me the rate was two rupees.

BAHADUR. Two rupees is what we charge the local villagers. You are an outsider. We don't know you. Outsiders have to pay five rupees.

KING. (*giving her the money*) Here you are. Will this do?

BAHADUR. Yes, it'll do.

KING. Okay then, I'll leave now.

UNCLE. Won't you stay a few days more, Maharaj?

Washerman enters.

KING. Actually, I was thinking, I like it here. The forest is dense in these parts, there's lots of game to hunt. I've come to know you all, I've got a companion to talk to. I think I will camp here for two or three days. Okay then, I'll be off.

BAHADUR. Once you sample the wine in our village, wait and see, you'll be stuck here. You won't be able to leave.

KING. Even better!

UNCLE. Let me know how I can be of service, Maharaj.

KING. We'll meet again.

UNCLE. I touch your feet, Maharaj.

KING. Ram Ram!

BAHADUR. Jai Shankar!

KING. Jai Shankar!

Bahadur and King exit.

UNCLE. Hridayram, were you here when Maharaj came?

WASHERMAN. No I wasn't. But Bahadur was up to her usual mischief.

UNCLE. Will she ever lose her childish ways? She's always been a handful.

WASHERMAN. Don't I know it. Clothes in the well is nothing new.

UNCLE. She and that well—all her troubles are connected with the well. Whenever she acts up, it's something to do with that well.

Uncle exits.

WASHERMAN (*to Washerwoman*). What have you been doing all this time? Give me that hook! It's been over an hour. Really, you're totally useless. Can't do a thing. Who does the cooking? Me. Who handles the provisions? Me. I grind the spices, I shush the baby when it's crying, I even have to remove the clothes from the well!

Bahadur and King enter.

Song.

Come twilight we'll go to the hillside, beloved
Just as I dreamed last night,
The hillside is our palace of pleasure
Our garden of delights.
Come twilight we'll go to the hill.
The woods where lovely peacocks dance,
Woods lit with birdsong bright
From koel, mynah, dove and more,
Our senses do delight!
Come twilight we'll go to the hill . . .

Girls dance around Bahadur and sing a folk song.

Ree reena reena, oh dear friend
Your man will win you yet!
The toe ring on your pretty foot
Is slip sliding away, my pet.
A candle lit in the palace glows,
The breeze's soft caress
Sways willing blossoms to and fro,
Dear friend, can you do less?
The girdle from your slender waist
Is slip sliding away, my pet.
Ree reena reena, oh my dear
Your man will win you yet.

SCENE TWO

GOVIND. What shall we do? The shop isn't open yet.

HRIDAY. Ever since that girl started going around with the King she doesn't seem bothered about home.

GOVIND. Isn't the old man here either?

HRIDAY. He must be searching for her. What other work does he have?

GOVIND. Shall we wait?

HRIDAY. What else to do?

GOVIND. How can the shop run like this?

HRIDAY. True. Arrey, when the Raja has become your son-in-law, why would the shopkeeper care whether it runs or not? Why are you so worked up?

GOVIND. I want my wine, that's why.

HRIDAY. You're right, there's no other wine shop near Sorar, not for miles. So just sit and wait, what else.

GOVIND. Isn't that old man even a bit worried about his girl?

HRIDAY. Arrey, why do you take on the worries of the whole world? The old man himself escorts the girl to and from the Raja's camp.

GOVIND. Here comes the old fellow.

UNCLE. That girl has forgotten all about the shop! She still hasn't shown up. Shall I give you wine, bhaiya?[6]

GOVIND. Give me one measure.

HRIDAY. Don't worry about Bahadur, she's a lucky girl.

UNCLE. Pray God your words are true.

GOVIND. They make a good couple.

HRIDAY. They're as inseparable as a pair of swans.

UNCLE. I like the match as well.

GOVIND. Arrey, not just you, the whole village likes the match.

UNCLE. Why don't you both sit here and drink your wine, I'll just be back— I'll go look for her.

HRIDAY. Well, we had thought of drinking this at home, but since you ask I suppose we could stay here instead.

GOVIND. Yes, that's okay.

UNCLE. Sit and drink here, that way you can keep an eye on the shop as well.

Uncle exits.

GOVIND. They won't be at the Raja's camp, they'll be near the pond.

HRIDAY. What is it to you where they are?

GOVIND. I think the old man has allowed the girl too much freedom. You talk about the King becoming his son-in-law—the likes of kings don't become sons-in-law of wine-sellers. It's just a moment's infatuation. When he loses interest, he'll leave.

HRIDAY. And if he leaves—will you become a widower?

GOVIND. He's fallen hard for her. It's been quite a few days already.

Bahadur and King enter.

BAHADUR. Isn't dadda here?

GOVIND. He went off to look for you. Left us to mind the shop.

HRIDAY. Since you're here now, we'll be off.

GOVIND. Now that we've started, we may as well carry on drinking here.

BAHADUR *(to King)*. Come, today you run the shop—why don't you sit?

KING. That's a great macholi my dear, but I don't see any customers?

BAHADUR. I'm your customer.

GOVIND. And we're your customers as well, Maharaj! I'll take a serving of wine and give me back the change! He doesn't know how to handle a shop— why don't you show him?

KING *(handing Govind his change)*. Here you are.

BAHADUR. This must be how you sit and run your kingdom! But you can't be looking as good as you do on my macholi.

KING. Sitting on your throne, I have no worries. But sitting on my own throne I'm surrounded by worries.

BAHADUR. Well then, you stay in my kingdom. Who's asking you to leave this throne? What are you looking at?

KING. I'm looking at the sun.

BAHADUR. Where is the sun?

KING. Can't you see it? Right in front of me.

BAHADUR. Liar! If you look at the sun you get blinded, you can't see a thing.

KING (*laughs*). It's because I'm blinded that I've lingered here so long. See, I was planning to spend a few days but it's already been three months.

BAHADUR. Oh, so you're counting the days, are you? I never felt that so much time was passing.

KING. I think I'll leave today.

BAHADUR. Where will you go?

KING. Gangrel.

BAHADUR. That's why you've been a bit different these past few days.

KING. I've been thinking about this.

BAHADUR. Suddenly you're talking of leaving right away. You've never spoken like this before.

KING. I was thinking about whether to take you with me, or to settle down here in Sorargarh. Today I have decided, so I'm bringing it up.

BAHADUR. I want to go too. How will you go?

KING. I'll ride.

BAHADUR. You can take me up behind you. I want to see what your kingdom is like.

KING. You'll feel too alone.

BAHADUR. I won't get bored if I'm with you.

KING. If I go alone, I'll come back sooner.

BAHADUR. So you've decided to go.

KING. I should go.

BAHADUR. When will you return?

KING. In a month.

BAHADUR. A month is too long. I can't live without you.

KING. But I'll be back forever.

BAHADUR. Stay for a few days more.

KING. Why? It'll just delay my return.

BAHADUR. So what?

KING. Since I have to leave anyway, what difference does a few more days make?

BAHADUR. I'm just coming.

KING. Where are you going? I don't want a drink now.

BAHADUR. Won't you accept a last drink of wine from my hands? (*She hands him wine, then takes off her necklace and clasps it around his neck*) A keepsake.

KING. Now I must go.

BAHADUR. Sit for a bit.

UNCLE. Look at that, you're here and I've been looking for you all over. Sit, I'll take over the shop now.

BAHADUR. Can't you come back before a month?

KING. If I can finish my work sooner, I will for sure. Now I must leave. (*Puts a ring on her finger*) This is from me.

BAHADUR. You are my memento.

KING. This is my pledge.

BAHADUR. Come, let me see you off. Dadda, I'll just be back.

UNCLE. The Raja can't bear to be parted from Bahadur for even a minute.

GOVIND. True love!

HRIDAY. It's all karma. What's written in one's fate can never be changed.

Bahadur returns.

GOVIND. Bahadur, I'd like a helping of wine please. (*She gives him the wine*) Don't you want the money?

BAHADUR. I forgot.

GOVIND. And you've given me extra change. Anyone else would have kept quiet and taken it.

UNCLE. What is it, child?

BAHADUR. Nothing.

UNCLE. Nothing? Then why so sad?

BAHADUR. He's gone.

UNCLE. Did he just leave without saying anything, my dear?

BAHADUR. He'll come back.

UNCLE. When?

BAHADUR. A month.

UNCLE. Who knows, my child, with Rajas and Maharajas. He may come back, or he may not.

BAHADUR. No, he's gone to finish some work at home, then he'll come back. He's a man of his word.

UNCLE. If you say so, child. But I have my doubts.

GOVIND. What's the matter?

UNCLE. Bahadur says the King has left, saying he'll be back in a month or so. But who knows, I for one don't believe it.

GOVIND. If he's said he'll be back then he'll come for sure.

HRIDAY. Baba, one day this King was out hunting, and I met him on the way. He asked me, do you eat poultry? I said, if I get it I eat it, Maharaj. The next day he actually shot three birds and had them delivered to my house. He is true to his word. He doesn't make false promises. If he has said he will, then he definitely will return.

He exits.

UNCLE. Look, my dear, you must put your mind to your work. I'm an old man now. Soon you'll be getting married, your responsibilities will increase.

BAHADUR. I'm already married.

UNCLE. Married? How? What are you saying?

BAHADUR. We got married in the temple.

UNCLE. How come you didn't tell me about this?

BAHADUR. It's hardly the kind of thing one tells one's parents!

UNCLE. Never mind. But he will come back, won't he?

BAHADUR. Yes, he will.

OLD MAN. Look, my dear, I'm an old man. Who knows how long I'll be around. Here today, gone tomorrow. You will have to shoulder all the responsibilities. What's the matter? Aren't you feeling well?

BAHADUR. I feel like throwing up.

OLD MAN. How long have you felt like this?

BAHADUR. Four or five days now.

UNCLE. All right, go and lie down, rest. I'll manage the shop.

BAHADUR. No, it's okay, I'll stay.

UNCLE. It appears as if you're in the family way, my dear. Is there anything you want to eat?

BAHADUR. I feel like eating sour tamarind.[7]

UNCLE. All right.

CHORUS (*song*). The blossoming bud has come to flower
>The seed is bearing fruit
>The one who plucked the virgin flower
>To Gangrel has gone, forsooth!
>Tell me whatever shall I do?
>Oh tell me what I should do.

MALA. The Raja has sent Bahadur some gifts

UNCLE. Bahadur, see what the king has sent! Go put it all inside the house, if you please.

Song continues.

CHORUS. The blossoming bud has come to flower
>The seed is bearing fruit
>The one who plucked the virgin flower
>To Gangrel has gone, forsooth!
>Oh what shall I do, dear friends of mine?
>Oh tell me what I must do.

>He won my heart and went away
>Leaving me behind
>How can I even message him
>When he sends me no sign?
>Without the gardener this flower wilts
>Deep sorrow fills her mind.

>Oh Ram, a Kalarin's necklace doth
>The Raja's neck adorn

A silver ladle in her hand
A golden stool, her throne
Pay the price and down your wine
Drink up! The night's still young.

Tana re hari nana, Tana re hari nana,
Tana re hari nana, Tana re hari nana,
Don't kill the gently nurtured bird
Oh Ram, don't you kill.

My field of grain the river beside
The fair one will carry my pitcher of wine
She won't stray here, she won't stray there
Swept away by floods e'er she's aware
My field of grain the river beside.

SCENE THREE

BAHADUR. Bhulwa, this wine is my treat. (*To Chhachhaan*) Quickly, put this there and come back, my son.

BHULWA. What's the occasion for today's gathering, Bahadur?

BAHADUR. What, have you forgotten? Today is my Chhachhaan's sixteenth birthday. To celebrate I've brewed something really special. You've never tasted anything like this. I buried ripe mahua underground for months, and today I'm serving it specially for the feast.

BHULWA. Arrey, Chhachhaan turns sixteen today! How fast the years have flown! God bless you, my child. He must be a couple of years younger than my younger one?

CHAIT. No, my mother said he was younger by four months.

GOVIND. Ram Ram!

BHULWA. Arrey, Ram Ram Dauji![8]

BAHADUR. Ram Ram Dauji.

BHULWA. He's the Dau of Mohara.

BAHADUR. To me they're all Daus. I think I recognize him.

GOVIND. See, she recognizes me.

BHULWA. This Devilal is a Gautiya[9] from Nawapara.

GOVIND. Ram Ram

HRIDAY. Ram Ram

DEVILAL. Who's this?

BHULWA. This is the Gautiya of Mohara.

GOVIND. No, I'm not the Gautiya of Mohara. I belong here but I used to live in Mohara for a long time. Now I'm back.

HRIDAY. So, Chhachhaan, you're all grown up, are you?

BAHADUR. Go on, son, touch his feet. What, you won't touch Dau's feet?

DEVILAL. Get away!

BAHADUR. I've brought him up with such difficulty, Bhulwa! I handled everything singlehandedly, like a man. Just like my dadda brought me up, I've brought up my child. Today I've been really missing my uncle since the morning, Bhulwa. (*She weeps.*)

BHULWA. Don't cry, Bai. It's not good to shed tears on such an auspicious day. Chhachhaan, take care of your mother.

GOVIND. Crying, is she?

BHULWA. Who?

GOVIND. Bahadur.

BHULWA. Yes.

GOVIND. What's the matter?

BHULWA. Her uncle passed away before Chhachhaan Chhadu was born. He died over sixteen years ago. Thinking of all this has made her cry.

GOVIND. She was remembering her uncle, was she?

HRIDAY. He died leaving her a huge burden of debts to pay off.

DEVILAL. Never mind all that now.

HRIDAY. But Bahadur paid off each and every debt to the last paisa.

DEVILAL. Yes, she paid off mine, too.

BHULWA. She lacks for nothing now.

GOVIND. How can she lack for anything? When hordes of people come from near and far to drink her wine! Or so I had heard. Today I have seen it for myself. So much so that their bullock cart wheels have carved deep grooves in the stone path to her door! What a festive atmosphere. And for sure she doesn't look like the mother of a sixteen year old. I've heard that she lives alone?

DEVILAL. What's the matter with this rogue—ever since he's arrived he's done nothing but sing praises of Bahadur. A tight slap and he'll forget all about her.

HRIDAY. You drink up and forget about him.

GOVIND. Who is he talking about?

BHULWA. He's not talking about you.

GOVIND. How long has she lived alone?

BHULWA. Who?

GOVIND. Bahadur.

BHULWA. Sixteen years.

GOVIND. Sixteen years! That's a very long time for such a beauty to live all alone.

DEVILAL. What rubbish is that bastard saying?

HRIDAY. You just keep your mind on your liquor. Why are you bothered?

DEVILAL. You shut up. Where's the booze? Here you, Chhachhaan, bring me some wine.

CHHACHHAAN. Dauji, You don't know how to speak politely when you've been drinking.

DEVILAL. Are you saying I don't know how to speak, you bastard!

CHHACHHAAN. Get out of the shop!

GOVIND. Arrey, what's happened, son? No need to fight.

DEVILAL. Oh look, the bastard's found his father today!

GOVIND. No, the boy's right. This is not the way to behave, Dauji!

DEVILAL. Shut your mouth! Dauji indeed!

Bahadur enters.

GOVIND. Arrey, look at how he's talking! He really doesn't know how to behave.

BAHADUR. He's not abusing you, Dauji, he's cursing someone else.

CHHACHHAAN. If he abuses me again I'll hit him!

BAHADUR. Come away! Now what is it, Chhachhaan, what's the matter?

CHHACHHAAN. He keeps calling me a bastard.

DEVILAL. I spoke the truth.

BAHADUR. Sit, sit, Dauji. How often have I explained, Chhachhaan, when men are drinking they say any old thing that comes into their head . . . Don't pay any attention. When you're running a shop you just have to take the good with the bad, my son.

CHHACHHAAN. He abuses me and asks for more wine!

BAHADUR. Okay, you sit here. (*To Devilal*) Here you are, Dauji. Here's your wine. He's just a young lad, Dauji, please excuse him.

DEVILAL. You sit down.

BAHADUR. Here, I've sat down, now drink up.

DEVILAL. Why won't you give me an answer? Did I say something wrong? Why don't you answer me?

BAHADUR. Drink up, Dauji. The lad has spoilt the taste in your mouth. I'll explain to him.

DEVILAL. Where are you going?

BAHADUR. Lots of household chores pending, Dauji.

DEVILAL. Give me my answer before you go.

BAHADUR. I'm right here, Dauji. Now you drink this lovely wine and let me manage my shop.

DEVILAL. I insist on getting your answer today. Tell me before you go.

BAHADUR. Forget it, Dauji. Rid your mind of this idea. Whatever happened in the past has happened. It's just me and my son now. That's my life.

DEVILAL. Don't talk about that boy, I forbid it. I refuse to be served by him!

BAHADUR. He's just a child, Dauji. Let's not talk about him.

DEVILAL. I'm telling you, either you serve me yourself or I'll stop coming to your shop.

BAHADUR. Why will you stop coming here, Dauji? Arrey, you liven things up here. With you around there's some laughter, some chatter. If you stop coming, what is left in my life?

DEVILAL. It is unbecoming for a woman to live alone. Your son cannot handle you. There, I've said it.

BAHADUR. Oh, you haven't had anything to eat, Dauji. Let me get you some bhajiya.

She fetches some fritters.

BHULWA. What news from your area, Dauji? How are things there?

GOVIND. There have been huge losses due to the floods, so I've shifted here.

CHHACHHAAN. I won't stand for any more abuse.

BAHADUR. Let him say what he wants, my son.

CHHACHHAAN. That dau's always calling me a bastard. I demand to know, who is my father? You tell me that he is a good man, a big man, a king then why do you hide it?

BAHADUR. You have nothing to be ashamed of, Chhachhaan. Your father is not someone to be embarrassed about.

CHHACHHAAN. If it's nothing to be ashamed of then tell me who he is.

BAHADUR. It's getting late, go on, eat something.

CHHACHHAAN. I won't.

BAHADUR. Eat up, my son, don't be angry.

CHHACHHAAN. I told you I won't eat.

BAHADUR. Not even if I feed you with my own hands? Look at me, my darling boy, my precious one, sit down.

DEVILAL (*to Govind*). Which village did you say?

GOVIND. Mohara.

DEVILAL (*in a sing-song style*). My younger brother's in-laws are there!

BHULWA. Bahadur, another helping of wine, please!

CHHACHHAAN. Chait, let's go to the pond for a walk.

CHAIT. Come, let's go.

BHULWA. Don't go into the fields, the chana[10] hasn't ripened yet.

CHAIT. We won't.

BAHADUR. The two of them are good friends, Bhulwa.

BHULWA. Yes, they're inseparable. Here's your money. Tell me, Bahadur, it's been sixteen years. Hasn't the king sent a message, a letter, any news at all?

BAHADUR. No, nothing.

BHULWA. Is he in Gangrel?

BAHADUR. I have no idea. Must be in Gangrel, where else?

BHULWA. And you never got in touch with him either?

BAHADUR. Why should I? He'll come if he wants to come.

BHULWA. Now he won't, not after sixteen years.

BAHADUR. What can I do if he doesn't? My life carries on. So many years have passed, the rest of it will also pass the same way.

BHULWA. Who knows if he's even alive. He may be dead; you should find out.

BAHADUR. I don't like talking about this. Let's change the topic.

BHULWA. That Dau from Mohara was saying that you don't look like the mother of a sixteen year old. I'm just repeating what he said.

BAHADUR. Stop being sly, Bhulwa. I've told you often enough that I'm not interested in being with another man. Why don't you heed what I say?

GOVIND. What is this, what are you doing over there, Bhulwa? Are you planning to drink up everything sitting there by yourself?

BHULWA. Coming, Dauji.

GOVIND. Something holding you up over there?

BHULWA. No. (*Sings 'Matey rahiye'*)

Hriday sings 'Matey rahiye, matey rahiye'.

DEVI. These idiots can't even sing properly! (*Goes up to them*) Here, follow my lead, like this: 'Matey rahiye' etc.

DWARKA. Come inside.

RAVI. A half measure.

DWARKA. You'll again cause trouble here! Don't drink so much!

RAVI. Okay, a quarter measure then. And we'll sit here and drink it.

DWARKA. Why here?

RAVI. Then where?

DWARKA. A drop to drink and you act like a tiger!

RAVI. I didn't do anything! They're the ones who picked a fight with me.

DWARKA. Now keep your mouth shut.

DEVI. Are you fighting over Bahadur?

DWARKA. We're not fighting.

DEVI. Come, sit.

RAVI. Not here.

DEVI. You've come to see Bahadur, haven't you?

DWARKA. What on earth are you talking about?

DEVI. Sit, sit. I was talking about Bahadur. What was I saying? Why did she refuse me?

HRIDAY. Talk about something else, why don't you. The poor woman is managing her life somehow. Leave her alone, you'll find plenty of others.

DEVI. I already have one wife, I don't need a second. I just feel sorry for her. She's not just managing her life somehow, don't say that! That's not true.

No, she's actually managing to lead her life very well, even though a single woman is a target for gossip. But that bastard son of hers is all grown up now. Who is going to marry the mother of a boy like that? Still I said I'd keep her.

DWARKA. Come, let's leave.

DEVI. Arrey, why are you leaving?

DWARKA. You're all busy with grownup talk, Dauji. Young lads like us have no place here.

HRIDAY. No, actually, we're talking about the woman who runs the shop.

DWARKA. Whom did you call a bastard?

HRIDAY. Her son.

DEVI. Don't you know Chhachhaan?

DWARKA. No I don't.

DEVI. Aren't you from here?

RAVI. We live in Navapara.

DEVI. Navapara? Liar! I'm the Gautiya of Navapara and my forefathers are from there, but I've never seen you before.

DWARKA. We just moved there.

DEVI. When?

DWARKA. A few days ago.

DEVI. Just a few days? Which village have you come from?

RAVI. Gangrel.

DEVI. Gangrel! I've heard that a big dam has come up on the Mahanadi River?

DWARKA. Yes, we owned the twelve villages that were submerged by the dam. So we decided to sell our home and move here, to Navapara.

DEVI. Are you the ones who have bought the big house?

RAVI. Yes.

DEVI. Arrey, why didn't you say so earlier? My fields and orchards were bought up just yesterday by the Raja Sahib.

BAHADUR. Babu, a moment. Are you the sons of the Raja of Gangrel?

DWARKA. Yes.

BAHADUR. Call that babu over here too. Please sit.

DWARKA. Ravi, come here.

BAHADUR. Have some wine.

DWARKA. We've come to drink wine—please may I have some? And here's the money.

BAHADUR. No, no, no money. It's on me. Today my son has turned sixteen, and in celebration of that it's my treat.

DEVI. Arrey, you've settled down that side! Bring the wine here. Just because you're the sons of the Raja of Navapara, does that mean you won't drink with the Gautiya of Navapara?

BAHADUR. Here's a measure of wine, please go give it to him.

DWARKA. Ravi, go give it to him. (*To Bahadur*) Here's the money.

BAHADUR. No, didn't I tell you—today's an auspicious day for me. So tell me, how many brothers and sisters are you?

DWARKA. We're two brothers. We have a sister who is married and lives with her in-laws.

BAHADUR. And how old are you?

DWARKA. He's twenty or twenty-one years old, and I'm about seventeen.

BAHADUR. Arrey. You're drinking on an empty stomach—that's not good. Here, let me fetch you something to eat. Drink slowly, okay? If you drink the wine too fast it'll make you ill. (*To Bhulwa*) Bhulwa, listen.

BHULWA. Now what's happened? Why are you crying?

BAHADUR. You see those two boys? They're my sons, Bhulwa.

BHULWA. Your sons?

BAHADUR. Weren't you saying that it's been sixteen years, hasn't Maharaj sent even a message or a sign? Well, he has just set up home in Navapara.

BHULWA. So why are you crying?

BAHADUR. I asked those boys how old they were. One of them is around twenty-one and the other is about seventeen. They have a sister who is married. I didn't know any of this, Bhulwa!

BHULWA. Don't worry, everything will be all right. Go, those boys are watching you.

Bahadur leaves and Bhulwa returns to his place.

GOVIND. Why was she crying again?

BHULWA. Oh, let it go. What else is there in her life but tears and sorrow?

GOVIND. Did she ask about me?

BHULWA. She asked which side Mohara was.

GOVIND. Really? And what else did she say?

BHULWA. I said it was near Rajnandgaon.

GOVIND. Then?

BHULWA. We talked of other things.

CHHACHHAAN. What! They're sitting here and drinking, and you're serving them?

BAHADUR. Arrey, what's the matter with you?

CHHACHHAAN. Get up, come on, up you get.

BAHADUR. Aaii! what are you doing?

CHAIT. They've been fighting with us. They entered our fields and beat us up. Look, they hit him so hard his head is bleeding.

BHULWA. Why did you go to the fields? Didn't I forbid you to go there?

DEVI. That damned bastard is back to pick a fight! Let's go.

HRIDAY. Yes, let's be off. The boy's very moody.

DEVI. No not moody, he's dumb. Arrey, no fighting!

GOVIND. Bhulwa, we're also going. (*To Bahadur*) Ram Ram!

BHULWA. I'm asking you again—how did you dare enter the fields!

CHAIT. The fields are ours! Why can't I go there? They attacked us for no reason. They said the fields belonged to them!

BHULWA. They're not ours anymore. I've sold them.

CHHACHHAAN. To whom have you sold them?

BHULWA. To Chakbandhi Sahib.[11]

CHHACHHAAN. Then why did they say the fields belonged to them?

BHULWA. How so, babus?

RAVI. Those fields are ours.

CHHACHHAAN. So the whole village belongs to your father!

BAHADUR. Chhachhaan!

DWARKA. Why are you talking about fathers? You don't even know who your father is, you bastard!

CHHACHHAAN. What did you say?

BAHADUR. Chhachhaan!

BHULWA. Keep quiet, don't make it worse. Don't fight.

CHHACHHAAN. I'm not the one fighting! These bastards started it, they hit us first. In the fields, the bastards!

DWARKA. Don't you dare abuse us!

BAHADUR. Chhachhaan!

BHULWA. Arrey, let's get to the root of the matter. Explain yourselves, babus.

DWARKA. The fields were bought by our father just yesterday.

BHULWA. From whom did he buy them?

DWARKA. From Chakbandhi Sahib

BHULWA. Now it's clear.

CHAIT. Why did you sell the fields?

BHULWA. Arrey, those fields were totally useless! And I got a good price for them, too.

CHAIT. Did you ask us?

BAHADUR. Arrey, one's elders can't check everything with their children. He's your father. If he decided to sell, it must be for your good.

CHAIT. It doesn't belong to him alone. All us brothers and sisters have a share in it. If he was selling he should have asked us. Now what will we live on?

CHHACHHAAN. Their father is working hand in hand with the officers to take over all our land!

BAHADUR. Chhachhaan!

BHULWA. What do you mean?

DWARKA. If you abuse us again, we'll fix you!

CHAIT. These bastards are set on beating us up!

CHHACHHAAN. Go on, get out of here! This isn't your father's house, you bastards!

DWARKA. Achchha, beta! Wait till we get you!

RAVI. Yes, we'll see to you, just you wait! Bastards!

CHHACHHAAN. Oh go on, get lost!

CHAIT. One kick up your backside!

BHULWA. Come away, this has gone too far. Showing off like anything!

BAHADUR. Chhachhaan, you've grown too big for your boots.

CHHACHHAAN. I'm asking you again to tell me what my father's name is.

BAHADUR. I won't tell you. (*She exits.*)

CHHACHHAAN. I alone can take on both those two bastards. I'll make mincemeat out of them and their dad. I'm telling you.

BHULWA. Shut up.

CHHACHHAAN. Leave me alone.

BAHADUR. Bhulwa, don't make it worse.

CHHACHHAAN. I'll settle those bastards! Come, Chait, let's go.

BAHADUR. Chhachhaan, please listen to me!

CHHACHHAAN. No, I won't.

BAHADUR. What was Chhachhaan saying, Bhulwa?

BHULWA. He was raining abuse on his own father. That's why I shut his mouth. He was committing a sin.

BAHADUR. What is all this, Bhulwa? What's happening? I don't know what this boy will do, where he'll go, I can't control him. In this maddened state he's capable of anything! Bhulwa, please go and pacify him, calm him down. Please!

BHULWA. Okay.

BAHADUR. Hey Bhagwan, who knows what my future holds. What else will I have to endure? I don't know what to do.

She exits.

CHORUS (*song*). Women and land have been the cause
of warfare down the ages
If you want proof you'll find the source
in myths and history's pages.
Old friends turn enemy over land
Hence the Kauravs' and Pandavas' strife;
While battle for a fair lady's hand
Lost Bali and Ravana their lives.
It's true—so say the scriptures all
As do all the sages
If you want proof you'll find the source
in myth and history's pages.

SCENE FOUR

SARPANCH. So tell us, Chhachhaan, why have you called for a Panchayat sitting?

CHHACHHAAN. The Raja of Gangrel has decided to settle in Navapara, and is buying up all the land in Sorargarh and Chirchari. And you are selling the land. We need to put an end to this. This is why we have called the Panchayat. Isn't that so, Chait? Speak up.

CHAIT. My father sold our fields without even asking us.

BHULWA. What choice did I have? I was going mad trying to pay the land revenue. I had to sell the fields.

CHAIT. My brothers and sisters and I all have a share in that land.

CHHACHHAAN. What about you, Brij? What do you have to say?

BRIJ. My land too was sold, bhaiya.

CHHACHHAAN. Sukhru Mandal's land is also being sold, and before that they bought the land belonging to the Gautiya of Navapara.

DEVI. Yes, I sold it to them, that's how come they bought it.

SARPANCH. You young hotheads are trying to teach your elders! When your parents and elders take a step, it's after due thought and consideration. Aren't you aware that for the past two years there has been a drought affecting the fields?

CHAIT. You'll see that the Raja's land won't suffer from drought.

BHULWA. The fields are sold now. What can you do about it?

CHAIT. They will have to return them.

SARPANCH. How can they return them?

CHHACHHAAN. If they don't agree to return them, we'll take them by force.

DEVI. And how do you plan to take them by force?

BHULWA. I've already got the money for the land.

CHAIT. We'll return the money.

CHHACHHAAN. Money doesn't last. Land lasts forever.

CHAIT. How much money did you get?

BHULWA. I got good money for the land.

CHAIT. So you say, but I see no sign of it.

DEVI. Babu, you visit Baalod every day, is that for free? You sit and drink every day in Bahadur's wineshop—is that for free?

CHAIT. Ask my father if he gives me any money for that?!

SARPANCH. Tell me, how do you make money? You don't get out of bed till ten in the morning.

CHAIT. Why don't you ask my father what time he wakes up, and if he smokes ganja every day or not.

BHULWA. Shut your mouth.

DEVI. Arrey, forget all this—why are you getting misled by that Chhachhaan, he only looks for excuses to pick a quarrel.

CHACHHAAN. Who picks fights? Do I, or do you start it first?

GOVIND. Arrey, no more fights. Every time this Dau of Navapara opens his mouth he says something wrong.

DEVI. Yes, and you have the sweetest tongue in the world.

GOVIND. I don't mean that. I am talking about those lads. Now take that Sukhru Mandal's case.

CHHACHHAAN. He has five children.

GOVIND. That's what I'm saying. He has five kids but what are they doing?

BHULWA. What work can those good-for-nothings do?

GOVIND. Exactly. Those boys don't do any work and go around getting into fights. What do you say, Dau?

DEVI. Leave me out of it. You speak.

GOVIND. Yes, I'm speaking, so listen, won't you?

DEVILAL. Are you speaking just for my ears? Everyone is gathered here, go ahead and talk to them.

GOVIND. I'm talking to them only. Now look at Sukhru Mandal's orchard. It's in the middle, surrounded on three sides by the Raja's land. Tell me, how will Sukhru water his orchard?

CHHACHHAAN. Yes, exactly—it's by stopping the water supply that he pressurizes the owner to sell the orchard. Same story with Bhulwa's land. Why don't you village elders understand what I'm saying?

King enters.

KING. Ram Ram Bhai ho! Greetings!

ALL. Ram Ram!

JAIRAM. Go, go, fetch some milk!

KING. No I don't want milk thanks, let it be.

HRIDAY. No, Maharaj, please allow us to be of some service to you! Go you guys, fetch some milk. To what do we owe the honour of this visit, Maharaj?

KING. Well, I'd come to meet Sukhru Mandal, and I just thought, I've come to Sorargarh for the first time, and the village elders of this area are all gathered here, so why not take this chance to meet you all and talk face to face.

ALL. That's wonderful, Maharaj. Come, please sit. (*All sit*)

KING. I have the larger plot of land, and the canal waters will reach it first; only after that will the canal be extended to Sukhru Mandal's orchards. With this in mind I thought I'd buy his land at a good price. What do you think?

SARPANCH. That's right, Maharaj.

BHULWA. That's right.

HRIDAY. You've done well, Maharaj. Here, drink some milk.

KING. Then tell me, why are his boys causing trouble? And there's another thing, you may or may not know this . . .

DEVI. What, Maharaj?

GOVIND. We don't know?

DEVI. First listen, then speak.

GOVIND. Okay, I won't speak.

KING. I'm not naming any names.I don't know their names anyway. But this I do know—some young men are inciting these boys.

(*King's sons enter.*)

What is it?

DWARKA. Sukhru Mandal has gone to Durg. His boys were there. They were about to attack us.

KING. Did you go the hospital?

DWARKA. Yes.

KING. How is he?

DWARKA. They're saying it's not serious. He's out of danger.

KING. Just yesterday some boys beat up the agent Chakbandhi Sahib. He's lying in hospital. It would have become a very serious case, but I managed to suppress it.

BHULWA. Some local men beat up Chakbandhi Sahib? We didn't know this!

GOVIND. That's what I was saying. We just heard about this.

DEVI. You've heard, but have you understood?

GOVIND. We've all understood.

DEVI. Go on, tell us who the attackers were.

GOVIND. I have no idea.

KING. I too don't know who did it, or who's behind all this, but it's wrong.

CHHACHHAAN. We did it.

CHAIT. And we'll do it again if need be.

KING. You all heard that?

CHAIT. From now on we won't allow any land to be sold off.

CHHACHHAAN. Have these guys have come armed with lathis to attack us?

CHAIT. Achha! Quite a few men have arrived!

CHHACHHAAN. Come on, pick up your lathi!

DWARKA. Ravi, take your lathi!

CHHACHHAAN. Come on then!! We'll take care of you!

CHAIT. We'll see to them all right!

CHHACHHAAN. Come on, saala![12]

KING. Arrey Dwarka, go there—come Ravi.

BHULWA. Chait, come here! What are you up to?

GOVIND. Chhachhhan, beta, don't fight.

KING. I came here to stop all this fighting, and to say to you all that it's up to the older and cooler heads to make the young hotheads see sense. They are hot blooded, they take offence over minor issues. This will not benefit the village in the long run.

DWARKA. If we have to fight we'll benefit everyone. How's that?

RAVI. These bastards are itching for a quarrel.

CHHACHHAAN. Chait, come, let's give these swines a thrashing they won't forget!

CHAIT. They'll curse us.

KING. Arrey, arrey, arrey!

BHULWA. Chait!

SARPANCH. You keep quiet.

DEVI. Don't cause trouble.

GOVIND. Dau, explain to these youngsters!

DEVI. What are *you* doing about it?

Song.

Tar na ko nana oh subedar
There's fighting at Nanga Ghat!
There's fighting yes there's fighting
Fighting at Nanga Ghat
From left to right sways old sardar
There's fighting at Nanga Ghat!
He flails his legs the old sardar
There's fighting at Nanga Ghat!

SCENE FIVE

KING. Who are you?

CHHACHHAAN. Chhachhaan.

KING. What?

CHHACHAAN. My name is Chhachhaan Chhadu.

KING. Oho! So that's why you're inciting all the young lads.

CHHACHHAAN. I'll kill you and drink your blood.

KING. Why are you spreading unrest in the village?

CHHACHHAAN. Pick up your lathi, then you'll know.

KING. I'm the Raja of the Gonds.

CHHACHHAAN. First deal with this Kalar, and if you survive then you can talk about rank and caste.

KING. So you're a Kalar, are you? From which family of Kalars?

CHHACHHAAN. There's only one Kalar family in this village.

KING. Are you from Bahadur's family? Is your mother called Bahadur?

CHHACHHAAN. You dare take my mother's name!

KING. How old are you?

CHHACHHAAN. What has my age to do with you?

KING. What's your father's name?

CHHACHHAAN. Father! I'm searching for my father. My father came here sixteen years ago. I'm sixteen years old. Maybe you are my father—that's why I'm saying, pick up your lathi!

KING. You're good with the lathi, but you won't be able to take me on.

CHHACHHAAN. You can call your two sons! I can take on all three of you! Go on, call your whole family!

KING. You don't know my mettle.

CHHACHHAAN. I'll know soon enough—pick up your lathi.

KING. You're my blood. You have my spirit.

CHHACHHAAN. Just pick up your lathi!

KING. You'll raise a hand to your own father!

CHHACHHAAN. If you're my father, either get ready to fight, or else come along with me.

KING. Not now.

CHHACHHAAN. Then fight. Come on.

KING. I will not lift my hand against you.

CHHACHHAAN. Take your pick, you have to do one or the other.

KING. The right time to go with you will come, my son, but not now.

CHHACHHAAN. You've been waiting sixteen years for the right time?

KING. You won't understand. Let it go.

CHHACHHAAN. I understand all right.

KING. You don't understand a thing. This is *my* problem.

CHHACHHAAN. Problem? The problem is mine alone. You think about that.

KING. Why do you think I've come here? It's to meet you. And also a question of my name, my honour . . .

CHHACHHAAN. Our honour matters too.

KING. I am respected all over.

CHHACHHAAN. We have respect too!

KING. That's why I have to think this through carefully. Give me some time to think it over.

CHHACHHAAN. You keep right on thinking about it for the rest of your life but now come on, lift your lathi and defend yourself.

KING. Calm down, beta, calm down. What will you gain from fighting with me?

CHACHHAAN. I don't think about gain or loss.

KING. You must think about it. I'm only thinking of your own good. I don't want to harm you. Look, you've just met me, that's enough happiness for me. Now go home.

CHACHHAAN. No, today I won't let you off. Today we'll settle things once and for all between us. Come on, pick up your lathi.

Song.

Tar na ko nana oh subedar
There's fighting at Nanga Ghat!
There's fighting yes there's fighting
Fighting at Nanga Ghat!
He kicks his legs does old sardar

There's fighting at Nanga Ghat!
He makes wild moves does old sardar
There's fighting at Nanga Ghat!

King dies. Bahadur enters and sees this. Villagers gather.
The Chorus sings.

CHORUS (*sings*). Oh Rama a Kalarin's necklace doth
The Raja's neck adorn!
The heavy clouds they weep with rain
The east wind blows anon
Oh tell who drove you from your land?
Oh tell who'll lend a helping hand?
The golden tongue speaks honeyed words
The lips in a smile do part
Yet in the guts a dagger twists
A weight sits on the heart.
Oh Rama a Kalarin's necklace doth
The Raja's neck adorn!

(*King's funeral procession exits. Chorus continues to sing.*)

Dear guest, will you not stay awhile
and share a smoke with me
The guest leaves, more's the pity!
I say more's the pity!
The Peepul leaves are all aflutter
This body awaits its mate
The guest leaves, more's the pity!
I say more's the pity!

SCENE SIX

Song.

> Mother, O mother, give me rupees full eighty
> And I will bring home as bride a beauty!
> Give up all thought of your beauty, my son!
> Her home is too far for her to be won!
> For you a young woman to cook and to serve
> A lass like a gem that our home does deserve
> Yes, mother, a jewel indeed.
>
> I have sown mustard seed in half of my land
> Green paan[13] on the other stretch
> But now from the paan all colour has fled
> And I hang my head like a wretch.
>
> The earth for a lehnga,[14] the clouds for a scarf
> The breeze for a bodice I'll have
> Beloved, prepare me a bed of soft cotton,
> The breeze for a bodice I'll have.
>
> For the dark-skinned maid a scarf of black and yellow
> For the fair-skinned maid one of print
> For the olive complexioned a striped one's best
> How lovely when old friends meet!

The wedding procession enters with the bride and groom. Bahadur welcomes them with a ritual arti.[15]

BAHADUR. This hearth and home is now yours, my daughter! May you prosper and be happy. You have no brothers or sisters in law. There is only me and I am an old woman now, I have few needs—just a handful of rice and a cot to lie on. Listen, my dear, a woman's glory lies in hard work. Life brings its ups and downs, its good times and bad, but work is what sees us through. No one else can help. That's why I'm handing you this pestle, consider it as precious as a jewel, and every morning at daybreak you should open the granary and start pounding the grain . . . Chait, Dharamsingh, seat our guests for the wedding feast. (*Bahadur takes the bride into the house and gives her new clothes*) Have the gifts been distributed properly? Is the bride's family satisfied?

GOVIND. You've found a pretty daughter in law.

BAHADUR. The boy has been wanting to get married for two years. I didn't agree because I thought he was too young. But he couldn't leave her alone, always hanging around her, couldn't bear to be without her, wasn't eating properly, so I thought it best to get him married.

GOVIND. We will never forget Chhachhaan's wedding. We've had the time of our lives.

BAHADUR. Well, I only have the one son. If I don't spend on him, who will I spend on?

She distributes clothes among them.

BHULWA. Have you seen the gifts that the bride has brought?

BAHADUR. Yes, I have . . .

GOVIND. Achha, bai, we'll be off. (*The guests leave.*)

BAHADUR. Dharamsingh, place the new utensils inside and go eat your food. Chait, take Chhachhaan inside.

BHULWA. Here, take these papers. The dowry includes a piece of land.

BAHADUR. Yes. How much land?

BHULWA. Twelve acres.

BAHADUR. That's fine.

BHULWA. It's in the bride's name

BAHADUR. Yes, so what, it belongs to her. Where is the land?

BHULWA. Beside the pond.

BAHADUR. Yes, he was saying it is fertile land.

BHULWA. Okay, I'm off to rest awhile. (*Bhulwa leaves.*)

Bahadur lies down to sleep. Chhachhaan comes and sleeps beside her.

BAHADUR (*starts awake*). Arrey, Chhachhaan why have you come here? Go and sleep in your room!

CHHACHAAN. I won't. I am sweating too much. My hands and feet are cold.

BAHADUR. What? You're sweating? Feeling cold? You must be exhausted from all the hard work you did for the wedding—here, let me press your limbs. Is that better? Now run along.

CHACHHAAN. I won't go.

BAHADUR. My son, wise minds say that the wedding night is very auspicious, it sets the tone for the future. If you act improperly on the first night you won't get on well in the years ahead. Go on, go.

CHHACHHAAN. I'm telling you I won't go!

BAHADUR. You've brought home a bride to cater to your needs and look after you. Don't keep running to your mother. If you feel uneasy, she will press your limbs. Please go.

CHACHHAAN. No, I won't go.

BAHADUR. Go sleep in your own room.

CHACHHAAN. I'm telling you I refuse to go there.

BAHADUR. How long will you stay in your mother's lap?

CHHACHHAAN. I told you I'm not feeling well.

BAHADUR. Look, you've worked hard all day long making the wedding arrangements, that's why you're feeling unwell! Go and rest, my son. Go on now.

Chachhaan keeps protesting as he is made to leave.

Song.

Thakur Devta, my Lord God, I first bow deep to thee
Our society holds you above all, none higher can there be
Sahra Devta and Burhwa Devta your companions are
They too acknowledge that your status is higher by far.

SCENE SEVEN

CHAIT. Chhachhaan, the Baiga[16] is here

CHHACHHAAN. Ma, the Baiga has come.

BAIGA. Bahadur, Ram Ram!

BAHADUR. Ram Ram! I touch your feet.

BAIGA. Are all the arrangements in order?

BAHADUR. Yes.

BAIGA. Then fetch all the necessary materials.

BAHADUR. Listen here a minute. My son keeps complaining that his hands and feet turn cold. Can you check him out and please fix this?

BAIGA. I'm here to fix everything, just fetch the materials quickly. I have another appointment. In fact I was on my way there when I was asked to come here. So I came here first.

BAHADUR. Chhachhaan, Bahu,[17] bring everything quickly, my children.

Chhachhaan and his bride bring a platter with the required items. Chait and the Baiga's aide bring a goat and a rooster.

BAIGA (*examining the materials*). Where are the incense and vermilion?

BAHADUR. Tied in the bundle

BAIGA. How many lemons?

CHHACHHAAN. Twenty-one.

BAHADUR. Baiga Maharaj, does my bahu have any role to play?

BAIGA. Well, since she's here let her stay. Let me see . . . Here, the two of you, pick up a pinch of rice each and place them separately.

(*Chhachhaan and his bride start counting out grains of rice.*)

Bahadur, your bahu has nothing to do, she can leave.

BAHADUR. Go, bahu, go and look to your chores. You can wash the utensils, they've piled up.

BAHU. Why should I go? I also want to hear! It's a question of my life too.

BAIGA. What kind of a bahu is this, who won't obey her elders?

BAHADUR. Go along with you, tie up the calf.

BAHU. All right, I'm going. You all go ahead and listen to everything. (*She leaves.*)

BAIGA. Arrey, how could I speak of such a serious matter in front of your bahu?

BAHADUR. What serious matter, Maharaj?

BAIGA. When your son counted out the rice grains, two were broken in half, and three were whole. And of the ones your bahu counted four are broken and only one is whole.

BAHADUR. What does that mean, Maharaj?

BAIGA. Hidden in the ceremonial basket that came from your bahu's maternal home was a powerful ghost spirit. We call it Sawra Mawra. It . . .

BAHU. What did you say? Are you accusing my mother and father of practising magic?

BAHADUR. We aren't talking about your mother and father. Baiga is only telling us what came from your maternal home.

BAIGA. What kind of a bahu is this! She dares to argue with her elders!

BAHU. Huh, you come here acting like a big shaman! Sawra Mawra indeed! You just want to incite my mother in law and my husband against my family!

BAHADUR. Chhachhaan, handle her.

CHHACHHAAN. Go on, go home.

BAHU. Yes, yes, you keep sitting, I'm off.

BAIGA. Very strange sort of bahu this—doesn't respect the qualities of a Baiga!

BAHADUR. What can I say, Baiga Maharaj! The daughters and bahus of today just don't listen. Please don't be angry.

BAIGA. Well, let's start. Place the pennant here. Anoint with vermilion. Take out the lemons. Pass it thrice over the body. Utter these words: 'return from whence you came' and place the lemons to one side. Pluck a feather from the rooster and some fur from the goat's tail. Touch their feet and then offer it to the sacred flame. (*To the Devta*) What did you say? I've brought you everything you asked for. Here, hand me the lemon and the knife. (*Baiga cuts the lemon.*)

Song.

Thakur Devta, my Lord God, I first bow deep to thee
Our society holds you above all, none higher can there be
Sahra Devta and Burhwa Devta your companions are
They acknowledge that your status is higher than theirs by far.
Oh Thakur Devta my Lord God!

BAIGA. 'Get me married again, I don't get on with this wife!'

BAHU. 'Get me married again!' Then what's to become of me? Where will I go? I'm killing myself with household work, and she will sit and eat in comfort? I'll live out my days like a widow?

She weeps.

BAHADUR. What is this, she's weeping as if she's a widow, while my son is still alive! Don't talk like this, it's not right. Go on, get out. Go do some work.

Bahadur pushes the bahu away.

BAIGA. Bahadur, did you hear the Devta's verdict?

BAHADUR. He wants a second marriage.

BAIGA. Devta is correct.

BAHADUR. How can there be a second marriage while my bahu is still around?

BAIGA. You're crazy! Will you disregard Devta's mandate?

BAHADUR. Yes, Chhachhaan's been saying the very same thing.

CHACHHAAN. I've been saying the same thing, Baiga Maharaj!

BAIGA. Did you tell me that?

CHHACHHAAN. Yes.

BAIGA. When?

CHHACHHAAN. When I asked you to come.

BAIGA. And what did you say?

CHHACHHAAN. I said I want to marry again.

BAIGA. Shut your mouth, you big fat liar! Arrey, it's the Devta who gave this verdict, and it's stuck in your head. So you're repeating it. And you're saying you told me before! (*Lifts Chhachhaan to his feet*) Place five lemons in his hand. Make him take two steps back and turn around. Turn him that side and push him. Forbid him from looking back. Okay, Bahadur, I'll be off. Be sure to call me when you have the second marriage.

BAHADUR. Do you know Sukhru Mandal?

BAIGA. Of course I do. I live in Sorargarh, we all know Mandal. He has only one daughter. If you like I can act as the go-between. His fields and orchards will all become yours. His land is in the middle of yours as it is.

BAHADUR. Has the evil spirit left my household, Maharaj?

BAIGA. Don't worry. What I've exorcised will never return.

Baiga leaves.

SCENE EIGHT

Song.

> The branch of the Mahua sways and sways
> Flowers blooming red as sindoor my dear
> The chief of our village has plucked a bloom
> It is time to go fetch your bride my dear
> Make haste and fetch your bride.
>
> A bride to be loyal and true always
> In exchange for a cow and a bull, my dear
> And a necklace of value beyond price
> Gifts to be bestowed my dear
> Gifts to be bestowed.
>
> The cow and bull must die one day
> And the necklace soon will break, my dear
> But my bangles and my sindoor[18] red

Will last for all our lives
Will last us all our lives.

May your dharma always be upheld
You'll hold your head up high, my dear
You've eaten the mango and chucked the seed
Brought home a lovely bride
Brought home a lovely bride.

May you live a hundred years
May you win name and fame, my dear
A thousand blessings on you we shower
May you be happy ever more
Happy ever more . . .

The second wedding. Bahadur takes the bride aside and advises her.

BAHADUR. Here, take this pestle, my daughter. Rise at dawn and start pounding the grain. This is your daily duty. Older bahu, take her in. Chhachhaan, you also go. (*To the guests*) Please go and eat now.

CHACHHAAN. Has my elderly mother in law eaten?

BAHADUR. Are you the only one capable of looking after our guests? Go on, you go. (*Chhachhaan leaves*) I hope you all have eaten well?

DOKRI. Yes, we've eaten our fill, thank you.

BAHADUR. What to do, saga.[19] As you can see, there's no elder, or head of the family. As a woman I have always managed everything myself.

DOKRI. I have thoroughly enjoyed coming to your place, saga.

BAHADUR. What to do, I have just the one son and he's the apple of my eye. My son has no faults or flaws.

DOKRI. None at all, saga, none at all. I have found a son in law as faultless as my darling daughter. She has no vices either. I have brought her up so lovingly! Never been harsh with her. And she is hard working too. She can work in the fields, pound rice, she's no shirker.

BAHADUR. Just like my beloved son. He doesn't take scoldings from anyone!

Chhachhaan hits his bride. She runs to her grandmother and clings to her, crying.

DOKRI. Did you two have a fight, my child?

BAHU. No.

DOKRI. Did he hit you?

BAHU. Yes.

DOKRI. Hai, hai, just see, saga, what your son has done.

BAHADUR. These things happen, what can one do . . .

DOKRI. You were praising him to the skies!

BAHADUR (*turning towards Chhachhaan*). Look, Dai, the boy is sitting there crying. Oh god! What happened? Did he hit you?

BAHU. Yes.

BAHADUR. Wait, I'll teach him a lesson (*goes to fetch Chhachhaan*).

DOKRI. Why did he hit you, my child?

BAHU. I don't know. I had fallen asleep. He was sitting there crying. So I wiped his tears and comforted him. He began pushing me and thrashing me.

BAHADUR. Chhachhaan, what's come over you? Did you two have a fight?

CHHACHHAAN. No.

BAHADUR. Did you hit her?

CHACHHAAN. Yes.

BAHADUR (*to her bahu*). Go to him, my dear, talk to him.

BAHU. He'll hit me again.

BAHADUR. No, he won't. Go on, my dear. (*To Chachhaan*) Take her with you, my son, be nice to her.

CHHACHHAAN. I won't (*he walks off in the opposite direction*).

BAHADUR. Older bahu, please take her inside.

OLDER BAHU (*roughly*). Come on then.

BAHADUR. Dai, you take her aside and explain things to her. I'll talk to my son. What's happened to you, Chhachhaan. You know very well what wise elders say - that the first night of a marriage is the most important and auspicious one. If you start fighting from now, what's going to happen in the years ahead? You have your whole life ahead of you. Did you hit your bride?

CHHACHHAAN. Yes.

BAHADUR. But why?

CHACHHAAN. I feel angry.

BAHADUR. But why do you feel angry?

CHACHHAAN. Just looking at her face makes me angry. She's not right for me, dai. I want to marry a third time.

BAHADUR. How many brides am I to get you? You'll make a laughing stock of me. Don't behave like this, beta,[20] come on, go to your room.

CHHACHHAAN. I won't go. I've told you. Let her stay there. When I get remarried I'll stay at home. (*Chachhaan leaves.*)

BAHADUR. Chhachhaan, Chhachhaan, come back, my son. All right, I'll arrange a third marriage for you.

Chhachhaan does not return. Bahadur turns pensive, goes in.

SCENE NINE

Women sing.

> Pick up the pestle and pound the rice
> A curse on such in-laws, sister!
> Counting the hours we pass our days
> Weep the nights away
> Our crazy man brings home new brides
> Each and every day
> Pick up the pestle and pound the rice
> A curse on such in-laws, sister!
> One is fair and one is dark
> And one is olive-skinned
> One by one the village girls
> Have all been counted in
> Pick up the pestle and pound the rice
> A curse on such in-laws, sister!
> May he die a horrid death
> Crippled, blind and lame
> Our youth he crushed into the mud
> No one but him to blame.
> Pick up the pestle and pound the rice
> A curse on such in-laws, sister!

Gathering of the Council.

BHULWA. All the young men of the village are angry.

BABUDAS. Why just the young men, even the older men are upset.

GOVIND. We have good reason to be angry. Call him and sort it out.

RAVI.[21] What is it? I'm busy working. Why are you disturbing me by showing up to stop my daughter's marriage? Want to start a fight about it? You've all married off your own daughters, and now that my girl has a chance you've called a meeting over it!

BHULWA. We're not here to fight. We're here to make you see sense.

DEVILAL. Arrey bhai, our daughters are suffering in that house. We're here to caution you, to save your daughter from the same fate. And you're turning around and accusing us!

VILLAGERS. You should be careful not to rush into anything out of greed.

RAVI. I've been there for each and every one of you. Always supported you. And today, when I'm arranging a marriage for my daughter, you're trying to stop me.

VILLAGERS. Our society won't accept this blot upon it. Every marriage is just a pretext to gain more land. That fellow is plotting marriage after marriage, and cornering land like his father. Here the poor are starving due to drought, and he says that there's no crop. Just like a poor craftsman blames his tools.

GOVIND. Whether it's a programme to get land, or some other reason, Bahadur has found 126 brides for that son of hers. She herself has known only one man.

DEVILAL. Yes, your programme failed, didn't it!

GOVIND. I'm not talking about my programme or your programme. I'm talking about that boy!

DEVILAL. You all don't know that boy. I've known his mentality since he was a child. The way he's going, one day he'll ruin his own home.

BHULWA. Not just his own home, he'll ruin the whole village.

GOVIND. His mother just gives in to whatever he says.

DEVILAL. It's the boy who's at fault, not his mother.

GOVIND. I didn't say she was to blame, I was talking of the boy. He answers back all the time.

DEVILAL. if his mother doesn't give in to him he raises his hand against her. One day they were quarrelling and I heard that he shoved her really hard.

GOVIND. Yes, I heard that too.

DEVILAL. Not just you, the whole village knows of it.

BHULWA. In that case, we should blame the mother not the son.

GOVIND. That's exactly what I've been saying!

DEVILAL. You're the only one with something to say, are you? What are the rest of us here for? No reason?

GOVIND. And do you come to the panchayat just to pick on me?

DEVILAL. Yes, because I've abducted your wife, right?

GOVIND. Don't talk warped rubbish.

DEVILAL. You talk such rubbish.

GOVIND. Okay, you speak then. But stick to discussing Chhacchhan, don't bring me into it.

VILLAGER. One day I was trying to water my fields and he stopped me. I told him I was in the right and he said, let the police sort out your rights!

MURLI. D'you know why Chhachhaan is mentioning the police? Because he has the authorities in his pocket.

RAVI. You are all trying to run down Bahadur and speak ill of her. Have you forgotten what happened three years ago? When the famine hit us, this very Bahadur went from door to door distributing rice and dal. She saved us from starving to death. And you're making such a big deal out of a small matter.

VILLAGER. That happened long ago. Talk about today. Things have changed.

RAVI. Arrey bhai, we can only give our children life, we cannot ensure their fate or decide their actions, can we? You elders all look for a good mate for your sons and daughters, consult pundits about their horoscopes. Who know why, their horoscopes[22] don't match. I have faith in my daughter. She is educated, she knows how to run a household, so much so that my wife goes off to work every morning and leaves everything in her hands. I have two or three little children, and she bathes them, feeds them, in fact, they don't miss their mother at all. I am sure that my daughter's horoscope will match with Chachhaan, and then Bahadur's home will be blessed.

BABUDAS. Well spoken. Your daughter's horoscope may be perfect but in all the 125 failed marriages that boy has made, don't tell me no one's horoscope was favourable!

RAVI. My daughter is not their only option. They can get any number of girls. There are so many willing to offer their daughters. How many will you fight with? How many will you stop?

BHULWA. He has made up his mind! This won't do.

RAVI. Be frank! You have come here to fight with me.

GOVIND. He won't listen to us. We should ostracise him.

MURLI. There is only one way to stop this marriage. Pick up your lathis and destroy his house!

ALL. Yes, yes! You're right!

ELDER. No, no, what are you saying!

BABUDAS. Arrey, why are you attacking his house! It's Bahadur's house you should be attacking!

DWARKA. Yes, why lop the branches, you should go for the root of the problem. And the root of all this is clearly Bahadur. Come on, let's go attack her place.

ELDER. No, no!

RAVI. Look I don't want any bloodshed or violence over this. No firing of guns. You all don't want me to marry my daughter to Chhachhaan? All right, I won't. Even if you ask, I won't go ahead. Are you at peace now?

BAHADUR. What is this meeting about? Why are you so quiet? What's happened, Ravi?

RAVI. What can I tell you, Bahadur, I'm trapped on all sides.

BAHADUR. They've convinced you to come and tell me you won't give your daughter to us in marriage. It's fine, do as you wish. There's no shortage of young women, after all. If not from this village, I'll find a bride in some other village. Come, Chhachhaan!

CHHACHHAAN. No, I will only marry his daughter.

BAHADUR. Ravi, Chhachhaan has fallen in love with your girl.

CHHACHHAAN. When Chakbandhi sahib came, who was the first to stand up to him? When irrigation of your fields was stopped, who got your fields watered? They are threatening to attack with lathis, are they? I'll see to them.

BAHADUR. Did you hear what Chhachaan said, Ravi?

RAVI. Yes, I heard him.

BAHADUR. Then go, make your preparations for the marriage. Don't let what they say stop you and me from doing what we have to do. You go prepare for the ceremony, and I'll take care of this end.

RAVI. All right, I'll go and make the necessary preparations. (*He leaves.*)

BAHADUR. Think about what you're doing. After all, my son has not done anything underhand! The Raja of Khairagarh, Raigarh and Patiala married so many times no one said anything to them! Go ahead, do what you have to. I'll handle it. Come, beta.

They leave.

GOVIND. Did you hear what she said!

VILLAGER. Sure did, bhaiya!

DWARKA. I feel there's a curse on this village. Soon it will be reduced to nothing but dust and ashes.

ALL. What can we do about it?

CHORUS (*sings*). This body made of clay, hey Ram!
This body made of clay.
We can't depend on it, hey Ram!
This body made of clay.
Wise Drona went, generous Karna went,
And so did heroic Bali,
Arrogant Ravana went, hey Ram!
This body made of clay.
No one can last beyond his time
Not king nor beggar nor pauper
Death will come for all, hey Ram!
This body made of clay.
Take Hari's name and live your life
This world is but illusion
Seek release from worldly woes
This body made of clay.

Chhachhaan's final wedding. During the song, Bahadur lies down to sleep. Chhachhaan bends over her.

BAHADUR. Chhachhaan, what's the matter?

CHHACHHAAN. I made a big mistake.

BAHADUR. What mistake? Why don't you speak clearly?

CHHACHHAAN. I won't say.

BAHADUR. Why not?

CHHACHHAAN. Just like that.

BAHADUR. Chhachhaan, you're overstepping your limits.

CHHACHHAAN. You don't love me anymore.

BAHADUR. Achha! Really!

CHHACHHAAN. You've changed a lot.

BAHADUR. How?

CHHACHHAAN. You don't talk to me like you used to. When you see me you turn your face away. If I enter a room you leave it at once. You're fed up with me!

BAHADUR. You've wedded 126 brides and you still lack love in your life!

CHHACHHAAN. I told you, didn't I, that I made a big mistake?! All these marriages were useless, they brought me no happiness, no relief at all. I'm very unhappy.

BAHADUR. Will I have to find you a divine apsara[23] for you to be happy! I have an entire village-load of girls as my daughters-in-law, and I'm sitting here nursing my shame. Why, beta? (*She touches him; he shakes off her touch*). What's bothering you, my son? What are you looking for?

CHHACHHAAN. Don't call me son.

BAHADUR. Don't talk like that, Chhachhaan, my little one.

CHHACHHAAN (*clings to Bahadur and weeps*). My happy days are over. I can't find pleasure anywhere any longer. I've realised this now. My happiness vanished with my very first marriage. I remember my childhood, how when I was a child you would feed me with your own hands. I've never felt that joy again. I don't know what has happened to me. I can't even tell you how I feel.

BAHADUR. Won't you tell me? Talk to me. Shall I pluck you the stars from the sky, my beloved son?

CHHACHHAAN. I've been married to so many women, but I've never found a woman like you.

BAHADUR. Never found a woman like me!

CHACHHAAN. I can't live away from you. There, I've said it.

BAHADUR. Do you know what you're saying?

CHHACHHAAN. I know what I'm saying.

BAHADUR. Have you gone crazy, Chhachhaan?

CHHACHHAAN. Yes.

BAHADUR. Sit. Come, sit down. Are you hungry? It's very late. Won't you eat something? Come, today I'll cook specially for you and feed you with my own hands. Making laddoos of the food, the way I fed you as a child— you'll eat, won't you?

CHACHHAAN. Yes.

BAHADUR. My prince, my little king! Today I'll tell the bahus to take the day off. Today, I'll cook all your favourite dishes myself and feed you.

Song.

Fetch me the branch, oh my son!
Fetch the branch to me
I'll use it to reach the little munga[24]
High up on the tree
Oh, fetch the branch to me.

As Bahadur feeds her son, the Chorus sings.

The clever woman feeds her son
Tempting dishes many
Curried potato, squash and greens
Shrimp, dumplings, lentil curry
Fried brinjal, radish, so much more
Hot, spicy, sour and tangy.
But not a drop of water to
Cool his palate fiery

BAHADUR. Have some more?

CHHACHHAAN. No, I'm full. Water, please.

BAHADUR. Come, just another mouthful.

CHHACHHAAN. Today your cooking has been fabulous.

BAHADUR. I've used only pure ghee.

CHACHHAAN. Nice and spicy.

BAHADUR. Not too much chilli, I hope?

CHHACHHAAN. That's what made it so tasty.

BAHADUR. Have a little more?

CHHACHHAAN. No, just some water, please.

BAHADUR. There's no drinking water. The bahus are all away, and I find it difficult to draw water from the well now. Why, is your mouth burning?

CHHACHHAAN. Yes, I'm dying of thirst.

BAHADUR. You love sesame seed laddoos. Have some, it will cool the burning in your mouth. Come, take this—isn't it good?

CHHACHHAAN. Yes, very tasty.

BAHADUR. Have a little more, just a little. All the household chores are lying undone, the dirty dishes . . .

CHHACHHAAN. Forget about the household chores!

BAHADUR. No, today I'll do everything myself. Why don't you take a stroll around. I'll clear up the pending work.

CHHACHHAAN. I don't want to leave you.

BAHADUR. There's too much work, let me go and finish the chores. (*She weeps.*)

CHHACHHAAN. You're crying?

BAHADUR. There, I'm not crying any more. Go, my darling, do as I say. (*She kisses Chhachhaan's hand tenderly; he goes.*) Bhulwa! Oye, Bhulwa!

BHULWA. What is it?

BAHADUR. Will you do something for me?

BHULWA. What do you want?

BAHADUR. Look, don't say no. Nowadays the village people don't heed what I say. If you explain, maybe they'll listen to you.

BHULWA. What is it, tell me.

BAHADUR. Go and tell everyone that if Chhachhaan comes and asks for water to drink, not to give him any.

BHULWA. Oh, they'll easily agree to that request. Everyone is angry with your son. But why are you denying him water?

BAHADUR. To bring him down to earth.

BHULWA. That's it? That's your plan?

BAHADUR. Leave that to me. I won't say anymore. You'll do as I say, won't you?

BHULWA. Yes.

BAHADUR. And if Chhachhaan pesters them too much, they should just shut their doors . . . but he mustn't get even a drop of water!

Song sung by the Villagers.

Though he howl like a dog in torment
Not a drop of water to drink!
At the height of his pride in his wealth
Not a drop of water to drink!
His atrocities beyond count
Not a drop of water to drink!
Drop by drop his pitcher of sins
Has filled right up to the brim
He eyed his mother with lust
His father he slew in the dust
The ruin of so many lives
Slit his throat with knives
But not a drop of water to drink!
Like Kansa of Mathura his time has come
Like Ravana, Duryodhana his hour is up
Ramkrishna is here to avenge
And there will be no regret
Not a drop of water to drink!

CHHACHHAAN. Water! Just a drop of water!

BAHADUR. Get up, make some effort. You're not a little child any more, you're a hefty young man. Take the rope and bucket, go draw water from the well and drink. Go on, go on and drink.

> *She pushes Chhachhaan into the well and rolls a rock over the opening to block his escape.*

BAHADUR (*sings, mourning her loss*).
The light has gone out of my world, my prince!
My darling son, what went wrong?
My womb is withered, I am undone,
My precious one, what went wrong?
In the prime of life my beautiful boy
Has left my side and gone.
No greater sinner than I, my heart
My enemy hard as stone.
I'm crying out to you, my son
Oh, tell me, what went wrong.
Thunder and lightning rage within
I have committed the ultimate sin
It pours with rain and floods my heart
A curse is upon me, my sight is dark,
The light has gone out of my world.

> *Bahadur stabs herself in the stomach and falls dead.*

CHORUS (*sings*). My lovely parrot whatever you crave
I promise to feed you
My lovely one till the end of my days
I will always love you.

Go tell them about this village Sorar
Spread the message about the tree
The tree, the well, the temple, the pestles
As well as the golden seat
All part of the myth around her name
Bahadur Kalarin

This magical tree which offers its shade
To soothe the wearied soul
Which flowers with multi-coloured blooms
Stunning to behold
Turning this village of Sorar
Into sheer Paradise
Spread word of this miracle in Sorar
A wonder for all eyes.
As beautiful as Bahadur
Whose legend never dies.

So go speak of her far and wide
Do not let us forget
This strange and wondrous story
Dear parrot, my lovely pet.

THE END

NOTES

1 Mahua is a local tree, the flowers of which are used for food or fermented to prepare an intoxicating drink.

2 Meaning 'brave'.

3 A low stool woven out of local material.

4 It is customary for water to be poured into cupped hands rather than to be sipped from a glass or tumbler; a practice linked with caste and pollution taboos.

5 Large metal pitcher.

Brother. Term of address.

7 A typical sign of pregnancy is the longing to eat something sour.

8 Term of respect.

9 Prominent village landowner and moneylender.

Chickpea crop.

Middleman or agent.

Used as a term of abuse, though technically it refers to an in-law.

Betel leaf.

A typical full long gathered skirt worn by women.

A ritual in which the one being worshipped, welcomed or propitiated is greeted with a lit lamp.

16 Shaman.

17 Daughter-in-law.

Vermilion powder used by women in the parting of their hair as a sign of marriage.

Respectful term of address.

Son.

Not the same Ravi as the King's son in an earlier scene.

The word used here is 'rasi'.

23 In mythology, a celestial nymph, epitome of a desirable female.

24 Type of monkey, or a form of wild cotton.

THE LIVING TALE OF HIRMA

Translated by Anjum Katyal and Prabha Katyal

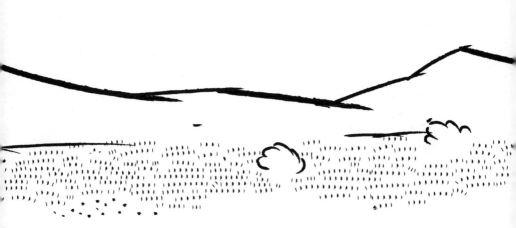

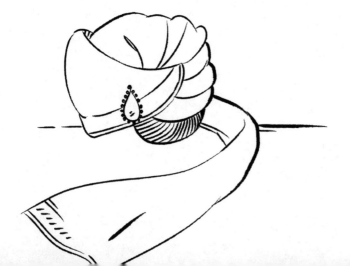

A DILEMMA OF DEMOCRACY

HABIB TANVIR

Hirma, messianic, wayward, headstrong ruler of a tribal state called Titur Basna, comes into conflict with a system representing so-called democratic developmental ideas. This gives rise to a sustained tussle between the adivasis and a host of officials, with disastrous results.

If the reader finds that there is similarity between the story of Hirma and the late Pravir Chandra Bhanjdev, erstwhile ruler of the former state of Bastar, he or she would not be mistaken.

I had seen Pravir Chandra on occasion during my Raipur days. He was a stunningly handsome man of wheatish complexion, tall, with long jet-black silken hair and large, luminous eyes. He was revered, nay, adored by the tribals of Bastar.

He was their Raj Purohit—the royal priest. Not only did he participate in every important tribal ritual but when he was informed that cattle had been afflicted by some epidemic disease, he went to the affected village, arranged Anga-Dev Puja and led it for days. In times of drought, he opened his granary for his subjects. During sowing season, he would dole out seeds to thousands of them. The Dussehra festival in Jagdalpur, the state capital, was as spectacular as the famous Mysore Dussehra, and as Raj Purohit he led the Dussehra procession in an enormous chariot. The visitor can still see, near the old palace, a huge wooden car, now immobilized. You can still find on the palace wall the numerous bullet marks made by the guns that fired and killed Pravir Chandra like an animal at bay, and made short shrift of hundreds of adivasis who were naive enough to believe that their arrows could out-match guns. They believed it when Pravir Chandra declared that he was Ishwar and if he was shot at, the bullets would turn into water. In fact, he wrote a little book in English titled *I, the God*.

This is not an uncommon phenomenon in the tribal world. Birsa of the Munda tribe of Bihar, who gave battle to the British for years in the nineteenth century before he was jailed and finally killed by slow poisoning, believed himself to be Birsa Bhagwan. He was Christian and had changed his name to Birsa, which rhymed with Isa, the original Biblical name of Jesus.

Tribal chiefs frequently believed themselves to be messiahs. Raigadh in the past had one such chief. The tribes of Africa and Latin America have experienced similar messianic movements.

Pravir Chandra, all said and done, was a simple man, and on the whole a kind man, though not without a trait of extraordinary cruelty in his vicious passion for virtue. He was both ostentatious and unassuming. He was educated, like most other princes of yore, at the Rajkumar College of Raipur. During his teens, he had an English woman as his English tutor. She was beautiful and far more mature in years. She initiated him into sex, and some say was responsible for turning him into a womanizer. He was a frequent visitor to Raipur, to which he was quite attached. There is a modest lodging above India Coffee House near the old bus stand where he would always stay whenever he came to Raipur. There, from the balcony of his room, which overlooked the main road, he would rain down hundred-rupee notes galore, and there would be a scramble of beggars and poor people for money.

He was whimsical, some say a bit mad. There was the case of a rickshawpuller who in his greed for dole came to him again and again, expecting alms. Pravir Chandra took his sword and cut off his begging hand. He was sent to jail for this. All his life he fought for his property which was taken into government custody after the Princely States were demolished by Sardar Vallabhbhai Patel. He fought State Legislative Assembly elections and won by universal consensus. Then he left the Indian National Congress and fought the government from the outside.

In fact, all the events in the play are more or less true to his life. For instance, the Collector, who was reluctant to follow government orders to kill him, was one Akbar. After the event he went away to Jabalpur, went into a coma and died after a month. The episode of the diamond ring, which plays an important role in the plot, was narrated to me by a friend, a Sessions Judge, who knew him well. He upheld the Manjhi system of tribal governance: giving the adivasis autonomy in administration, law and order, jurisprudence, and keeping a regard for tribal taboos. He was a patron of the arts and crafts practised by his people for centuries.

This too was not so uncommon among Indian princely states. The others —Patiala, Baroda, Sachin, Raigadh, Khujji, Khairagadh, Sarguja—all patronized classical and folk music, dance, arts and crafts. Yet they represented exploitative systems, being feudal. The life of luxury the princes led was based on extortion from the people, of course. The royal coffers owed their abundance to the people. In short, the feudal system had to go. Therein lies the dilemma.

The dilemma becomes more complex when we consider whether we are giving the tribal people a better alternative for governance. When we witness

state elections fought, for instance, in Gujarat recently and won by an over-
whelming majority almost immediately after genocide, not unlike the German
national election fought by the Nazis in Hitler's times during the 1930s, then
we get startled by the fact that the democratic system as we know it today also
carries within it seeds of fascism, which ominously sprout forth every now and
again, though they may remain under wraps most of the time.

That is the real dilemma of the play *Hirma ki Amar Kahani* (*The Living
Tale of Hirma*)—not immortal in the heroic sense, but living nevertheless
because Hirma never dies. Narangi-wale Baba, the reincarnation of Hirma, is
as real as Hirma himself. This rogue, who made the simple people of Bastar
believe that he was none other than Hirma resurrected in a new avatar, is a
notorious character who surfaced in recent times in all kinds of disguises all
over the country—in Orissa, in the north and other places, and finally in
Bastar. The politicians knew him, his deceptive methods, and the devastating
consequences that followed, but could not touch him. Had he chosen to fight
elections, he would have won hands down. In fact, he did become a king-
maker and helped many a candidate win. He was all over the front page in all
the national newspapers, just as the episode of Hirma's assassination in 1964
was taken up by the Press in a big way and for a long time. The findings belied
the official figure of deaths. Truckloads of dead adivasis were thrown overnight
into the Irawadi river.

Need I say more? The play does not, cannot, offer a solution. But I think
it does present the dilemma in its naked form. Safdar Hashmi, after watching
many rehearsals and as many shows, and after copious discussions with me
on the issue, wrote a long review: the only one which seemed to suggest an
understanding of the conflict between democracy and feudalism, democracy
and fascism (see Appendix).

The story represents the adivasi lifestyle and history. It focuses on a clash between two contrasting lifestyles. It would seem to have occurred and repeated itself on innumerable occasions, at least during the last two centuries in almost all regions of the country where tribals have existed. It highlights the process of assimilation of a primitive people—a terrible process which has precedents all over the world.

At the end, it is for you to answer the questions posed: who is the victor? What is development? Does development mean the same thing for all societies, including the tribals?

Bhopal, 1 October 2004

Hirma ki Amar Kahani was first performed in September 1985 at Railway Stadium, Bilaspur (then Madhya Pradesh, now Chhatisgarh) by Naya Theatre, with the following cast and crew:

HIRMA DEV SINGH GANGVANSHI *ruler of Titur Basna*	Bhulwa Ram Yadav
BAIGIN BAI *his consort*	Fida Bai Markam
BIRA DEV SINGH GANGVANSHI *his younger brother*	Ravi Lal Sangre
KALHAN, COLLECTOR OF RAINPUR *later chief secretary of the state government*	Deepak Tiwari
RENUKA *his wife*	Poonam Sonwani
LORMA *an adivasi*	Ram Charan Nirmalkar
SAHEBA *another adivasi*	Brij Lal Lenjvar
LAL SAHIB DUMRAJ DEV SINGH *Hirma's protègè, later additional district magistrate*	Dileep Barua
RICKSHAWPULLER	Sachidanand Bhajan Ram
GOVT. OFFICIAL SUPERVISING HIRMA'S AFFAIRS	Tarun Thakur
SUPERINTENDENT OF POLICE (SP)	Udai Ram Srivas
COLLECTOR PANDE	Shahnawaz Khan
POLICEMEN	Rajesh Ganodwaley, Yog Mishra, Vasudev, Mahadev, Parasar
STENOGRAPHERS	Mahadev, Parasar, P. K. Thakur, Yog Mishra
SPEAKER OF THE VIDHAN SABHA	Anil Sharma

MINISTER	Naushad
MLA 1	Habib Tanvir
MLA 2	Ram Charan Nirmalkar
MLA 3	Vasudev
BIRA'S HENCHMEN	Anil Sharma, Tarun Thakur
WOMEN AGITATORS	Agesh Nag, Mala Sonwani, Poonam Sonwani, Tribal girls of Bastar
CIRCLE INSPECTOR	Naushad
ADIVASI TOWN CRIER	Brij Lal Lenjvar
ADIVASI TOTEM-HOLDER	Ram Shankar Rishi
ADIVASI DANCERS	Tribals of Mokhpal in Dantewada,Bastar; Tribals of Remawand in Narainpur, Bastar; Tribals of Kanker.
CHORUS	Fida Markam, Mala Sonwani, Poonam Sonwani, Nageen Tanvir, Brij Lal Lenjvar, Bhulwa Ram Yadav, Ravi Lal Sangre, Habib Tanvir
HARMONIUM PLAYER	Devi Lal Nag
CLARINET PLAYER	Ram Shankar Rishi
TABLA PLAYER	Amar Das Manikpuri
COSTUMES, PROPS	Moneeka Misra Tanvir
DIRECTION, SET DESIGN, MUSIC,LIGHTING DESIGN, LYRICS	Habib Tanvir

PROLOGUE

Song.

My feathered friend,[1] for a ring denied
All was lost was lost was lost

For the sake of that ring, a throne was lost
Was lost was lost a throne was lost

Not just a throne, a country was lost
For the sake of that ring, was lost was lost

Not just a land, life itself was lost.
For the sake of that ring, was lost was lost

Not just life, bhagwan was lost
For the sake of that ring, was lost was lost

Devotion and worship itself was lost
For the sake of that ring, was lost was lost

For the sake of a ring on a finger worn
That finger was lost was lost was lost

Oh my winged friend, for a ring denied
All was lost was lost was lost!

*It is the season when the first seedlings have begun to sprout. The Marya adivasis
are dancing. Kalhan enters.*

KALHAN. This is a story about the adivasi state of Titur Basna. A few months
after Maharaj Hirma Dev Singh Gangavanshi came to the throne, this state,
like so many others, was merged with the Indian government. In the capital, Rainpur, the Maharaja began to rule his state through a government
ministry. Actually, I've known Hirma Dev Singh for a long time. We're old
friends. Which is why, in 1953, I was posted here in Rainpur as Collector.
I have played an important role in the history of Titur Basna. I am an old
ICS man. I know the ins and outs of politics well. Before this story began,
the biggest issue facing me was how to replace the system of feudalism
with democracy. This question faces me even today. The entire population
of the state of Titur Basna is adivasi. This is a fact. Its whole life is according
to the adivasi system, and one cannot label the adivasi system a feudal
system. But we saw feudalism in the adivasi rule of Titur Basna, and we
began to work hard to introduce democratic values into this rule. In the
course of this struggle, I saw many ups and downs. And this is the subject
of our play.

PART ONE

SCENE ONE

Palace, place where puja is done.

CHORUS (*sings*). Know your goal, oh my heart, know your goal
   Jai jai Ram, jai jai Ram, jai jai Ram

   There was dark and there was light
   And the light was dark as night
   Tell me, how would you describe it?
   Know your goal, oh my heart, know your goal
   Jai jai Ram, jai jai Ram, jai jai Ram

   Both wide awake and fast asleep
   Now moved to laugh, now made to weep
   Tell me, what harvest was to reap?
   Know your goal, oh my heart, know your goal
   Jai jai Ram, jai jai Ram, jai jai Ram

   From night's long sleep with a start I arise
   The memory of a dream behind my eyes
   An unnamed dream, as I surmise

Know your goal, oh my heart, know your goal
Jai jai Ram, jai jai Ram, jai jai Ram

I forgot the night of the long, long sleep
I forgot the dream with its message deep
Then whom should I blame, how can I weep?
Know your goal, my heart, know your goal
Jai jai Ram, jai jai Ram, jai jai Ram

Maharaj Hirma Dev Singh, Kalhan and Mrs Kalhan enter together. Hirma is dressed in a red dhoti, saffron kurta, silk shawl and has a red tilak on his forehead. The adivasis, upon completing their dance, prostrate themselves before him, addressing him as 'Mahaprabhu!'

HIRMA. Now go and put the seeds into the *devguri* and then come back. (*Adivasis leave*) Baigin, please open the *devguri*. Distribute the prasad, and inform all the retainers. The villagers are to deposit their share of seeds in the *devguri*. Then they can come to me and collect their *inam*.

BAIGIN. Yes, yes, I'll feed them their soaked rice and then send them off. (*She leaves.*)

HIRMA. Yes.

RENUKA. Baigin Bai is managing things very well.

KALHAN. And why not? She's the woman of the house, after all. Maharaj has taken five pheras with her.

HIRMA. I consider Baigin Bai my wedded wife.

RENUKA. So why did you suddenly stop the wedding ceremony after doing only five pheras instead of the full seven?

HIRMA. I heard a voice from the skies ordering me to stop. So I stopped right there.

RENUKA. Then how can you claim that she's your wedded wife?

KALHAN. What business is it of yours? Why're you so interested all of a sudden?

RENUKA. Well, it's been two years now and she still hasn't borne an heir.

HIRMA. Renuka, I'm not destined to have a child.

KALHAN. According to Maharaj's horoscope he'll be childless.

RENUKA. You have nothing better to do than to pore over people's horoscopes.

KALHAN (*to Hirma*). Didn't I tell you, after looking at your horoscope, that your *mangal* lay in the second house?

RENUKA. What d'you mean?

KALHAN. Those whose *mangal* is in the second house have a tough life, but a blessed one. Didn't I tell you, Maharaj? You must keep it in mind. This is a very difficult period for you. You must be very, very careful. Think twice before you speak or act. Even Gandhiji's *mangal* lay in the second house.

HIRMA. Baigin, did you open the *devguri*?

BAIGIN. Yes, and I've also stored the seeds. They are eating. They'll come to you when they're through.

HIRMA. Yes. Kalhan, yesterday you saved my life in the hunt. How can I repay you?

KALHAN. My life was in danger too, not just yours.

RENUKA. Why, what happened?

HIRMA. I missed my aim. The tiger attacked.

RENUKA. And he must have dropped him dead with one shot!

HIRMA. Yes, indeed! We had tied anklebells to our jeep!

RENUKA. What?

HIRMA. Kalhan had tied anklebells to the tyres of the jeep. He was driving it himself, slowly, at the speed of a bullock cart. The tiger thought the jeep *was* a bullock cart. He attacked, thinking he was attacking bulls.

RENUKA. So even a cunning animal like the tiger can be fooled.

HIRMA. Absolutely. That's exactly what happened. The moment he saw the tiger, Kalhan told me to shoot. I pulled the trigger, but missed. The tiger roared, leapt onto the jeep, Kalhan shoved the barrel of the gun into his mouth and killed him.

RENUKA. My god! I would have had a heart attack! I would have passed out along with the tiger! I know all about his hunting ways. He would rest his gun on my head and practise target shooting. He never missed, but in the process I was reduced to a terrified quivering mass of jelly.

HIRMA. That's what happened to me yesterday!

All laugh.

KALHAN. Listen, the Rashtrapati arrived at four o'clock.

HIRMA. Yes?

KALHAN. I've made an appointment with his secretary for seven o'clock.

HIRMA. Fine. Seven is a long way off.

Dumraj enters.

DUMRAJ. Namaste, sir. Namaste Mrs Kalhan. Maharaj, the *majhi* of Komalnaar has come.

BAIGIN. Lorma's here?

DUMRAJ. Yes.

HIRMA. Send him to me.

DUMRAJ. Right.

KALHAN. Haven't seen you in a while, Dumraj. Where've you been?

DUMRAJ. I stay in Jabalpur, sahib.

HIRMA. He was studying in college there.

BAIGIN. Now just look at him, he wears full pants and knows a lot!

Dumraj leaves.

RENUKA. I've always seen him here, working at your place.

HIRMA. He used to live here. When he completed his schooling, I sent him off to college. Kalhan, you know that vacant post of nayib tehsildar under you? I want this boy to be given that job.

KALHAN. What is his qualification?

HIRMA. He is BA pass.

Lorma enters.

LORMA. Mahaprabhu! I touch your feet, maharaj!

HIRMA. May you live long.

LORMA. I touch your feet, mother.

BAIGIN. May happiness be yours.

HIRMA. What's the matter, Lorma?

LORMA. All the cattle in my village are dying, maharaj.

HIRMA. What's the reason?

LORMA. Who knows? The Parma says they've got *chhai*, others say *chapka khurha*. We've tried all kinds of remedies, but nothing works.

HIRMA. What remedies?

LORMA. Raw turmeric, gur, *phitkiri*, made into a paste, rolled into balls and fed to them. And for the foot and mouth disease, we tried a solution of buttermilk. Still no improvement.

BAIGIN. What about chopping off the ear and beating the animal?

LORMA. Tried that as well

HIRMA. What does Leska say?

LORMA. Leska says unless we do an Angadev puja, this ill omen won't pass and things won't get better. That's why I'm here, maharaj.

HIRMA. All right, I'll bring the Angadeva from the *devguri* and reach Komalnaar today. We'll start the puja tonight itself.

KALHAN. You have an appointment with the Rashtrapati at seven. Don't forget.

HIRMA. I remember. I'll leave after that.

RENUKA. How can you travel by night? It'll get very late. Komalnaar is quite far from here.

KALHAN. It must be about forty to forty-five miles away. And you'll travel on foot.

BAIGIN. Maharaj can't be stopped. He will go.

RENUKA. And when will you return?

KALHAN. The puja lasts about eleven days. Eleven days and eleven nights, nonstop. Isn't that so, maharaj?

HIRMA. Kalhan knows all our customs.

KALHAN. It's part of a Collector's job. If, after living in a place for so long, one can't even familiarize oneself with the local customs, then one's no good at all.

HIRMA. Lorma, go and make all the preparations for the puja.

LORMA. Very good, Maharaj. Maharaj, you remember Saheba of Bharanji village? He's here, he says his land is totally arid. Here he comes.

SAHEBA. I touch your feet, Maharaj.

HIRMA. Yes, what is it, Saheba? Lorma tells me that your land has become infertile?

SAHEBA. I've been farming the same spot for four years. Now it can't yield new crops, Maharaj.

HIRMA. Is that so, Lorma?

LORMA. Yes.

HIRMA. Between Lohriguda and Bharanji, it's all jungle, isn't it?

LORMA. Yes, Maharaj

HIRMA. Measure ten acres of land from the boundary of Bharanji, and let's give it to Saheba, shall we?

LORMA. Sure. Why not?

HIRMA. Sahiba, take that land, clear the jungle and start cultivation from this year itself.

SAHEBA. That will solve all my problems, Maharaj.

HIRMA. And listen. Take your share of the *inam*.

Baigin enters, carrying the treasure chest. She places it before him.

LORMA. *Inam*? What for, Maharaj?

HIRMA. The essence of adivasi life is tantrik power and tantrik power alone. Through the power of Tantra, the goddess appeared to me. She told me that very soon my rule would be freed of this government council of ministers, and I would regain control over my kingdom. In honour of that, I am distributing this gift.

He opens the treasure chest and distributes hundred rupee notes. Many adivasis come forward to take the inam.

RENUKA. So many people have gathered! From so many villages! If you carry on giving away money like this, how long before this treasury gets empty?

KALHAN. Maharaj's bounty never falls short.

RENUKA. One needs a large heart.

KALHAN. Absolutely,

Bhajanram, a minister, enters.

BHAJANRAM. Namaskar

ALL. Namaskar, Bhajanram-ji

BHAJANRAM. Maharaj, what's all this?

HIRMA. Why? What d'you mean?

BHAJANRAM. Lorma the *majhi* was saying that you've decided to give ten acres to a farmer?

HIRMA. Yes, indeed.

BHAJANRAM. And you're distributing the treasury money amongst the peasants?

HIRMA. Whom else should I give it to?

BHAJANRAM. Surely you should have consulted me, Maharaj!

HIRMA. What, do I have to ask your permission for every little thing now?

BHAJANRAM. Maharaj, after all the council of ministers has been appointed to help you.

KALHAN. Now, now, Bhajanram-ji, just keep the paper work in order. You're the head of the council of ministers. As the head, your signature should appear along with the Maharaj's on all documents.

HIRMA. Okay, now go, get on with your job.

BHAJANRAM. One more thing—

HIRMA. What is it?

BHAJANRAM. As you know, there's an acute shortage of resthouses in Rainpur. In my opinion the bungalow near the palace gates should be given to the government to use as a resthouse.

HIRMA. That bungalow is within the palace compound.

BHAJANRAM. So is the entire wing you've given over to government offices! Only this bungalow has been left out.

HIRMA. That bungalow has been reserved for Baigin Bai to stay in.

BHAJANRAM. Collector-sahib suggested the same thing as me.

HIRMA. Why not just tear the clothes off my body? Here, this kurta, dhoti, shawl, take it all, it's yours!

KALHAN. Bhajanram-ji, Maharaj is busy at the moment. Bring up these matters at some other time.

BHAJANRAM. Very well, sir! Namaste.

KALHAN. Namaste, Bhajanram-ji. This evening at seven we have to go to the circuit house with Maharaj. To meet the Rashtrapati.

BHAJANRAM. Of course. Namaste.

He leaves.

KALHAN. What Bhajanram-ji was saying is right, Maharaj. These people are here to help you. There is no harm in taking their advice. After all, how can they hinder your work? Just mention your plans to them. They will concur, and it will keep them happy.

HIRMA. Oof, Kalhan, why are you forcing me to employ these senseless ploys?

KALHAN. This is what politics is about. One has to do all this. I'm saying this for your own good.

RENUKA (*peeking inside the treasure chest*). Wow! What beautiful jewellery! May I take a look at this necklace?

HIRMA. Of course.

RENUKA (*trying on the necklace, then placing it on Baigin's neck*). It looks lovely on you.

HIRMA. It's meant for her.

Renuka takes out a ring.

RENUKA. Is this a diamond?

BAIGIN. Yes.

RENUKA. May I try it on? See how it looks? (*She tries it on*) How beautiful! As if it's made just for me. It's mine now, a gift. Okay? Everyone's getting an *inam* today. Let this be my present. Thank you so much for the gift!

KALHAN. What are you doing! Is this some kind of a joke?

RENUKA. No, it's not a joke at all. You saved Maharaj's life, and he gifted me this ring. Now it's mine. What d'you say, Maharaj?

Bira rushes in.

BIRA. Dada, I need two thousand rupees.

HIRMA. I don't have it.

BIRA. Bhauji!

HIRMA. I've told you I don't have it!

BIRA. The treasury's full and you say you don't have money?

HIRMA. This money is not to be wasted on your drunken orgies.

BIRA. So who doesn't have a drink now and then? Don't you?

HIRMA. Silence! The royal treasury is not meant to be frittered away on family indulgences.

BIRA. Oh, I suppose it's only meant to be thrown away on villagers!

BAIGIN. Bira!

BIRA. See, Bhauji, Bhaiya has never spoken to me like this before!

HIRMA. It has become necessary for me to speak to you like this. Now leave this place.

BIRA. Achchha, so be it.

HIRMA (*to a man*). Who are you?

BAIGIN. What is it?

HIRMA. He's not from around here.

BAIGIN. So what?

HIRMA. He drives a rickshaw in Rainpur.

RICKSHAWPULLER. I never denied that, Maharaj!

HIRMA. How many times have you taken a share already?

RICKSHAWPULLER. Once or twice, Maharaj

HIRMA. Four times. Now why are you here?

RICKSHAWPULLER. I heard you were distributing *dakshina*, so I came. I'm a poor man, Mahaprabhu!

HIRMA. Achchha, put out your hand, I'll give you *dakshina*!

RICKSHAWPULLER. Forgive me, Mahaprabhu, I was in the wrong! (*He tries to run.*)

HIRMA. Where do you think you're going?

(*Hirma chases him offstage with drawn sword. Baigin Bai also runs after him. There is a roar of anger from Hirma and a shriek from the Rickshawpuller.*)

Take your alms! Here! here is your reward!

Hirma re-enters with Baigin Bai following.

BAIGIN. You cut off the poor man's hand?

HIRMA. Now those hands will never beg again. (*To three or four* inam *seekers*) You people had better go. The distribution is over. (*The adivasis leave*) All right, I'm off to Komalnaar. They're waiting for me, Kalhan. (*He shakes hands with Kalhan.*)

KALHAN. It's almost time to meet the Rashtrapati. You should get ready.

HIRMA. Of course.

KALHAN. But you're off to the puja.

HIRMA. Yes, I am. It is more important. And then it's not as if I'm a mukhtar, an independent, raja. Why should I go and meet the Rashtrapati? It would be foolish. And he's bound to bring up some new scheme, and ask me for more money, what else? Take Bhajanram-ji with you. I won't be coming. Renuka Devi, bye bye. (*Hirma proffers his hand, she offers her hand in return, he takes the ring off her finger and turns and hands it to Baigin.*)

CHORUS (*sings*). No more friendship with the king, my dears
Against him I will sing
Oh the wicked king
The rogue king
I've fallen out with the king

The crocodile dwells in water, dears
The tiger on dry land
Where do I go? Oh I fear
To exile I am damned
I just want my life secure
Safe I wish to stand

The king his mansion towers high
And higher still his glory
His gold and riches are so vast
He doesn't have to worry

His treasury full is more than enow
To make Kuber[2] feel sorry

The king is fierce, the king is harsh
He rules with an iron hand
He is a refuge when times are hard
To all throughout the land
A friend he is in times of need
Beside you he will stand

A charming and romantic man
A man to wed and bed
A man to roam the wide world with
and a measure tread
The king is more than man enough
To turn a woman's head

So sweet to taste, so fair of face
Is the gallant king
Just like a chilli smooth and green
He burns with fire within
Bittersweet my feelings
His praise no more I'll sing

SCENE TWO

Office in the palace.

KALHAN. I was able to gauge the actual situation in Rainpur only after I left
Rainpur. While I was there, all I could see was the palace. It was only after
gaining some distance from the place that I could clearly see both the

palace and its close relationship with the people of Titur Basna. The Chief Minister made me his chief secretary and summoned me to the capital. On the basis of my report, the government concluded that if somehow the palace could be weakened, then Titur Basna's path to development would be clear.

Hirma's palace. Superintendent of Police (SP) and Bira enter. SP is inspecting some goods placed there.

BIRA. It shouldn't be difficult to catch him. Lorma was inside the palace, I sent him off to fetch cigarettes from the shop at the gate. And I've told Dumraj to wait at the cigarette shop with some sipahis.

Dumraj enters.

DUMRAJ. Good morning sir.

SP. Mr Singh, have you got Lorma and Saheba?

DUMRAJ. Yes. They're in the next room.

SP (*to the sipahi*). Send them here.

DUMRAJ. Bring both the men here.

SP. Mr Singh, I hear that you stopped visiting the palace a while ago?

DUMRAJ. Not really, sir.

SP. Then, when you were ordered to fetch Hirma, why did you send others and not go yourself?

DUMRAJ. I was waiting for Lorma at the gate.

SP. Sipahis were good enough to apprehend Lorma. And you could have entered the palace after catching Lorma.

DUMRAJ. Sir, the truth is, Maharaj still treats me as if I'm a house servant. And for me, it's difficult to forget that I'm one of his men.

SP. One of his men? How?

BIRA. Arrey bhai, he's lal sahib.[3] Grown up with us. Lal Sahib Dumraj Dev Singh, isn't it so?

DUMRAJ. Yes, sahib. That's the reason. I can't speak against him, nor can I help him. Also, when Maharaj talks badly about you all, I feel terrible. I feel as if he's speaking against me.

SP. What does he say?

DUMRAJ. One day Maharaj was sitting with his guru.

SP. What guru?

BIRA. Dada has brought a tantrik guru from Lucknow.

DUMRAJ. I had gone on government duty. Maharaj got annoyed when he saw me and started cursing all of you.

SP. What did he say?

DUMRAJ. He said, go and tell your sahibs that one day my tantrik power will overthrow the whole government. Burn down all the offices.

BIRA. Why didn't you inform me of this? I would have tackled him.

LORMA. Liar!

SP. Lorma, Komalnaar adivasis have refused to pay the *lagaan*. Why?

LORMA. No idea, sarkar.

SP. Aren't you a leading member of the Adivasi Seva Dal[4] started by Maharaj? One of Maharaj's trusted men? A *majhi* from Komalnaar? And you don't have a clue about what's happening in Komalnaar?

LORMA. Sure I know. But I'm not involved.

SP. I'm not suggesting that you're involved. I'm asking who has a hand in this.

BIRA. Tell him, go ahead, don't be scared.

LORMA. No idea, malik. Here, take your cigarettes. I forgot about them.

He hands Bira the pack of cigarettes. Bira takes it.

SP. Saheba, who does the Lohriguda jungle belong to?

SAHEBA. The sarkar.

SP. Then why did you burn it?

SAHEBA. To farm.

SP. But you just said it belonged to the government. It's not yours. So with whose permission did you burn it?

SAHEBA. I was granted ten acres of land.

BIRA. Who gave it to you?

SAHEBA. Sarkar. Ask Lorma.

BIRA. Which sarkar?

SAHEBA. Maharaj Mahaprabhu.

SP. Don't you know that the state of Maharaj Hirma Dev has been merged with the government of India? (*Pause*) When my sipahis tried to prevent you from burning the jungle, your people chased them off with arrows. Aren't the police the sarkar's representatives?

SAHEBA. Raja is the sarkar, he is our Mahaprabhu.

SP. Lorma, isn't all this being done on the orders of the Maharaj?

LORMA. No.

Hirma enters.

HIRMA. SP-sahib, did you send for me?

SP. Yes, to apprise you of this government order.

HIRMA. Go ahead.

SP. Mr Singh?

DUMRAJ. Yes, sir.

SP. Read out the order.

DUMRAJ. It is hereby ordered that from today the entire estate of Maharaja Hirma Dev Gangavanshi is to be given in custody to the Superindent of the Court of Wards. (*Hirma slaps Dumraj*) And it is further ordered that from today he is forbidden to call himself the Mahapurohit of Danteshwari Devi. Nor is he permitted to participate in the Dussehra procession on his royal chariot.

SP (*to the sipahi*). Look here! Lock these people up. They have to be produced before the Collector tomorrow. (*Sipahi leads away Lorma and Saheba*)

HIRMA. Why are you arresting my people?

SP. On the charge of forcibly usurping government property.

HIRMA (*to Bira*). So this is why you sent Lorma off to fetch cigarettes? Very well. I'll sort you out, all of you.

SP. A minute, please. Your signature is needed on these papers.

HIRMA. Signature? For what?

SP. To acknowledge that you have received the information from the Court of Wards. (*Hirma signs a document. Another document is presented to him.*)

HIRMA. Now what's this?

SP. Sign here, please, and take the summons. Read it at your leisure.

HIRMA. Summons? What summons?

DUMRAJ. That rickshawpuller has filed a case against you. The man whose hand you cut off.

HIRMA. Namak-haram! Ingrate!

SCENE THREE

Hirma's palace.

KALHAN. Despite the Court of Wards, Hirma continued to squander monies. His brother Bira Dev kept complaining that he was forced to beg for every paisa, that his older brother refused to relinquish his hold on the estate and all its wealth. Then one day, Hirma came to the capital to meet the Chief Minister in connection with his estate. The Chief Minister sent him back with the assurance that he would arrange something immediately. He summoned me and gave me his orders.

Adivasis are sitting on the palace verandah. Baigin Bai enters.

BAIGIN. Mahaprabhu has been at puja for quite a while, he'll be here any moment.

ADIVASI 1. This is the second year running we've had no rains in the village.

BAIGIN. You're Kesarpaal's *majhi*, aren't you?

ADIVASI. *Panch mukhya*, bai, I am Kesarpaal's *panch mukhya*. Kesarpaal, Khursipaal, Tokapaal, all three villages are in a bad way. Drought all around.

ADIVASI 2. People are dying like flies in my village, ma.

BAIGIN. Which village?

ADIVASI 2. I'm the *majhi* of Nagarnaar. Seven or eight days ago a buffalo died, and two elderly villagers. People are rooting for whatever they can find, leaves, bark, shoots, and that's what they're eating.

Hirma enters.

HIRMA. This famine is man-made, my brothers. The government is responsible. For two years in a row, there has been a scarcity of rain, but there are other reasons, many reasons, for the shortage of grain in Titur Basna. Firstly, the government has imposed an unnecessarily high levy on grain. Secondly, although we are facing a shortage, grain is being despatched to other regions where it is freely available. Thirdly, all the grain of the government levy—hundreds of sacks of it—has been lying in the government godown in the eastern wing of the palace for two years now. That entire wing has been requisitioned by them. The roof is leaking, it has not been repaired, but the government has bothered neither to remove the stocks to a drier place, nor to give us back our own grain. I'm tired of reporting this to the Collector over and over. Either give back our ancestral property, or at least move the grain out, otherwise it will rot and go to waste. Finally, yesterday I sent the Collector an ultimatum. If he did not unlock the godown by twelve o' clock today, then I would break it open and distribute the grain to needy farmers. Come on now, break open the doors. I will distribute the grain personally.

Bira enters.

BIRA. Dada, don't break open the godown. It is an illegal act.

HIRMA. The government has acted illegally by giving my estate to the Court of Wards. You fool, how come you don't realize this? You dare to try and stop me!

BIRA. An order has just come. Collector-sahib has brought it.

HIRMA. What order?

BIRA. I don't know. Collector-sahib has just informed me of your decision to break the lock at twelve o' clock. I'm to stop you, and he will be here with a government order for you.

HIRMA. All right. There, he's come. Achchha, wait here. I've talked to the Chief Minister in the capital about my estate, and he's given his word that he'll do something about it at once. Let's see what he arranges.

Collector Pande enters with some sipahis.

COLLECTOR. I have brought a government order. Please read it.

HIRMA. Why don't you read it to us?

COLLECTOR. It is hereby ordered that His Highness Hirma Dev Singh Gangvanshi is to be deposed from the throne, and in his stead his younger brother His Highness Bira Dev Singh Gangvanshi is appointed Raja of Titur Basna. (*Hirma advances on Bira with a drawn sword. Two sipahis step forward and arrest him.*) It is further ordered that His Highness Hirma Dev Singh Gangvanshi be placed under arrest.

HIRMA. The reason for this order?

COLLECTOR. There is some doubt about your mental balance.

HIRMA. Really?

COLLECTOR. For instance, take the case of the rickshawpuller. That wasn't the act of a normal man.

HIRMA. Are you aware that the six month sentence given to me for that case was withdrawn and the case dismissed after an appeal to the High Court? Or perhaps you have some other information that makes you doubt my mental balance?

COLLECTOR. There are other charges against you.

HIRMA. For instance?

COLLECTOR. In the month of January you toured Delhi, Lucknow and Cuttack and everywhere you gave a statement to the press that unless your estate was released from the Court of Wards, you would take the reigns of the administration into your own hands, and declare your self independent.

HIRMA. You consider this an act of insanity, do you?

COLLECTOR. I will say nothing further on the subject. If this is not insanity, it is certainly rebellion.

HIRMA. Are these the arrangements the Chief Minister vowed to make?

BAIGIN (*to Bira*). Bastard, may you rot in hell! (*Collector gestures to the sipahis to remove Hirma. Collector exits*) Go ahead, obey the orders of Maharaj. Break open both the godowns. I'll distribute the grain amongst you all.(*Simultaneously, Bira exits swiftly, and returns with his gun. He takes aim*)

BIRA (*to Baigin*). Bhauji, stop where you are! Come on, move! From this moment on, Baigin will be our guest in this room. (*Baigin snatches the gun from him*) Arre-re-rey! Take it easy, Bhauji, relax, sit down! You'll come to no harm, I'll make sure you're ve-r-y comfortable, keep you in the state to which you're accustomed! After all, I'm the Raja now! If I don't look after the Rani, who will? (*Baigin aims the gun at Bira*) Oh, ho, watch it! It's loaded! Maasey! Munga! (*Calls his goondas.*)

BAIGIN. Stuff your bloody gun down your throat! (*Throws down the gun and walks off.*)

SCENE FOUR

Lohriguda maidan.

SP. The crowds gathered here at Lohriguda are growing by the minute. This is the season for sowing seeds, but it doesn't look as if they are here to sing or dance. I was informed correctly. These people are intending to march in procession to Rainpur.

BIRA. I'll just find out.

COLLECTOR. Find out what the programme is, and also talk to them and explain.

SP. I don't think it is advisable for Maharaj to go there. Let me send some of my men to find out.

BIRA. No, you won't be able to handle the situation, Sharma. Collector-sahib is right. The people want to see the Raja. Only I can calm them down.

COLLECTOR. Why not take Mr Sharma with you? He and his sipahis will observe from a distance.

BIRA. Fine. Come on, Sharma boy, let's go.

COLLECTOR. Mr Singh, you stay here with the sipahis.

DUMRAJ. What's the harm in shifting Hirma Dev to Rainpur Jail, sir?

COLLECTOR. Why?

DUMRAJ. The unrest may settle if we do.

COLLECTOR. Or it may increase with his presence here. I talked to Kalhan-sahib on the phone, he agreed with me. Okay, I'll be off. Mr Sharma, there may be no need for police action, still—be very very careful. Mr Singh!

DUMRAJ. Yes, sir.

COLLECTOR. These people must on no account be allowed to progress further! Understood?

DUMRAJ. Yes, sir.

COLLECTOR. Well, I'm off. Good luck. (*He leaves.*)

DUMRAJ. All the adivasis are heading this way, towards Usriguda. Come, let's join the police contingent.

SP. Come, Maharaj, let's go.

DUMRAJ. Please stay out of sight, Maharaj.

BIRA. You people go, I'll wait for them here.

SP. It's better if you make yourself visible a little later. First let's get a sense of the situation.

BIRA. No worries, Sharma! I'll just talk to them and be with you.

sp. As you wish, but be careful, please.

Bira sits down; SP and Dumraj exit.

LOHRIGUDA. The adivasis continue to swell in number. They have broken into groups. Some are standing and conversing, others roaming about.

ADIVASI 1. Which villages are here already?

ADIVASI 2. Lohriguda, Dharaur and Mendri.

ADIVASI 3. Komalnaar and Bharanji folk have also shown up.

ADIVASI 1. Good, let's get ready to leave for Rainpur.

ADIVASI 2. All the people from Parapur aren't here yet. Let's wait here a little longer.

Bira enters, reeling, drunk.

ADIVASI 1. Arrey, look, look!

ADIVASI 2. Who's it?

ADIVASI 1. Arrey, Bira, who else?

ADIVASI 2. This is Bira, is it?

ADIVASI 3. What's he here for? What does he want?

ADIVASI 1. He's totally drunk.

BIRA. Brothers, why have you gathered here?

ADIVASI 2. We're going to Rainpur.

ADIVASI 1. To see Mahaprabhu. To get Mahaprabhu's darshan.

ADIVASI 3. Let's go to Rainpur. (*Some more adivasis enter*) To Rainpur!

ADIVASI 2. Let him speak! Let Bira speak! We'll hear him out. We want to see how he performs!

BIRA. What are you all doing here? This is the planting season. Time to dance and sing. Time for the hunt. You should all return to your villages, peacefully. Celebrate, be happy! And I'll celebrate with you! Dance, sing, I'm your Raja, your Mahaprabhu!

ADIVASI 3. We don't accept you as Raja.

ADIVASI 2. You've snatched the crown from Mahaprabhu.

ADIVASI 4. You've murdered Mahaprabhu!

BIRA. Says who?

ADIVASI 4. Says I.

BIRA. Believe me, I am your Raja. Hirma-dada is not dead, he's locked up in jail.

ADIVASI 4. No, he's not in jail. He's been killed. If he was alive, he would still be on the throne, no one would have been able to remove him from the throne.

BIRA. If Dada had been killed, everyone would have come to know.

ADIVASI 4. If he's not dead, how come we don't see him?

BIRA. Dada is in the capital, that's why.

ADIVASI 1. Why in the capital? Why not in Rainpur Jail?

ADIVASI 2. They must be scared of keeping him in Rainpur Jail!

ADIVASI 1. Who're they afraid of?

ADIVASI 2. Of us.

ADIVASI 1. Why? Can't we go to the capital to see Maharaj?

ADIVASI 2. If we have to go to Delhi to see Maharaj, we'll do so!

ADIVASI 4. I am convinced they've killed off Maharaj.

ADIVASI 3. No one can kill Maharaj.

BIRA. Absolutely right! Who can kill Hirma-dada? He's in jail. When he's set free, I myself will inform you. Then you can all get his darshan.

ADIVASI 1. Yes. And for now, get Bira's darshan.

ADIVASI 2 AND 4. Bira's darshan! Bira's darshan!

ADIVASI 2. Bira-bhaiya! Don't we get a drink?

ADIVASI 3. Why not?

ADIVASI 2. He'll give us a drink and come along with us.

ADIVASI 1. Yes, let's take Bira to Rainpur!

BIRA. Come, let's go. I'll come with you, but we must be peaceful, bhai, no trouble.

ADIVASI 1. We'll sing and dance as we go, Bira-bhaiya.

BIRA. Good, let's begin, start the singing.

ADIVASI 2. Lift up Bira-bhaiya! Let's go!

ADIVASI 3. To Rainpur! Come, let's go!

ADIVASI 2. Yes!

ADIVASI 1. Get in line! All of you! It's time to go.

Bira is lifted onto their shoulders, they advance singing. Dumraj arrives with two sipahis bearing guns. One of them aims and orders them to stop. Bira falls to the ground. Adivasis retreat. The second adivasi lifts Bira and pulls him back.

DUMRAJ. Please disperse to your own villages. Do not proceed any further!

Adivasis move forward. A gun is fired. Adivasis shoot arrows. More firing. Some adivasis fall dead. Firing continues in the dark.

CHORUS (*sings*). Go on, shoot, shoot your gun!
Go on, shoot your gun
A murderer who's full of fear
A coward who's turned murderer
Go on, shoot your gun!

The bullets whine, the bullets roar
Fear spreads the silence of terror
Go on, shoot your gun

The coward's face, the tyrant's face,
Is blackened, harsh and cold
With cruelty, with lack of trust,
And with fears untold
Half his face it twists with fear
The other half with distrust
It has become a funeral pyre
It sears, it burns, it rusts

For fear of losing his own life
A man takes that of another
The coward has all the weapons he needs
He turns them on a brother
His face is scarred with ugly lines,
Cruelty mars its shape
He looks on all with cold dead eyes
That no one can escape

The hero brave he faces up
To the tyrants of this world
Snatches the weapon from their hands
Defies their power untold
Half his face a glowing sun
The other half the moon
See his glory shining forth
Like the Sun God at high noon

The hero brave his face is smooth
Unlined with hate or fear
No lowering clouds of grief darken
His visage gleaming clear
His eyes burn not with cruel fire
His beauty is a boon
His face a blessing on us all
His presence our fortune.

SCENE FIVE

Inside the jail.

KALHAN. In the Lohriguda firing, twelve adivasis were killed. Cases were started against fifty-nine people, but they were all released by the court. Still, the unrest spread. The demand for Hirma's release spread like wildfire. Finally, the government decided to release him.

Hirma is sitting in jail. Kalhan enters.

KALHAN. Hirma, the government has decided to release you, but on one condition.

HIRMA. Which is?

KALHAN. You will have to leave Titur Basna.

HIRMA. Why are you people playing games with me? You speak of democracy, and in the name of democracy you destroy a princely state. You depose a rightful king whose right to rule goes back for generations, and replace him with a man who cannot take my place as long as I'm alive. And today, you come and tell me that I should get out of jail and exile myself? And this, while the entire populace is clamouring for me? They consider me their maharaj, mahaprabhu, Mahapurohit and bhagwan! You tell me, if Bhagwan leaves their midst, who will the people call on, who will they turn to?

KALHAN. I'm just conveying the government orders.

HIRMA. I asked you a question.

KALHAN. You haven't eaten for two days. When will you end your hunger strike? I've brought you some sweet lime juice.

HIRMA. Kalhan, all this because you didn't get a diamond ring?

KALHAN. Both of us are trapped in the web of politics. What's this got to do with diamond rings? I have to carry out my orders. I am not here to account for myself. I'm still waiting for your reply.

Pause.

HIRMA. I accept the condition.

KALHAN. You will leave Titur Basna?

HIRMA. Yes, but on one condition.

KALHAN. What's that?

HIRMA. Dussehra is round the corner. Let me preside over this Dussehra in the age-old manner.

KALHAN. What's the good of that? It's just likely to incite people further.

HIRMA. If I was to slip away quietly without going back to Rainpur even once, and you were to announce that I had left, do you think you would be believed by the people? I made this suggestion not in order to incite the people but to give them reassurance. Let the people see me as act their purohit once again, during Dussehra, and it will definitely allay their fears, it will calm them down. I give you my word that after Dussehra I will leave Rainpur and Titur Basna at once.

Pause.

KALHAN. All right, I agree. In fact, I'll accompany you to Rainpur. Now come, let's go.

SCENE SIX

Dussehra. Adivasis enter singing and dancing. Hirma is seated on the rath, distributing daan. People surround the rath.

KALHAN. With the beginning of Dussehra, Hirma set off a veritable conflagration all around. He spent the whole day closeted inside Danteshwari Devi's temple, and then sent word from within the sanctum. He claimed that he couldn't ignore Ma's command. Ma had ordered him to take her with him. As it was, thousands of adivisasis were gathering for their Mahaprabhu's darshan. When the people heard this, village after village was in uproar. They all began to clamour that they would leave Titur Basna. Word spread like wildfire. Thousands began to converge on Rainpur. The roads are teeming with people. All with the same aim. To leave Titur Basna. We'll go wherever Danteshwari Devi goes. We'll follow where she leads.

BIRA. Kalhan-sahib, I'm telling you for the umpteenth time, don't let Bhauji go free.

KALHAN. Why can't you understand? At a time like this, keeping Baigin Bai prisoner is not advisable.

BIRA. Don't underestimate Dada. He's already caused such upheaval, if Bhauji joins him, who knows what sort of a storm they'll unleash!

KALHAN. I realize this. I've gauged the situation correctly. Now, don't delay. Release Baigin Bai at once. I'll try and have a word with Hirma.

BIRA. That's if he'll agree to talk to you.

KALHAN. Why won't he? Here, he's coming this way. You go. Release Baigin Bai.

BIRA. As you wish.

Bira leaves. Hirma enters from the opposite side

KALHAN. Hirma, what's all this?

HIRMA. Why? You didn't order me not to remove Danteshwari Devi, did you? I am obeying your orders. But it is also essential to obey the Devi.

Hirma exits. Bira enters.

BIRA. I've released her, but I'm telling you again, this was not well done.

KALHAN. Namaskar, Baigin Devi.

BAIGIN. Where is Maharaj?

KALHAN. He's gone this way. He's making preparations to leave Rainpur. Why don't you go and explain to him that if he stays, perhaps arrangements can be made to restore his estate?

BAIGIN. Even I'm going with him.

She goes within.

BIRA. What can Bhauji say to influence him? I know Dada well. He is very stubborn. Once he's made up his mind, he won't listen to anyone. There, both are coming this way. I'll be off.

Hirma and Baigin enter.

KALHAN. It would be better if you didn't leave Rainpur.

HIRMA. What, are you reversing your orders? This is no longer possible.

KALHAN. I'm taking back my orders. You're not to leave.

HIRMA. Restore my estate and I'll stay.

KALHAN. That's beyond my jurisdiction.

HIRMA. Think it over seriously.

Pause.

BIRA. What did I tell you?

HIRMA. Bira!

BIRA. What?

HIRMA. When I get my kingdom back, what'll become of you?

KALHAN (*gestures for Bira to leave*). Hirma, why are you acting like a child? This is all a matter of politics. Court of Wards is a Central Government order. It can only be changed by the high command. I'm just an ordinary government servant. How can I help in this case?

HIRMA. You or the high command. I only know that all your schemes have failed, and your politics has been a failure. If even a small fraction of the huge budget of two crores which had been allocated for the development of Titur Basna had been used, we could have built a road of pure silver from Rainpur to Raipur!

KALHAN. Hirma, the entire populace of this huge kingdom, consisting of lakhs of people, dances to your tune. God knows why you don't take advantage of this to serve your own purpose!

HIRMA. My politics is based on tantric philosophy.

KALHAN. A politics of confrontation. You cannot win.

HIRMA. So am I to bow before your tyranny?

KALHAN. Fight tyranny from within.

HIRMA. You mean become a member of the ruling party?

KALHAN. What's the harm? The elections are not far off. You have seven constituencies under you. If you want, you can win them all.

HIRMA. And after that?

KALHAN. Talk it over and see.

HIRMA. Will I get my estate back?

KALHAN. Of course. After all, this is politics. At least talk to them and see.

Hirma looks at Baigin and she nods in approval.

BAIGIN. Thik hai. All right.

HIRMA. Well, I guess I might as well try it.

CHORUS (*sings*). She is our mother, this earth so dear
    Our mother dear is she
    Our mother, this earth both far and near
    Beautiful to see

    Proud she is in her mountains tall
    In her rivers she delights
    She's the one who summons the sun
    Mirrors the moon in her sights
    Enchants the gathering bright of stars
    Sings songs of the wind all night

    Laughing, she scatters the colours of joy
    She rains down perfumes sweet
    With the burgeoning clouds she'll dance and sway
    Sing along with the murmuring leaves

    The infant clasped to her breast grows strong
    He grows up brave and tall
    She nurtures and feeds us with her own food
    And clothes us, big and small
    She scolds us, makes us laugh and cry
    And play, she does it all

    Champa, chameli, roses pink
    Flowers of different types

Rabbits, monkeys, bears and beasts
Of different shapes and stripes
Each and every one of these
Our playmates from childhood times

SCENE SEVEN

Vidhan Sabha (Legislative Assembly).

KALHAN. In the Assembly elections Hirma won six out of seven constituencies. Six of his nominees entered the Assembly as members of the ruling party. The party won by a large majority and formed the government once again. Before the elections, Hirma had been assured that when the government was formed, his estate would be released from the Court of Wards. But you tell me, can any government fulfil such a promise? So the unrest started again.

A member of the Assembly is giving a speech.

MLA 1. Honourable Speaker, sir. Many promises were made to us before the elections. Ten months have passed since this government was formed. Not one promise has been kept to date. Instead, the people are being subjected to all kinds of torture and oppression. Even the one or two incidents I am aware of are enough to make the blood run cold. For hundreds of years, the adivisasis have considered the land on which they live their own, and they have thought of the jungles as theirs by right. For ages, they have been settling their own domestic, property and land disputes through their panchayat. But now their lands have been snatched from them, and their right to the jungle and its produce has been taken away. It has been said that they cut down the jungle. And destroy the jungle. We demand our land back, we demand our jungles back!

CHORUS (*continues to sing*).We are the children of mother earth
Her soldiers and sentinels too
We are the natives of the jungle
Guard the forest is what we do
Of these trees we are the servants
And the masters too!
She is our mother, this earth so dear
Our mother dear is she
Our mother, this earth both far and near
Beautiful to see

MLA 1. Traditionally, the adivasi held full rights to all the riches of the forest: Lac, *harra*, honey, gum, mango, berries, *tendu*. They subsisted on the sale of this produce, a little cultivation, and some hunting. Now all this is forbidden to them. Yet a few middle men and contractors are legally permitted to profit from the forest. Illicitly, hundreds of contractors and complicit government employees and forest officials are hacking down trees on a large scale. They are embezzling lakhs from the government funds. Doesn't this harm the forest? But let a single adivasi attempt to cut down a few trees and cultivate land according to his traditional way of life, and he is punished. It is said that he is destroying the forest. As a result he is being forced to turn from agriculture to manual labour. And all the while, his own jungle, his own wealth, is being swallowed by rich seths. And the sarkar is totally indifferent.

Earlier, the villages used to resound with the music of *mandar* and *manjira*. Now they are as silent as graveyards. For ages, the songs and dances of the people have been flourishing in the districts of Titur Basna. Instead of giving them the chance to develop further their art and culture, which is inseparable from their way of life, their farming and hunting and daily routine is being destroyed. Instead of creating a healthy environment for these arts, which are linked to their daily life, they are being reduced to mere exhibitions in big cities once or twice a year. Adivasi cultural wealth is being wiped out, in return for a smattering of awards to a few individuals. Shri Hirma Dev Singh had started an adivasi dance and music school for children. The government gave it no financial support, just let it close down. And from Shri Hirma Dev Singh's estate—

MLA 2. Honourable Speaker Sir, the respected member is not the sole representative of Titur Basna. I too have been authorized by the people to represent them. The respected member wants our adivasis to remain preoccupied with singing and dancing and pay no attention to their own progress. This cannot be allowed, I will not allow it. Our poor adivasis shall attend school and college, shall get education—

MLA 3. An education that is not part of our culture?

MLA 1. You've opened schools enough. So why aren't the adivasis sending their children to these schools? They say, if the teachers can be paid to teach, why can't we be paid to learn? His interest in teaching is that he gets paid for it; what is our motivation for studying when we get nothing for it? Give us a share of the teachers' salary, then we'll send our children to school. Otherwise, what do we have to do with reading and writing?

SPEAKER. Please sum up your address.

MLA 1. Honourable Speaker sir, it is commonly held that the adivasi is an ignorant savage. That he refuses to work even when offered a job. Refuses to educate himself despite plenty of schools. All the paths to progress lie before him but he prefers to lie around drunk, squabble and fight and outright refuses to progress. But what is our idea of progress? Do what we think is good for you, break stones, make roads for us, don't try and look for a path suited to your own idea of progress. And who are 'we'? The same handful of educated city folk, some bureaucrats, some merchants and traders! And of course a few leaders like this honourable member here. You deprive an entire people of their way of life, their beliefs, their history and their tradition, and then in turn accuse them of being no-good idlers, of being sunk in apathy, of turning away from the path of progress.

MINISTER. Honourable Speaker sir, point of order. We were supposed to be discussing the matter of Sri Hirma Dev's estate. The honourable member is straying far from the point.

MLA 4. The discussion was on the Titur Basna adivasi's entire way of life.

SPEAKER. You have been allowed more than enough time. Kindly conclude your speech within a minute or two.

MLA 1. The Honourable Minister spoke of Maharaj Hirma Dev Singh's estate almost as if he was about to restore it to him. It is a matter of great shame that a decent, upstanding, sensible gentleman should be declared insane, and his personal wealth, his by right of inheritance, should be forcibly taken away from him. And what is more, that this should be propounded by taking advantage of this for the elections. He is promised that if he should help the government win the election, his property will be restored to him. And after all this, Sarkar Bahadur blatantly refuses to relinquish his estate!

Cries of 'Shame! Shame!'

MINISTER. Mr Chairman sir, I protest!

MLA 1. Who is protesting, you or I? It's a matter of deep concern, sir, that in a huge area like Titur Basna, the largest district in India, even larger than Kerala state, at least six out of seven representatives are unhappy with the policies of the government. And yet the Minister says, I protest?! I ask him—

Outcry; uproar; lots of members speak at the same time; confusion; the Speaker rings for silence and slowly the uproar dies down.

SPEAKER. Your time is over. Minister sir, please submit your reply.

MINISTER. Speaker sir, I don't feel duty bound to answer any questions which lie outside the purview of today's discussion. Most of them are wild allegations against the government. For example, regarding forest rights, the government stand on that is well established. If we were to allow even one adivasi to practise shifting cultivation, can you imagine the outcome? Think of it! The adivasis form a large section of the population all over India, they would all have to be granted the same right. How much of our forest would survive, tell me. As for the matter of Hirma Dev Singh Gangvashi's estate, the government has not reached any decision as yet. The matter is under consideration, and as soon as we reach a conclusion, it will be announced in this forum.

MLA 1. Your committees and your deliberations are nothing but a screen from behind which you hunt your prey. You can no longer hide behind them. We resign from the ruling party of Titur Basna. We are joining the Opposition.

Six members get up and join the opposition.

MINISTER. Speaker sir, this entire drama that has been enacted before us is nothing but a feudal conspiracy. The erstwhile Maharaja of Titur Basna, my good friend Shri Hirma Dev Singh Gangvanshi, is clearly behind this. He is fighting for his ancestral property. He wants to re-establish feudal rule in the state. And yet he claims that he's doing it for the people. If this had not been so, these worthy gentleman would have worked side by side with us, given us suggestions and advice, guided us. But these gentlemen are not interested in this. This is why they have played their trump card and taken us by surprise. I totally condemn this politics of floor crossing, after winning the elections on the ticket of a party! We should put a stop to this common political practice by making it a constitutional offence.

Uproar. Many members leave. Speaker adjourns the session.

Interval.

PART TWO

SCENE ONE

Street.

CHORUS (*sings*). Two kinds of people in this world
    Listen and hear us out
    Two kinds of people in this world
    Those with money and those without

    Heaven for one is hell for another
    A feast for one means famine for another
    Business for one means a jobless other
    Oh, listen and hear us out.

    Whose wealth powers the thriving markets of this world?
    Whose hunger fuels the flourishing commerce of this world?
    Whose beggary begets the governments of this world?
    Oh listen and hear us out.

    Without any wealth and without any power
    Life without God is nothing at all
    For the poor on this earth, God is all that we have
    For us life with no God is nothing

This world is theirs, they can make their own pleasures
Yes, it's all theirs, the whole world and its treasures
They make the poor, they both rob and they feed
For us, the poor, God is what we need
Life without God is nothing at all
For us, life with no God is nothing

Earth, sky, wind, water, fire, trees,
All of nature plus us, human beings
Belong to them, all in creation is theirs
The fire, the wind and water's not ours
Not the flowers nor the fruit nor the trees, not ours
Nothing belongs to us, and when nothing is ours
Life without God is nothing at all
For us, life with no God is nothing.

KALHAN. Hirma and his supporters joined the opposition party. There were new demands raised by their party. The issue of Hirma's estate was turned into a people's movement which spread throughout Titur Basna. Baigin Bai meanwhile organized a separate women's political wing. She dressed them all in red saris and soon the streets of Rainpur were filled with thousands of red-sari-clad women agitators. The new year brought fresh problems. Bira's habits began to disgust more and more people.As the people's discontent with his administration grew, so did their rebellion against the government.

A procession of women agitating and shouting slogans.

BAIGIN. We demand—

WOMEN. —our property back!

Bira enters, drunk.

BIRA. Bhauji, you've started a revolt against the government!

BAIGIN. You government lackey!

BIRA. Rubbish! I'm the ruler now. The government follows my orders!

BAIGIN. That's why the government has usurped our estate and you're doing nothing about it!

BIRA. And what are you doing? Just leading these women astray. You talk of 'estate'. But what has our estate got to do with you? When we get back our estate, it will be ours, and after Dada, it will all belong to me. Dada doesn't have an heir. And you're just his kept woman. When the time comes, he'll turn you out. You're not even married to him!

BAIGIN. Get out of here, you bastard!

BIRA. All right! All right! I'll speak to the Collector and get you all arrested.

BAIGIN. Oh, go to hell! Don't pay any attention to him, he can't do a thing to us! We demand—

WOMEN. —our property back!

BAIGIN. We demand—

WOMEN. —our raj back!

The women march out.

SCENE TWO

Collectorate. Collector, SP are present. Dumraj enters.

COLLECTOR. What's your report?

DUMRAJ. All I know, sir, is that when the chaprasi reached the palace to summon Hirma Maharaj, he was attacked and killed by a whole host of adivasis.

SP. You should establish whether this murder was carried out on the orders of Hirma.

DUMRAJ. I couldn't find out, sir. Perhaps if one or two people are arrested, we'll get to know, but at the moment, there are so many people crowded into the palace that it's difficult to arrest anyone.

SP. Please answer this question. I sent a search party with you to Bira Maharaj's *kothi*. How come they returned without taking possession of the gold bars?

DUMRAJ. I told you, the palace is swarming with people. And then, Bira Maharaj said, there's no need for a search, I myself am going to meet the Collector-sahib. He left at that point, and will probably be here any moment.

COLLECTOR. Any fresh evidence in the case of the sipahi's murder?

DUMRAJ. Sir had taken out a warrant and Sudru and seven others were arrested.

SP. Nothing important could be got from them.

DUMRAJ. Actually, so many people have gathered in Kilepaal . . .

COLLECTOR. Mr Singh!

DUMRAJ. Yes, sir.

COLLECTOR. Was the truck carrying the levy of paddy, which was coming from Kilepaal, burned? That's the rumour. What's your report?

DUMRAJ. That's what I'm trying to tell you, sir, this is false. The truck is still there. The paddy is still intact inside it. It's been surrounded by a crowd. Of those who led the gang in stopping the truck, about fifteen have been arrested by us. Nine men and six women. But the truck has not been burnt. This is for sure.

Bira enters.

COLLECTOR. Namaskar, maharaj.

SP/DUMRAJ. Namaskar.

BIRA. You people have done the division of the estate totally wrong. I'm going to sue the government. Both the State Government and the Central Government, and also those to whom Hirma-dada has sold buildings, the buyers.

COLLECTOR. What's the matter? What's happened?

BIRA. What's happened? The treasury is being looted day and night! Saris are being distributed, watches and gold rings are being given away in celebration of the restoration of his estate! Fifteen thousand rupees in cash has been given to this one and that one, and I am reduced to watching this spectacle helplessly, though I may be seated on the throne. I told you people long ago, if you have to restore the estate, let Dada get only his private inheritance. The public property should have been allotted to me. But the government handed Hirma Dev the whole palace, all the royal ancestral gold and jewellery, and left me languishing in a corner with nothing. And now I'm forced to watch it all being frittered away!

SP. Maharaj Hirma had registered a report against you.

BIRA. Yes, yes, that's what I'm saying! That business of two gold bars! They were state property, so I took them. And he accused me of stealing!

SP. He claims that they belong to Danteshwari Devi.

BIRA. Yes, they probably do. All I know is, they've been with us for centuries.

COLLECTOR. Several adivasis had come to us in delegation over this matter.

BIRA. I know. And you sent a police search party, which I despatched summarily. What was the need for a search party? If you had asked me for them I'd have given them to you.

COLLECTOR. So where are they?

BIRA. Yes, yes, I'll return them.

COLLECTOR. This is now an urgent matter, Maharaj.

BIRA. Yes, I know. After all, will Dada let me get away with anything? When I brought up the question of the palace and the palace grounds, he told me, take them, they're yours. Just clear it of all the adivasis who are roaming around here. Now tell me, how am I going to clear out thousands of adivasis from the compound? Dada has total authority over them. And then he dares me, saying I don't want the estate, take it all!

COLLECTOR. And what do you know about the sipahi murder?

Hirma enters.

HIRMA. Collector-sahib, am I now to be subjected to obeying a chaprasi's orders?

COLLECTOR. The orders came from the government, not the chaprasi or myself.

HIRMA. Couldn't you find anyone other than a chaprasi to send to summon me?

SP. Does that mean you turn him into a target and have him shot?

HIRMA. He turned himself into a target. My men asked him to identify himself, and he just barged in, insisting, 'Call the Maharaj!' They told him I was doing puja and asked him his business. The insolent fellow refused to answer, just kept repeating, 'I'll only tell Maharaj.'

SP. Those were his orders.

HIRMA. Then you are responsible for his death. He became abusive. When one of my men tried to stop the chap, he turned violent. Do you think my people will tolerate my being insulted? They shot him full of arrows.

COLLECTOR. Well, an inquiry is being held on that matter. At present, I've summoned you to discuss the matter of the levy. The truck carrying the levy has been stalled by the villagers for two days in Kilepaal and two constables have been killed in this connection. Please explain to the villagers that it is a government truck, and that they should not prevent it from reaching Rainpur.

HIRMA. Give me the throne and I will give the order. The Raja is sitting right here, tell him to have the truck released.

BIRA. Dada, this is becoming a very serious matter.

HIRMA. Quiet! Collector-sahib, I have just one thing to say. Either abolish the raj gaddi and take the reins of government into your own hands, or hand them to me. Let me rule. As long as I am alive, there is no way my younger brother can be the rightful ruler. As for the question of the levy, you have my answer. Okay, I'm off. Where are the gold bars? Hand them over! (*Bira hands him the gold bars*) You low-down thieving rascal!

Hirma leaves.

COLLECTOR. Maharaj, there is something else. Regarding the murder of the two constables in Kilepaal last week, I had asked you to please inform me if you have any reliable information or leads.

BIRA. What actually happened?

SP. Sudru, an adivasi from Kilepaal, was trying to prevent the farmers from paying the levy. When our men reached there to arrest him, the villagers killed them. We have arrested seven men in this connection. Sudru was carrying a gold ring. Perhaps Hirma Maharaj gave it to him?

BIRA. He must have. Goodness knows how many such rings and watches he has given away!

COLLECTOR. But this evidence is insufficient. I had asked you to investigate the matter thoroughly.

BIRA. What on earth can I find out? And moreover, why do you need an investigation? It's quite clear that Dada has a hand in it. After all, the ring can only have been given by him. How else would a villager get a gold ring?

SP. He's distributed such rings to goodness knows how many people.

BIRA. And those are the very people who are rebelling.

Baigin Bai enters with a group of women shouting slogans and gheraos the office.

BIRA. Mr Pande, please ask these women to fetch me my bottle of whiskey, at least!

COLLECTOR. They won't even allow us water, and you want whiskey!

BIRA. I have a severe headache, if I'm forced to stay in this room any longer, I'll die! Mr Pande, at least try and reason with these women! Ask them, in the name of humanity, to allow us to arrange some food and drink!

COLLECTOR. I've tried to tell them.

BIRA. I should never have come here! It's my mistake! I was trying to help you. I must have been mad to come here out of sympathy for you! It's been eighteen hours! How long must we be locked up in this room?! I'm dying of thirst, hunger, I can't sleep! And you're not doing a thing, just sitting here calmly! (*He looks out*) There are lots of policemen outside, and they're all carrying guns! Collector-sahib, this is not good. It won't be good if they start firing. Then there'll be no chance for us to escape alive!

COLLECTOR. Calm down, please. Don't shout.

BIRA. I'm telling you, this is wrong! Just arrest Baigin Bai, and everything will settle down. Wait, let me try talking to Bhauji one more time.

(*Bira exits. His voice, offstage.*) Bhauji, Collector-sahib is willing to listen to your demands. Why don't you come inside so he can talk to you?

(*Baigin pushes him back in.*) They won't listen to me. Mr Pande, why don't you go and offer them reassurance?

COLLECTOR. Don't drive us all mad, just sit down and be quiet.

BIRA. What's the use of staying quiet? I can't understand what's going on.

Kalhan enters, followed by some gun-toting policemen. Baigin bai and her companions bar entry to the office and block his path. Kalhan gestures to the policeman, who take aim with their guns. Hirma enters, Baigin Bai and the women surround him. Kalhan gestures to the police to lower their guns.

HIRMA (*to Baigin*). You go. Go to Kilepaal and stop the paddy truck.

BAIGIN. Yes, come on, sisters, let's go to Kilepaal and stop the paddy truck.

Baigin Bai leaves, shouting slogans, along with the women. Kalhan goes up to talk to Hirma. Hirma walks off without saying a word. Kalhan enters the office where the Collector, SP, Dumraj and Bira are sitting.

SP. Good morning, sir.

COLLECTOR AND BIRA. Namaste, Kalhan-sahib.

DUMRAJ. Namaste, sir.

KALHAN. Good morning, namaste Your Highness. Please sit, sit, what news?

COLLECTOR. Sir, the situation is just the same, in fact it has deteriorated. Your unexpected arrival is a pleasant surprise, sir.

KALHAN. Have you discussed the matter of the levy with Hirma?

COLLECTOR. Yes, sir. He refuses to help. He says, give me back the throne, then I'll get the trucks despatched from Kilepaal.

KALHAN. Achchha. Hey, come here!

POLICEMAN ONE. Yes, sir.

KALHAN. Do you know that one-armed rickshawpuller?

POLICEMAN. Yes, sir.

KALHAN. Please bring him here.

POLICEMAN. Yes, sir. (*He leaves.*)

KALHAN. Hmm, Dumraj, you've reached the post of ADM very quickly! Many congratulations!

DUMRAJ. Thank you, sir. When did you arrive, sir?

KALHAN. Hmm? Bas, just now, I've come straight here.

DUMRAJ. From the capital?

KALHAN. Yes, yes, where else?

BIRA. Kalhan-sahib, are you carrying any new orders?

KALHAN. Your Highness, I can tell you things won't continue like this for long.

BIRA. Ji?

Sipahi enters.

SIPAHI. Sir, I've found the cripple.

KALHAN. Cripple?

SIPAHI. The one you asked me to bring. Everyone calls him a cripple, sir.

KALHAN. Where is he?

SIPAHI. Standing outside.

KALHAN. Send him in. (*Sipahi exits. To Collector*) And listen, have you prepared a report on Hirma?

COLLECTOR. Ji? What?

KALHAN. Please prepare a full report on Hirma.

COLLECTOR. Certainly, sir.

KALHAN. How long will it take?

COLLECTOR. Oh, about . . . I'll try my best to do it fast.

KALHAN. Take Mr Sharma's help.

SP. Yes, I understand. The facts are known to everyone, the report should be ready in an hour or so.

KALHAN. Very good. I want to meet Hirma. Prepare the report and send it to me. I'll meet Hirma after I've gone through it. (*Rickshawpuller enters*) So? How're you doing? Managing to pull your rickshaw with one hand?

RICKSHAWPULLER. I manage, sir.

KALHAN. Given up begging? (*Laughs*) Come along with me. Mr Pande, come to my house after dinner, along with Mr Sharma. Let me read the report first, then I'll meet Hirma. When I get back from there, I'll phone you myself. It might be late at night, kindly remain at home. (*To rickshawpuller*) You— come along. Do you smoke? Here, take one.

RICKSHAWPULLER. Thank you, sir!

Kalhan steps aside and hands the rickshawpuller a bundle of notes which he shamefacedly accepts. Both leave.

SCENE THREE

The Threat of Death.

CHORUS (*sings*).

Tell me, why is the bitter gourd so bitter, why so bitter the gourd?
What makes the bitter gourd taste sharp, just like a slicing sword?
Turned lover and fell in love, oh yes, drank love's sweet sweet juice
But love itself destroyed the lover, oh what's a lover to do?
The elephant battles the lion, oh yes, the mongoose fights the snake
When water takes on burning coal then steam that match does make
The British killed Bhagat Singh, oh yes, by them killed was he
But Bhagat Singh he finished off the British eventually

Red spinach is red, oh yes, and green spinach is green
While green mango, though sweet, can be sour to the extreme.

KALHAN. It's hard for me to explain what I felt towards Hirma. Friendship, enmity, these words are far too threadbare to adequately express my feelings. They won't do. Perhaps love and hate are two names for the same emotion, one feels the same attachment, the same bond, in both. It's as if we are still locked into playing a game of tennis singles as we did so often in our youth, and that game is still continuing. Every set springs a new surprise. Both of us are concentrating on which way the ball will fall. Sometimes one of us wins a point, at times the other; but it is very hard to assess who won and who lost in the finals.

Adivasis are engaged in the worship of Danteshwari Devi. Hirma is amongst them. Kalhan enters and sits in the verandah. Stands up as Hirma approaches. Some men are with Hirma.

KALHAN. I've been waiting for you.

HIRMA. Tell me, Kalhan, have you come with some new plan for me?

KALHAN. Maybe. I'd like a word with you alone.

HIRMA. You all may go. (*His men leave.*) Go on?

KALHAN. Hirma, you must be knowing your own history.

HIRMA. Yes, somewhat.

KALHAN. Do you remember the revolt of 1910?

HIRMA. Why? What about it?

KALHAN. Hundreds of adivasis were killed at the time. Village after village was set on fire. There was a lot of bloodshed.

HIRMA. Is that what you want to see repeated?

KALHAN. Not me, it seems that you're the one who wants it.

HIRMA. As you say.

KALHAN. Chitrakoot, Sarjhanpuri, Kilepaal, there are meetings being held all over. In Kilepaal twenty-two people have been arrested.

HIRMA. This is an atrocity on your part.

KALHAN. Just recently in Kilepaal there has been an incident of a terrible murder of two constables.

HIRMA. For which you have already condemned seven men to life imprisonment. What more do you want?

KALHAN. For the past four to five days, the palace has been overrun by adivasis.

HIRMA. So what's strange about that? This is the time of seed collection. This congregation will stay for seven or eight days. Farmers are bringing their seeds to deposit in the *devguri*. You're perfectly familiar with the local customs, or else, you wouldn't have risen from Collector to Chief Secretary.

KALHAN. A blacksmith was caught carrying arrowheads into the palace.

HIRMA. Adivasis always get their arrowheads made by blacksmiths. Arresting that blacksmith is another instance of atrocity.

KALHAN. You have again raised the demand for an inquiry into the incidents of firing at Lohriguda and Kirandul.

HIRMA. And you're preparing for a third incident of firing.

KALHAN. Every man is bound to do his duty. Trouble starts when the duty of one man clashes with that of another.

HIRMA. What is it that you want?

KALHAN. Bas, just have the paddy truck despatched from Kilepaal. I've come from the capital to resolve this one issue. It is having a bad effect on the market, and the tension has spread to the markets in other areas too.

HIRMA. I cannot do this.

KALHAN. Think before you answer.

HIRMA. I've given it enough thought.

KALHAN. When all the paths are blocked, Hirma, there is only one path left.

HIRMA. The path of death?

KALHAN. If a mouse was trapped in a room, what would it do?

HIRMA. Exactly what I'm doing.

KALHAN. No, that which we're doing.

HIRMA. So you're carrying my death warrant, are you?

KALHAN. No, it's not like that.

HIRMA. You are forgetting that death is hovering over your heads too. Your writ is not likely to last very long. Don't think of killing me. You can't kill me. You have no idea of my power.

KALHAN. I know your power. That's why I've come to you. You are leading your adivasis down the wrong path. You've got entangled in party politics and I am caught in the web of bureaucracy. I wish to help you. But I can't. The tension that has built up is pushing us both towards a confrontation which will not be good for anyone. I am not asking you to stop your struggle. Just accept this request of mine, and despatch the truck from Kilepaal. I'll handle the rest.

HIRMA. I don't think even I can stop them now.

KALHAN. Perhaps you're right. This is a history which cannot reverse its course, but what about the future? Now see, a month ago your band of adivasi women told the officials of the Dandkaranya development authority to vacate Dharampur. Patwaris are being told to leave the villages. Government servants are being told to clear out their offices within the palace grounds. People are being told not to cooperate with the government.

Being stopped from paying taxes to the government. The clerks are being prevented from preparing the lists of the farmers who have to pay levy. At first, the demand was for ancestral property, then the throne, now for self-government. Tomorrow all government employees might be asked to leave. Moneylenders, traders, shopkeepers might be told, you are outsiders, you have no right to live here. If this is not a repetition of the 1910 story, then what is it?

HIRMA. You are preparing your notes with great zeal. Carry on. And when the time comes, recite it to those for whom you're preparing this long speech. There's no need to tell me about it. You know very well that ours is an economic and cultural movement, and totally nonviolent in nature.

KALHAN. I know. Your people listen to what you say. That's why I'm telling you. If you choose, you can stop them.

HIRMA. But what are you people doing? I had given the Collector some suggestions regarding the levy. Were they implemented?

KALHAN. Stop the levy, stop the requisition of paddy, rice at rupees four a kilo, what world are you living in?

HIRMA. The world that existed before you people came. If you leave us alone, even today it is possible to achieve. I didn't ask them to stop the levy, merely to reduce it. I didn't ask them to stop the requisition of paddy, merely to reduce it. I'm only interested in the throne to the extent that I can restore to the adivisasis their land, their self rule and their rights. Had you done that, I would have had no complaint against your government. You accuse me of hampering your work. I say that you are the one who has been continuously hampering me in my work, is still hampering me and will continue to hamper me in the future. Kindly leave. You are wasting your time here.

Hirma exits. Kalhan stays on for some time, thinking . Then he leaves.

SCENE FOUR

Outside the Palace.

KALHAN. Twenty-fifth of March. On that day, more than 3,000 men and women were in the palace. Section 144 had been imposed in the town. The previous day, Hirma Dev had left for the Danteshwari temple in the morning, and returned late at night. The next day, at 10.30 in the morning, Dumraj Dev Singh, ADM, reached the palace with a large police contingent. They were armed.

SP enters with a troop of policemen. He is accompanied by the Inspector.

SP. You know your orders?

INSPECTOR. Yes, sir!

SP. Okay, stay on duty.

INSPECTOR. Yes, sir! Hawaldar Chandanlal!

CHANDANLAL. Yes, sir!

INSPECTOR. Take your sipahis to the eastern gate of the palace.

Chandanlala salutes and leaves. Sound of sipahis marching off.

INSPECTOR. Hawaldar Khusram!

KHUSRAM. Yes, sir!

INSPECTOR. You go to the western gate.

Sub-inspector enters.

CIRCLE INSPECTOR. Sir! (*Salutes*)

SP. What's the matter?

INSPECTOR. The paddy truck has left Kilepaal.

SP. What?

INSPECTOR. Yes, sir. Hirma Dev went to Kilepaal and persuaded the people to release it.(*A procession of women enters and passes by silently.*) Sir, these women have come from there.

SP. Has Collector-sahib given any new order?

INSPECTOR. No sir, only that Hirma Maharaj has sent a message to stop police action, he is despatching the paddy truck.

DUMRAJ. Has the truck reached?

INSPECTOR. It's about to, any moment. My man has seen it on the road. This is confirmed, sir.

SP. Has Kalhan-sahib been informed?

INSPECTOR. Yes sir, Collector-sahib has spoken on the phone.

SP. What did Kalhan-sahib say?

INSPECTOR. Nothing. He disconnected.

SP. Disconnected?

INSPECTOR. Collector-sahib phoned again. Kalhan-sahib said, I've heard what you have to say. This conversation is over. And he disconnected again. Collector-sahib told me to tell SP-sahib.

SP. Anything else? Did Collector-sahib say anything more?

INSPECTOR. I asked him, sir. He said SP-sahib will act as per his powers. Just tell him this much. And tell him I have no fresh orders.

SP thinks for a while.

DUMRAJ. Perhaps Hirma Maharaj got worried when he learnt of the police arrangements.

SP. Idiot!

DUMRAJ. What?

SP. Sorry sir, what should we do now?

DUMRAJ. What action do you wish to take?

SP. What can I do?

DUMRAJ. Why? Didn't you hear Collector-sahib's message? He said, SP will act according to his powers. He didn't mention my name, did he? That's why I'm asking you.

SP. Sir, where's the question of my authority when you're present? Collector-sahib means that I should act according to your instructions. To my mind, the basis for police action was the stopping of the paddy truck. Now that the truck has been released, the reason for police action no longer exists. In this situation what action can we take?

DUMRAJ. Why not? Collector-sahib has not reversed his earlier orders. So how can we change it?

SP. You can change it if you wish.

DUMRAJ (to Circle Inspector). Even I can't change it, because what did Collector-sahib say about the old order?

CIRCLE INSPECTOR. He said, I have no fresh order.

SP. So tell us what to do.

DUMRAJ. What do you mean? I've given no order, the orders have come from Collector-sahib.

SP. Still, sir, in the presence of the ADM, how can I take responsibility for this action?

DUMRAJ. So you want me to be answerable while you fire the bullets?

SP. You will have to give the order.

DUMRAJ. Look, don't waste your time arguing with me. Neither can I issue new orders, nor can I change the old ones! Just do what you have to do. Do your job.

SP. As you wish. All of you, do as instructed. Keep your orders in mind. This is action till the end. Circle Inspector Biharidas!

CIRCLE INSPECTOR. No problem, sir!

SP. That's it, then, each of you to his post.

SP leaves.

SUB-INSPECTOR. Havaldar Sukhram!

SUKHRAM. Yes, sir!

SUB-INSPECTOR. Go to the north gate.

SUKHRAM. Yes, sir.

SUB-INSPECTOR. Havaldar Sunaruram?

SUNARU. Yes, sir!

SUB-INSPECTOR. You go to the south gate.

SUNARU. Yes, sir.

SUB INSPECTOR (*to Dumraj*). Please come, sir.

Exit Dumraj, Circle Inspector followed by Sub-inspector.

SCENE FIVE

Death of Hirma.

The adivasis are dancing. Hirma is with them. The police enter with a prisoner, the rickshawpuller.

HIRMA. When will you people stop walking in and out of the palace?

POLICE ONE. We are taking this prisoner to the lockup.

HIRMA. Can't you keep him in the police station for a day or two?

POLICE. There's no place in the police station.

HIRMA (*sees the rickshawpuller*). Who is this? Oh, it's you! What crime are you arresting him for?

RICKSHAWPULLER. I haven't done anything, Mahaprabhu, please save me, Maharaj, they're thrashing me black and blue, sarkar, please give me shelter, Mahaprabhu!

Police exit with rickshawpuller, who keeps shouting and pleading. Baigin Bai enters.

HIRMA. Listen, my people, my brothers, Devi's orders were that to see the real face of the government, we should first remove all their alibis and excuses. The paddy truck was a ploy and an excuse for the government, I removed that excuse. But still they insist on coming into the palace. As long as there are adivasis inside the palace, they will not leave. And if I send you out, you can't return home because outside, Section 144 is in force. In other words, the government is forcing us to break the law. If we busy ourselves with our own work here, just to provoke us, the police keep coming in and out under the excuse of carrying out their duties. You should understand what the police are up to. Be on your guard. Beware. Stay calm, and sit down here peacefully with me.

BAIGIN. Sit down, everyone, please sit down comfortably. Maharaj is beginning the meeting.

HIRMA. I want to know, on whose orders was the paddy truck stopped?

BAIGIN. On whose orders?

ALL. On Mahaprabhu's orders.

HIRMA. And on whose orders was it released?

BAIGIN. By whose orders?

ALL. By Mahaprabhu's orders.

HIRMA. Who does Titur Basna belong to?

BAIGIN. To the adivasi!

ALL. To the adivasi!

HIRMA. Whose is Rainpur?

ALL. The adivasis!

HIRMA. Who is the god of the adivasi?

BAIGIN. Mahaprabhu is our god!

ALL. Bhagwan!

HIRMA. Tell me, if God is above everyone, who can kill God?

BAIGIN. No one!

ALL. No one can kill you!

HIRMA. And if you shoot bullets at God, what will the bullet turn into?

BAIGIN. It'll turn to water!

ALL. Turn to water!

CHORUS (*sings*). Just lift your eyes and look at the sky
Beautiful in blue
Just lift your eyes and look at the clouds
Like a sheet all drenched through

Green, yellow, purple, blue, red, mauve, and pink
All these seven colours from a single drop they spring
Just one ray of sunlight, what a miracle it brings

Trees laden with so much fruit, the fruit it comes from God
Who then are these who stand between us, so as the fruit to guard?
A deeply painful tale, tell me, how can I put it into words?

The tree of oppression towers high, its branches slippery smooth
Its flowers are pleasing to the eye, in many hues they bloom
The tree of tyranny towers high, but poisonous is its fruit.

After a while, there is a sudden uproar and the adivasis run in the direction of the noise.

HIRMA. It's just a trick! Pay no attention!

BAIGIN. Listen to Mahaprabhu! Don't go there! Sit down!

Another outcry. Some prisoners come running. The rickshawpuller is with them. They are being chased by the armed police. The prisoners run away. The rickshawpuller hides in the crowd. The police take their positions, and aim their guns at Hirma and the adivasis. Hirma starts herding the adivasis inside. There is shooting, and some adivasis drop dead. Hirma shelters Baigin and takes her inside. The police hide on the other side. Hirma comes back with his sword, two adivasis behind him. The police fire from within. First both adivasis die, then Hirma is killed. The police run out. The rickshawpuller enters. First he steals Hirma's gold ornaments. He begins to leave, then thinks of something and stops, picks up the sword and cuts off Hirma's hand. He takes off the gold ring from Hirma's finger and puts it on. Then he takes it off and pockets it. He tries to shake off the hand and throw it away, and is astounded when the amputated hand sticks to his. He is petrified. Screaming, he runs inside. Baigin enters. She searches for Hirma amongst the corpses. Seeing him lying dead, she begins to lament and keen. She picks up the sword and sheathes it. Kalhan enters just then. Baigin looks at him, hands him the sword and the bunch of keys, and walks out. At the moment when Baigin hands over the sword to Kalhan, a group of adivasi women begin to chant a dirge.

EPILOGUE

KALHAN. The Rainpur Firing caused a furore in the Assembly, Parliament and the newspapers. A judicial enquiry commission was set up. The commission concluded that Maharaj Hirma Dev's death was the result of an accident. Anyway, after Hirma Dev's death, Bira fell ill and died within the year. His alcoholism had made his liver rot. Hirma Dev was dead, but the problem of Titur Basna was not. The question remained to face me: what was I to call this? How to define it? Do we term it a clash between feudalism and democracy? Or a clash between tribalism and democracy? Then the question arises, as to what exactly is tribalism? Have we been able to understand it? The thing is, we had assumed that with Hirma's death, the root problem of Titur Basna would be resolved. But two years have passed, and I am still caught up in the dilemma of whether we have managed to promote the development of Titur Basna or not. If not, then perhaps our ideas of development are wrong. Or else, it is the adivasis who are wrong in their basic approach and point of view. Where does the mistake lie? And what kind of mistake is it? I still have no answers. My problem is that till today, I kept thinking Hirma is dead. But after two years, I have come to the conclusion that Hirma is far from dead, he is very much alive.

A majhi enters carrying a bamboo with an order tied to it.

MAJHI. Listen, all you brothers and sisters. Listen carefully to what I say. Yogi Maharaj mahatantric Mahaprabhu Rajshri Maharaj Hirma Dev Gangvanshi's incarnation Paramguru Paramhans Mahaprabhu Narangi Wale Baba sends his orders. Within five days from today, all of you must gather within the grounds of the palace. On Friday, guruji will begin his mahayagya within the palace. (*Majhi hands the scroll to the adivasis and leaves. The adivasis gather in a cluster*)

KALHAN. Both this Narangi Wale Baba and the adivasis believe that Hirma can never die. That the police switched the bodies, and Hirma escaped into the jungle, to reappear when the time is right. So he has appeared in the form of this Narangi Wale Baba. Well, you can see how helpless we are.

Kalhan exits.

The adivasis take a full circle, singing as they carry the bamboo with the scroll. They fix it in one place. Singing, they gather in the middle of the stage.

THE END

NOTES

1 Typically, traditional folk tales and songs are often addressed to a parrot or mynah.

2 Kuber is the Hindu god of riches.

3 In feudal Bastar, this was the term used for the king's illegitimate offspring from maids, etc.

4 Adivasi Welfare Society.

GLOSSARY

chapka	disease of the mouth that afflicts cattle
chhai	skin disease that afflicts cattle
daan	largesse, donation
devguri	place where the idol of the god is kept, also used as the granary for security
harra	medicinal jungle fruit
inam	gift
khurha	cattle disease of the foot
majhi	administrator in tribal social system
mandar	percussion instrument
mangal	in the second house: *mangal* refers to the star that brings good fortune only if it is in an auspicious position. The second house is a reference to the astrological table, which has twelve divisions.
manjira	cymbals
Panch mukhya	Sarpanch, head of the panchayat, or local self-governing body
Parma	witchdoctor, *Baiga*
pheras	completing seven pheras (circles) around the sacred fire formalizes a Hindu wedding in North India.
phitkiri	a kind of disinfecting salt
tendu	jungle fruit

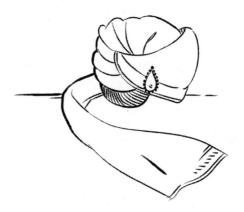

MY MILESTONES IN THEATRE

Habib Tanvir in Conversation

-

[This conversation with Habib Tanvir was spun out over several hours and two cities. It began in January 1995 in Delhi while I was working with him on the translation of *Charandas Chor* (which he subjected to minute scrutiny, testing it against the ear, so to speak, suggesting several changes and updating the text to the version currently in repertory). It continued in Calcutta some months later when Biren Das Sharma, a colleague, added his comments and questions to mine. What appears here is an edited version, aimed at providing a trajectory which culminates with *Charandas Chor*; and at talking 'theatre' more than anecdote and memory, though Habib Sa'ab's inimitable humour and conversational style inevitably weave those in. The complete version appears in *Seagull Theatre Quarterly* (*STQ*) 10 (June 1996): 3–38.—*Anjum Katyal*.]

Can you talk of your theatrical evolution, and the milestones that led to your, and Naya Theatre's, very distinct style of theatre?

You see, in these matters one just goes on and one has to suddenly pull one's thinking cap on and look back and analyse one's own self and how it went. All that I'm aware of is that some things started in *Agra Bazar* way back in 1954. My *yatra* is from *Agra Bazar* to *Mitti ki Gadi* to *Gaon ka Naam Sasural*, which paved the way for *Charandas Chor*, which was a hig hit and turned into a classic, almost. And then followed my other plays, but except for the story, there was no new ground broken.

Why don't you start with telling us about *Agra Bazar* and go on from there?

Well—this was in 1954. Athar Parvez, a writer, who was at that time in Jamia Millia Islamia University, approached me: Habib, can you do a feature or something, to celebrate Nazir Diwas? Nazir Akbarabadi was a very fine, a very interesting poet. I went and lived in Jamia with Parvez and there'd be food and a hookah and gallons of tea and I writing, reading, writing; reading all of Nazir's verses, all that was written about him, very little documented as hard facts. The one thing that did emerge was that the poetry of Nazir was spurned by the critics of the day who hardly considered him a poet, because they didn't like the people's language that he used; they thought it vulgar language because it was colloquial. It's fantastic, beautiful language; but they didn't like it. So in history books of Urdu literature he is brushed aside in two or three lines while lesser poets and writers get pages after pages.

He was a man of great humility and never bothered to get his things published or collected. He was known to respond to anyone wishing to get something written; maybe a vendor saying *turbooz pe kuchh likh dijiye* (please write something in praise of the water melon we sell). So he would, and they'd sing it and sell their fruit. And all of it is beautiful poetry. Nazir wrote about swimming and kite-flying tournaments; he wrote about all the indigenous flora and fauna of India. If you want to, you can trace them through Sanskrit literature, or through Nazir's poetry. Most Urdu poetry repeats Irani flora and fauna, at best trees which are found in Kashmir. Nazir has motiya, chameli, genda, all Indian flowers; tota, mynah, baya, gilehri—all these animals and birds; references to all the religions—Guru Nanak, Hazrat Mohammed, Ali, Baldevji ka mela, Ram—a very eclectic, open-minded man. True poet. Very sensual, very amorous poetry with some unprintable words, but beautiful, calling a spade a spade—that sort of poetry. But never collected.

As part of my research into the language, I looked up Mirza Farhatullah Beg, a writer of Delhi writing in Delhi language; or Ahmed Shah Bokhari, who wrote *Dilli ki Galiyan*—beautiful language. And the sounds of Old Delhi, the sellers, the vendors, they all have musical calls; there's a book called *Dilli ki Awazen*, it has all these things, *kaun kaise bolta hain, kaise pukarta hai* (who speaks in what way, who calls out in what manner). And then you go to Old Delhi and hear this language. And a lot that I heard then, of the people's language, has gone into *Agra Bazar*. Therefore it has that vigour.

When people read the play for the first time, they said, 'Where's the play?' It was just movement on stage—and the openness of the play, its form, the singing of the Nazir songs, came to me first as a feature. There was not enough material on Nazir to do anything more than just a feature. So I decided on collecting a few poems, the best, and making a feature of it with a thin narrative to describe Nazir; and I suddenly arrived at a dramatic form. Then I worked further on it, brought it to Delhi and it became a play. Now, that gave me great flexibility of form.

I didn't bring Nazir on stage because I felt—this became my inspiration—that there wasn't very much known about his life, except some anecdotes, but his poetry pervades the country, so let it pervade the stage. Poetry everywhere, which has his presence, but not the man. So I went about producing a bazar in which I created two poles, the kiteseller's shop with conversation about kites in colloquial, spoken languages, and the bookseller's shop where poets and critics and historians gather and speak an ornate literary language, spurn Nazir and uphold Ghalib and others; and the vendors who sing his poetry because they obtain it from him and their wares, which were not selling, immediately get sold when they begin to sing the songs of Nazir. That is the theme of the play. It was only about forty to fifty minutes long. But it was so lively.

This play was first done with students and teachers and the neighbouring Okhla villagers used to come and sit and watch rehearsals on the open air stage. So one day I told them that instead of watching from there, they could go on the stage and sit and watch, because *bhalu naach ho raha hai kabhi, kabhi bandar ka tamasha ho raha hain* (because at times there was a performing bear, or a monkey dance). So they did that, that's how they became part of the play. So there were more than 70 people who appeared on the Ramlila grounds with a *kumar* (potter), with a donkey—and the donkey even littered—so you had realism to the hilt, including the smells of a bazar!

And then I wrote into the play more and more nuances—the *kotha* (brothel) was introduced, a goonda was introduced, prostitutes and an inspector. At first it was a skeleton, then it developed into the full two hour version in which Nazir is talked of, he's here, there, but never comes on stage. It was taken up by some ladies of Delhi like Anis Kidwai and Qudsia Zaidi, and we took it to Aligarh. It went on and on.

In 1970 I was given the Sangeet Natak Akademi Award and they asked me to revive *Agra Bazar*. So I called all my Chhattisgarh actors (a thread I'll pick up later). They came and participated in the bazar scene, and I got the music compounded with many strains of music including Chhattisgarhi folk tunes and it became much richer. And it got a big ovation and I came back with the award, great jubilation! The play was so popular, that it went on and on—twenty shows. I went on getting dates and extending it. It had a momentum. Then the Information and Broadcasting Ministry took on the play for twenty shows in Punjab/Kashmir and twenty in UP. It was revived again and again till about two years ago. It still is very popular. I think already by 1954, in *Agra Bazar*, I had established my signature.

You are an Urdu poet, and yet you seem to have a fascination for dialect— did this interest in folk expression lead you towards the kind of theatre you do?

I remember in 1945, when the war-effort was still continuing, even though the war was about to come to an end, I was the supervisor in a factory. And I'd talk to the carpenters who were mainly from eastern UP—Benaras, Alla-habad—and they'd speak their dialect; they had a great facility for turning English words into Indian words, Indianizing them: like 'the *tapiya* has been made, now I have to make the *bottomiya*'—the 'top' and the 'bottom'. So my interest was also literary when I'd talk to these people. I was drawn to dialects, because of their richness; like the term for 'airconditioned compartment', I still cannot pronounce it in Hindi, it's a very long word, same in Urdu, but the Bombay coolie simply called it 'thandi gadi' (cool coach)—'*Kahan jana hai, saab? Thandi gadi mein chalenge* ?' (Where d'you want to go, sahib? To the *thandi gadi* ?)' And I thought, for a tropical country, calling an air-conditioned coach 'thandi gadi' was the most appropriate thing. Language is constantly getting coined by people who use it, who need it, who make their living off it. For words connected with horse and saddle, every part has a name, but who has given the names? Those who make those things. You go to the blacksmith, he'll give you all the names connected to the horse's hooves. Our scholars have taken recourse to books to coin words—an artifical, arduous and futile process—instead of going to the people and learning.

The Urdu masters in classical poetry have always insisted on idiomatic language and on how to make it polished, really beautiful. In Urdu poetry, you get a very fine sense of the use of language, Urdu has all kinds of nuances, it's a language of usage and I think that's one reason why I came to it.

You see, my involvement with Nazir Akbarabadi's poetry, which was mostly colloquial poetry, and my being in touch with the Chhattisgarhi folk songs and the graphic way they use language, are part of the same interest. Let me cite an example of two Chhattisgarhis, Munna and Ramcharan, fighting. Munna had left Ramcharan's *nacha* party and when I went to his village, there at the tea-stall both were sitting and arguing. Munna said something like this—if there are two bullocks to a cart and one wants to go one way and the other another, you can't pull the cart. In other words, without me the party can't run, and Ramcharan replied: Well, if you don't have milk, or even sugar, but you have some tea, there's always water you can boil, and even without milk and sugar you can still enjoy tea. That means—I can still have my group without you. These examples came to them as such graphic metaphors in Chhattisgarhi and with such fluency! This went on and on for a long time. And I was simply dumbfounded to see how civilized the fight was. There were no curt words at all. Also I noticed things of everyday usage, sensually used, so when you say my *karaonda*, my *khat-mit kharaonda*, it means a sweet-sour girl like a *karaonda*, far more enticing than a sweet-sweet girl. I'm mentioning all this because it became the basis of my theatre. The so-called dialects, *bolis*, sub-languages, are really the very source of mainstream language, just as the great traditions are fed by the little traditions that make them.

After this I went abroad to study theatre, and saw Brecht's and many other performances and came to realize that imitation doesn't take us anywhere. What the villagers do by way of simplicity of staging, the imaginative use of space with regard to make-believe, and the manner in which they deal with time, all that haunted me and I saw that simplicity in Brecht also. So I came right back to Indian-ness in the sense of realizing that you cannot possibly excel in imitating western dramaturgy and western methods, you must come back to our Sanskrit tradition and folk traditions.

That realization got translated into *Mitti ki Gadi* in 1958, another milestone, where I did use time and space according to my new understanding of Indianness. Blending folk with the classical, realizing that there are no barriers.

I was producing *Mitti ki Gadi* all over Europe on paper. I must've produced on paper something like twelve sets at least, drawings, and every time it obstructed the flow of the story. But my reading of the play never produced this obstruction. When you read it, you're not bothered about what the locale is. So long as the story is going on and you understand it, and the story flows. Let me explain the difficulty. There is a clash between Bharat Muni's dramaturgy which is followed by the Sanskrit playwrights, and the *Poetics* and Aristotle's theory of the three unities. When many Western scholars of Sanskrit—and I dare say great translators, through which medium alone I got these classics, because I do not know Sanskrit, and Hindi translations by and large were lousy till then—commented on those plays, they praised the authors as Mahakavya writers, with great poetic imaginations, a great command of words. Only somewhere you found a subdued apology—the poor chaps did not know their dramaturgy, because they failed to see the unities. That was bad enough. It was much worse when you came across books written by Indian pundits echoing the apology because they knew no better either. For all their knowledge of Sanskrit grammar and language, they had no clue as to what was going on, because they had no contact with theatre. And what do I read? I find, in the very first act of *Mrichchhakatikam* which is divided into ten acts, the stage-manager, the sutradhar and nati talking, introducing Charudatta; and Charudatta comes from outside somewhere and goes into his house, some scene takes place there. The scene continues on the road. Suddenly you find Vasantasena the courtesan, with Shakara and his retinue all over the road and somehow—without break of scene—she comes to the exterior of Charudatta's house and slips into the house—things going on outside the house, also inside, in and out—that's scene one. Scene two: a gambler's being chased, and he goes out on the road, comes back and moves into a mandir, becomes a murti on the pedestal, they chase him, fool around and he again gives them the slip and runs into Vasantasena's house, talks to her and she comes out and hears the shouting—all one scene. The locales haven't been changed.

Duncan Ross, my teacher of theatre at the Bristol Old Vic, had taught me an important lesson: it must flow. So I made those scenes on paper and everything seemed to obstruct the play because how could you have a very swift set for a particular locale and move on in the kind of fluent manner in which you read the play? And I wanted the play to come across exactly as I read it, not with those obstructions. So I ended up, after removing this, that and the other, with a bare, circular platform. This gave me space enough on the stage for the exterior and enough for the interiors, which was the circular platform on stage with a diameter of about 12 feet. And the play just flowed. I didn't have to explain the scene changes. Initially I used to hang things, which would keep dropping and going up to suggest a locale. Later on I thought it was fussy, I removed it. And also I felt another thing, quite candidly, I felt that the descriptions of the Sanskrit poets who wrote these plays are so vivid and so beautiful, so graphic, that in your imagination, before your mind's eye, any kind of picture of which you are capable can be thrown up. One differing from the other, in the auditorium, in the audience. Now that liberty, that faculty, will not be given full play if you paint the scenery on the stage. I find it presumptuous to paint, to translate the words in terms of paint. Either you'll fall short of the description or you'll exceed it. In either case, art has mastered poetry. And as one says in Urdu, 'Yeh zyada hai, yeh labz zyada hai (this is redundant, extra).' The poet and the poem, the two couplets, must be terse—one word added for the sake of the metre is bad art. We know it from Shakespeare, from the great painters—what one line, one stroke can do, many cannot. Therefore, to have both painted and verbal descriptions is meaningless. And to have a painting as a substitute is to have a poor substitute, because it deprives the viewer of access to the work. At least, I thought so.

In the play the vidushaka goes into Vasantasena's house and you see nine courtyards, one is painted with all kinds of beautiful pictures, in another there are monkeys and horses and cows and he describes them all. In the third, wonderful meals are being cooked and he describes the aroma. So each has a description. Suddenly, he comes to the eighth or ninth courtyard and he finds a huge woman seated there, and he finds out that this is Vasantasena's mother. And he wonders how she managed to enter the house. And then he comes to the conclusion that she was already seated there and the house was built around her. Now, such beautiful descriptions, what will we do? So, going by Duncan Ross, going by the internal evidence and the reading, I arrived at the conclusion that there were neither curtains, nor machinery, nor a revolving theatre in the classical theatre days. There was utter simplicity—it was an actor's theatre. Whether the actor danced it out or acted it out. Otherwise you would not get instructions like, actor enter, seated on a throne. How will you manage that? Actor enters supine, lying on a couch. How? Only a dancer can do it. Or a Kuchipudi curtain behind which the actor moves in rhythm, on drumbeats, rhythmically, and that by itself is a visual spectacle because the curtain is beautiful and behind it they reveal the actor, which is what I did in my *Mudrarakshasa*. So my shrewd suspicion was that though it is not written anywhere in the books about Sanskrit drama, there was this curtain, enter by whisking the curtain. The curtain comes down again and again. I recall seeing a great Kathakali dancer, and I was fascinated by the fact that he came in behind the curtain as Hanuman and took so long to reveal himself—naughtily he'd just lift the curtain to show his toes; then you'd see his crown, white, then you'd see his nails, gold, fingers. Gradually, he showed himself, bit by bit. To me, it seemed that he took twenty minutes just to reveal himself fully—finally he threw off the curtain and you saw the whole of him. So, this curtain fascinated me, held me spellbound.

Also, when I had come back from Europe after having spent three years there in 1958, before beginning *Mrichchakatikam*, I went home to Raipur to meet my family. It was summer. I heard that there was to be a *nacha* on the grounds of the high school where I was educated—*nacha* is a Chhattisgarhi form of secular drama: It was to start at nine o'clock. I saw it all night through, which is the usual duration for a *nacha*. They presented three or four skits. There was Madan Lal, a great actor, Thakur Ram, another great actor, Babu Das, a very good actor too, Bulwa Ram, a glorious singer: and what comedians, these fellows, like music hall comedy. They were doing *chaprasi nakal, sadhu nakal* (take-offs). I was fascinated. I went up to them and said—would you like to come to Delhi and join me in a production? They were happy to do so. So I enlisted Bulwa, Babu Das, Thakur Ram, Madan Lal, and Jagmohan, who was on the clarinet. Then I was to go to Rajnandgaon to speak on Indo-Soviet friendship or something. There they wanted to know about my European tour. I described my Hungarian travels and sang a Chhattisgarhi song as an illustration. At the end, a dark man with squinting eyes and a short, grisly black beard, came up to me and said, 'Come to my house.' This was Lalu Ram. He liked the folk songs. I went to his house. He offered ganja, we shared ganja, and he heard many songs from me. He sang many, one of the best singers in Chhattisgarh, glorious voice. The session went on all night. So I enlisted Lalu Ram as the sixth member of the troupe.

These six came to Delhi and participated in *Mitti ki Gadi*, with Bulwa and Lalu Ram playing chandals and singing at the top of their voices, Jagmohan playing the clarinet, Madan Lal playing the gambler, Thakur Ram playing Sarvilaka.

So anyway, *Mitti ki Gadi* I simplified till the play moved without a hitch. The pundits all attacked it. The Sanskrit scholars said, this has been done in *lokdharmi* and the play belongs to *natyadharmi*—that means that I did it in folk-style and it should have been done in the classical style. The same pundits, in the 1970s, when I sat with them in seminars, and I talked about the curtain, they paid attention to it. Then I talked about the rasa theory being the only unity which governs the Sanskrit classics—they paid attention to it, they repeat it now.

Mitti ki Gadi is a *prahasan* (farce) and many critics have criticized the play for its lack of harmony and mixtures of rasas, saying that it doesn't work, it is not a romantic story, it is not another gambler's tale, it has got the jewellery thing travelling around, and so many strands of stories and the play doesn't have that kind of unity of rasa. But the play works. It has a certain harmony— when I read it, I felt it was harmonious. It has a circular mood, like the nine courtyards of Vasantasena, nine public squares where Charudatta is taken, and it is repetitive—the same announcement made again and again. So I got a feeling that the treatment in music and elsewhere—let's take the example of music—is repetitive. Hardly four or five or six words in a line, sung for two hours, several hours, all night, in classical singing. Develop the raga and you get everything that you want, not so much through the words, although the words also help a bit, though they're just an aid. But the repetitiveness of it, cumulatively, finally, casts a spell on you—if you're so inclined. Keeps you riveted. So that repetition is important.

So you've used Chhattisgarhi actors from that production onwards?

Yes. Of course, they let me down too, saying: we want to go off for a short while, and producing some false telegram or something—they never came back. I got two or three of them in 1960 for my production of Molière's *The Bourgeois Gentlemen*. But in 1970, they all came—Madan Lal, Thakur Ram, Jagmohan, Devi Lal. Brij Lal I used to know as a child, they used to sit in Lalu Ram's paan-*thela* to sell paans. Most of them were female impersonators. Thakur Ram and Madan Lal were the only male actors. Otherwise, Bulwa Ram had never acted in a male role except in my theatre, Brij Lal always in women's roles, Devi Lal, who played the harmonium, all played female roles. So, it became a professional theatre by 1973 and we haven't looked back. Though the story of being let down went on making me very angry, there was a fellow from one of the local villages, who did some kind of travesty of *Charandas Chor*, and presented it as his own play and direction, etc. And this used to make me very angry. And they were making a lot of money in the village, they were showing it; so I went to Haider Ali Vakil, a neighour who was much older than me and my elder brother's friend. He was a social activist and writer, a leftist and a pleader with a difference. Not out to make money. So I went to him and asked him what to do. Haider-bhaiyya listened to my story; he said, 'Habib, you're working with folk actors. You know them by now. You know nothing about litigation. Let me tell you that these illiterate villagers know a lot more about litigation than you do. You will never win the case. You'll be grilled, you'll waste your time and you might lose the case because they know all the tricks of the game. But in any case, winning and losing apart, *why do you want to sue them?* You are a social worker also, you care for them. Forget it. Do a panchayat—go to them, call fifty people, talk to them plainly: Why do you cheat me? Why don't you announce it is my play? Give them the liberty to do it if they like. But ask them why they're telling lies.' It was very good advice. So I went to Rajnandgaon and in Lalu Ram's house, we did collect a lot of people, including these culprits. And I said, '*Aap logon ko kya cheez sata rahi hai, koi musibat hai? Jhoot kyon bolte ho?* (What's bothering you people, what's the problem? Why do you lie?)' *Maine kaha mujhe* royalty *nahin chahiye, paise nahin chahiye, kuchh bhi na kaho to bhi thik hai; par galat kyon kah rahe ho— tumhara* play, *tumhara* direction? ('I don't want any money or royalty, it's even okay by me if you don't credit anyone with the play, but why pass it off as your play, your direction?'). They all agreed before everyone and they went back and merrily continued to this day; and not one, several groups are doing it. Now it doesn't touch me.

But my understanding has changed now; these fellows let me down time and again, and I went pursuing them, again and again, and brought them back, till I came to the conclusion that it must be an open door policy, that if they wanted to go, I'd allow them. They always wanted to come back sooner or later—and I always took them back, without acrimony. Only last year Bulwa and Ramcharan said, 'We're too old now and we've got some domestic problems and we want to go.' Last summer Bulwa took his son as well. Then I called them to Raipur to meet and talk about a pension scheme which I'd discovered. So I called them, separately, and I said, 'Going like this isn't going to help. Fill up the form—it talks about how much land you have and earnings, etc. Then you have to sign it and I'll submit it. You must, because you've worked in the theatre for so long. But tell me,' I said, 'many of my old plays are constantly in demand. I wouldn't like to close them. In new plays I'll have the new cast. But in the old plays I cannot do without you. So for the shows of old plays will you come?' They said, 'Whenever there's an old play, we'll come.' What I'm trying to say is that this has been my handling in my mature years and it has worked very well.

So Naya Theatre is a professional company—they are paid actors of that company?

They're on a regular salary and it's this kind of a policy, no written agreement, nothing. And in my case, it seemed to work very well. As a matter of fact when Peter Brook came, he wondered how I have had them for so long, with no trace of staleness or being tired. He said, 'The history of theatre shows five years.' And suddenly it occurred to me, he's right. Stanislavsky—Actors Studio—five years, and roughly you'll see four to five years—*khatam*, finished. And no more innovation takes place. Peter Brook himself. Therefore there's one credit that I accept unabashedly, that I have held a group for so long. If somebody gives it, I'll lap it up, because it *is* a credit. I'm saying a great deal more than seems to be contained in these words. You've no idea how difficult it is to live with them and work with them. The tantrums, the scenes, the galis, I can't even go on record saying what else.

It took me time to realize two basic approaches to working with these folk actors: mother tongue and freedom of movement. Because what was happening with those six whom I'd brought in 1968 was, I'd pull my hair and fret and fume, stamp my foot and say, Thakur Ram, what the hell, I've seen you in the village and I know your strength as an actor; what is happening? Why can't you simply follow my instructions and give me that same strength? He'd also not know. He'd shout back and say, it's not your fault, it's my fault, my fault, my fault! So these kinds of scenes would be created without any one of us knowing what the fault was, except I realizing, after many years, that I was trying to apply my English training on the village actors—move diagonally, stand, speak, take this position, take that position. I had to unlearn it all. I saw that they couldn't even tell right from left on the stage and had no line sense. And I'd go on shouting *ki tum dahina haat se kya karte ho, baayen haat se kya karte ho, itna nahin samajhte* ? Don't you know the difference between the hand you eat with and the one you wash with?

I saw the *nacha* again and again, and what do I see? A big platform and they're performing; thousands of people or hundreds of people on a small platform or no platform, at the same level—still performing; and nothing was lost. Or a stage, and some who didn't get a place and considered themselves special, coming and sitting on the stage with the orchestra and the actors; and I'd get very annoyed over this, but not the actors. It didn't matter. I also stopped worrying about it. It didn't interfere with the audience. But what was happening was that the audience was sometimes on three sides, sometimes on all four sides. Entry through the crowd, in the middle somewhere a performance, actors all around, invariably three sides and wherever the response went, like a cow going through the audience, the actors would turn to that. Or a joke improvised, connected with some incident in the village which they'll come to know of, and a spoof. Or a line connected with it, and a response from a section, then they'd turn to that section. So I realized that those who were responding to an audience for years in this manner could never try to unlearn all this and rigidly follow the rules of movement and that was one reason why Thakur Ram, a great actor, wasn't being able to be natural.

Another reason was the *matrubhasha*—he wasn't speaking in his mother tongue, So it jarred on my ears, because he was speaking bad Hindi and not Chhattisgarhi, in which he was fluent, which was so sweet. This realization took me years—it was naïve of me, but still it took me years. Once I realized it, I used Chhattisgarhi and improvised, allowed them the freedom and then came pouncing down upon them to crystallize the movement—there you stay. And they began to learn. That quite simply was the method I learnt.

In 1970, when I revived *Agra Bazar* for the Sangeet Natak Akademi award ceremony, I used Chhattisgarhis and blended their music with Nazir. Till 1973, I went on in pure Chhattisgarhi idiom. I presented their own stock comedies for three years. And also pieces from the Mahabharata after working diligently on *pandavani*, the *sampurna* or complete Mahabharata, and then, having a grasp of what they had to say and having studied Mahabharata over again, in its abridged form by Rajagopalachari, I got the hang of it, and devised a production. *Arjun ka Sarathi* ('The Charioteer of Arjuna') was the name of a short piece of half an hour which I rehearsed for timing, saying you must talk only of *geet updesh*, and for half an hour; combining it with ritual which was not usually presented on stage in Chhattisgarh but in temples, and with the singing of fascinating songs with intricate, changing rhythms. Seven songs coming one after the other, blending into one another, a fascinating experience in the temples, during the weeklong Ramsatta festival, when these women start singing from their homes and go to the temple. Ramsatta had some lovely ritual tunes. I got all these women, eight or twelve of them. Then there is a ritual song which is on Shiva-Parvati, called Gauri-Gaura (Gauri is Parvati and Gaura is Shiva). Songs are sung around the idols of Gauri and Gaura. Intricate rhythms, with one song flowing into the other. It's beautiful. That was launched as *Gauri-Gaura* with *Arjun ka Sarathi* and a half hour skit, *Chaprasi*. This became an instant success in *pandavani*, which enable me to present Mahabharata in *pandavani* in many drawing rooms, and then in Karol Bagh, in the open, the *sampurna* Mahabharata, for a number of days. Though they would sing and recite in Chhattisgarhi, yet the ordinary householder men, women and children thronged the park where we were showing it.

But when I did the Gauri-Gaura ritual, two women, in two different songs, would come into trance. When I was trying to rehearse Gauri-Gaura we were all living in the Gandhi Darshan space. There was an open air stage and accommodation. And suddenly Janaki came into trance. I was in consternation because something had to be done to get her out of it. So we ran helter-skelter to the market to get incense, we needed alcohol, candles for the soles of the feet, and the skull. We managed somehow, but we weren't equipped for it. Janaki came out of the trance. I then realized that it was the rhythm which does it. Slowly, easily the rhythm must slow down and stop. When we launched it in Delhi, there were strange reactions. One drama critic came up and said, 'Habib, when these women get into a trance, is it acting?' I said, 'No. It's an actual trance. One girl gets into a trance in one song and the other in another.' 'But why show it on the stage?' I asked, 'Didn't you find it engaging, fascinating?' He said, 'Yes.' I said, 'You have the answer.' My answer is that I find in this drama in an embryonic form and I'm presenting it to you, not in an academic way, but as good theatre which fascinates you. Its magic is felt. I visualize the beginnings of drama in India like this, a semblance of the kind of hymns chanted around the fire in Vedic times; and this is dramatic because religion *is* dramatic.'

This kind of exercise, this show of three things, one piece from *pandavani* Mahabharata, then Gauri-Gaura and then a short comedy skit, was well attended, but never house-full. We were doing it from 1970–73. I continued with something or the other in Chhattisgarhi, giving them the confidence of doing something as actors in their mother tongue, and yet I couldn't draw more than fifty to seventy people per show, and I called that a failure. Not enough for successful theatre.

In 1973, I had a workshop in Raipur, month-long, one of the best I had, the first and best. I got many *nacha* parties to participate for as long as they wished, observe, be there, go away. There were some city boys, students, scholars, Surajit Sinha from Calcutta, Komal Kothari from Rajasthan, R. P. Nayak, an authority on Madhya Pradesh tribals, who at that time held some high post in the government of MP. And they wrote some good papers, and there were some professors of anthropology from the university; and city actors and lots of these folk actors of Chhattisgarh. Many *nacha* groups came as observers.

We had many things, make-up in the folk style—Thakur Ram who used to play the old bridegroom used to put some white chalk on his face and look very good as the old man, and he was also very good with jewellery, and with tying his turban, quite an artist in his own right in these things. So I asked him to conduct the workshop on make-up, how to use coal, chalk, all the local, inexpensive things, and teach the city boys one indigenous way of putting on makeup. Then I would take a dalda tin and put a bulb in it, to show them the difference between a flood and a spot, and I told them, if you have nothing else, you can use this, and that by itself is a kind of spot since it controls focus, which is all a spot does, and the reflection of the white tin inside will increase the light. You can increase it more by adding reflectors, or put a lens on it. So the workshop touched many subjects including these. It was a rich workshop.

I had auditioned and selected some of the folk actors whom I'd known, who'd been part of my team earlier and later became the nucleus of Naya Theatre, like Thakur Ram, Madan Lal, Bulwa, Latu Ram, Brij Lal, Devi Lal. And Fida Bai came for the first time. She had never acted before, though she had sung on stage and danced. The *nacha* form is three or four skits, which go on all night, and in between they have dances and songs by men dressed as women. Sometimes they would have Devar girls, like Fida, singing and dancing. I saw her just before the workshop in a *nacha* in the village, singing and dancing. A boy in the audience whistled and accosted her, making a pass. And from the stage, on the microphone, she abused him and stamped her foot, saying that 'I'll crush you like this', and he subsided. And I decided then, that's the girl who can act. I told Lalu Ram, the veteran amongst the actors of our core nucleus group, that she should be a good actress. He had had experience with her, also Thakur Ram, she had danced with them on the *nacha* stage. He said, no, no, she can't act, she'll be useless, Mohini can do it. She was one of the twelve women who came for *Gauri-Gaura*, and she was a good singer, with a sweet face, but I had noticed that she was slightly self-conscious. Still, I said, let's try it. So we did, and it didn't work. So I went back to my original request, let's go and find Fida Bai and get her. We got her. And the first day, I suggested what was to be done, and there she was an actress. I was very pleased. I was right. And then, as anticipated, trouble started. I had been warned by the others that she was a difficult person, trouble of all kinds, her family came, her husband came, her mother-in-law came, she herself refused to participate. But what an actress!

In the workshop I had welded three stock *nacha* comedies, blending them into one long play. I wrote some link scenes to connect the three apparently unconnected skits, but I made them into a story, and it had the Gauri-Gaura ritual too. I used 'Chher Chhera', the name of the first ritual: during *paus purnima* young boys go about calling out a few stylized lines, a call for donation for the *paus purnima* ritual. People give them grain, vegetables, etc. They collect it and go to the riverside where the festival takes place, and have a community picnic amongst the youth. So the stock comedy starts with two boys, then two girls who come to donate, and a flirtation takes place with jokes, remarks, song and dance, and that is the first skit. The second skit was 'Burwa Biwa'. Burwa Biwa was an old man who asks for the hand of a young girl, and the girl's father misunderstands, because they discuss dowry and other things and he makes it sound as if he's negotiating for some young boy of his household, then returns as the bridegroom himself, shocking the young girl's father, and then he says you've agreed, given your word, and he gets away with the girl. It's a satire, and hilarious, and a good musical. The third skit was 'Devar Devarin'. The very name suggests the Devar tribe, a nomadic tribe, they live in tents and keep on the move, they sing and dance, traditionally, with their cocks, fowls, pigs, a dog, a dholak and a kind of sarangi, and the girls sing on doorsteps, and a man or woman plays the dholak, even in melas. This is how they earn. They also catch snakes and ask for milk and money for the snake and make a living; or they drive monkeys off fields for farmers. Occasionally, they may have a performing monkey, though that's unusual. But the men, traditionally, are wonderful balladeers. They have long, beautiful stories in ballads, unrecorded and untouched to this day. I don't know if there are any left now, and with them go the stories, because the stories can't be related to any pauranic tales, the whole stock is separate. Adventure stories, love stories, in song, and they sing for long hours, like sagas. The other thing about the Devars is that they are kept as mistresses by rich people, landlords and moneylenders, anyone who can afford them. They can be gold-diggers, and as tradition goes, occasionally a Devar woman has become a householder and stayed with one man, abandoning her nomadic life and even her profession of singing and dancing, but this is very rare. Traditionally, they are taken as mistresses and either run away or are brought back home by their parents, and they go to another man. It is not prostitution. They make a profession of it, the singing and dancing, and a kind of life. Occasionally, if a woman likes to live on with a man she fancies, which is not common, but does happen, then the parents are unhappy, and sometimes they go and cook up a fake fight and create such a racket that the man gets fed up, and they bring the girl back. And not just the parents, but the relatives, a whole gang, goes. If the girl refuses, there's a huge racket and commotion, they tie up the girl like a bundle and bring her away. There's a monetary motivation, because each time the girl 'marries' there's a bride price for the family. These people are also very open about using abusive language. In anthropological books you'll find them described as a criminal tribe like the thugs, but of course, that is a totally wrong description. I've seen them fighting, sometimes splitting open heads, and yet I would not say that they are criminal or crime-prone tribes. I have a different understanding of it, but they do fight in that fashion, making of anything a weapon.

I've described the three skits. In 'Chher Chhera', one of the young boys falls in love with a girl, but her father inadvertently sells her to the old man and can't get out of the commitment, and the old man takes her with him. The boy lover, who was trying to find money for the bride price, upon going to the bride's father, is told it's too late. The father himself suggests—we can retrieve her, they can't have reached the groom's house yet, so let's go disguised as Devars. And that's where the 'Devar Devarin' skit comes in. There the Gauri-Gaura ritual is taking place, which was not part of the three skits, but which I had had experience of, and the beautiful songs are going on, and there the actress goes into a trance—dramatically, not a real trance—to fool the old man and beat him. He thinks there's a devi or goddess in her and the devi is beating him, and she beats him so hard he runs away. The priest who is looking after the ceremony is one of the disguised friends of the young lover—he had already cooked up a false fight to drive off the original priest and take over to help her elope with the hero, who is disguised as a Devar. But then the old man comes back in time. And the lover re-enters as a Devar boy, providing the excuse for the 'Devar Devarin' comedy, which is a spoof on the tribe, but their own thing, and it's brilliant, full of humour. It is in the Devar dialect, which is different from Chhattisgarhi, and they kick up a racket, pretending to be the relatives, and finally run away with the girl, just as the Devars do. So this I introduced by linking themes and connecting the story. And in the end celebratory songs take place, the young lover gets back the young girl who was betrothed to the old man, and there's a happy ending. This was called *Gaon ka Naam Sasural, Mor Naam Damaad.* This was a collage, the result of that one-month workshop in Raipur.

At the end of the workshop, we held a weeklong festival—tribal dancers from Raigarh and Bastar, other *nacha* parties and our own *Gaon ka Naam Sasural,* everything in the open, in the garden, thousands of people, a very successful festival. Of the folk actors from different groups, who had come to observe the workshop, Ramcharan belonged to another group from Baraonda and he came only to observe for one or two days. He noticed that we were buying authentic jewellery which the *nacha* players never had. *Mayapariksha* was the play he was to present at that festival. I had seen it before and I had selected it, saying you must show it because they were very good actors, Ramcharan and Ramratan, these two used to do it. It was both a comedy and a serious play. And they did it very well, including a murder scene in which suddenly a man is attacked, there's a splash and he's full of blood. I said, 'How d'you manage that?' They'd have a balloon filled and then they'd punch it and it would suddenly become flat. So he came and what do I see? More authentic than my production. He'd observed for two days, he saw the value of authenticity in terms of jewellery, real silver, real gold—everything was absolutely authentic, clothes and all. I'm just talking about the effect of things. Otherwise, *nacha* wouldn't care for this sort of thing, basically, they would give you any kind of costume, out of necessity, not design—any old coat, hat, jacket, sometimes not so good, sometimes fantastic, the colours combine and it looks very good. This was distinctive to *nacha*. They wouldn't have Chhattisgarhi tunes either. They would mostly have film tunes and hybrid things. But in the main, the songs were in the fields, at harvesting time, in the mandir, during rituals, in childbirth, good, authentic songs, death songs, marriage songs, all these existed in society, but on the rustic stage little of it was reflected. So this was the first effect I could see of the workshop, on one party anyhow.

So *Gaon ka Naam Sasural, Mor Naam Damaad* was the collage that I produced out of three different short plays, by adding link scenes and changing the story a bit. I presented it in Raipur in the open air. This was a turning point for me because when we brought it to Delhi and showed it for the first time it went on for at least twelve shows to packed houses, which was a big change from the fifty to seventy coming for just a few nights. We had transcended the language barrier. People came again and again for the wonderful musical quality of the play and for the clarity of expression we had gained by this time, despite the fact that it is a specially difficult play in terms of dialogue, full of improvisation. In 'Devar Devarni' they speak in words which are not easy to follow, for the Hindi belt. And yet they got a lot out of the slapstick and things became clear in a basic manner. In 'Burwa Biwa' and 'Chher Chhera' also, they have enigmatic and puzzling words, yet the *abhinaya* (acting) was clear, the jokes were followed in the main and the comedy came off. I realized that Delhi had accepted us.

This paved the way for *Charandas Chor* in 1974 and for all the other plays that followed. It was a turning point in my career, a breakthrough in introducing Chhattisgarhi as a language for a modern play. It gave me an all-Chhattisgarhi cast. Upto now I was combining them with urban actors. Now only folk actors. This play I consider my third milestone.

In 1974, came a workshop lasting about a month, in which I produced a number of small plays. Various groups came (all Chhattisgarhi), and I had a workshop in Bhilai. We produced six little skits of forty-five minutes to an hour. We got a very good response from the local village audiences. They were their own plays—I just did some work on them, injected some elements. Towards the end of the month's workshop, in the last four days, I began to work on a thief story, which wasn't called *Charandas Chor* at that time. I had tried it earlier at a workshop in Rajasthan, the story being from Rajasthan. I was holding a workshop with Rajasthani folk actors and I thought this was the best story to try; but the story failed. In three or four days I realized they were lacking in actors. There was only one good actor they had, a wonderful actor. Otherwise, their whole strength lay in music. Wonderful singers. And their form was opera—the little scenes that they enacted had feeble acting. So I abandoned the thief story.

Chhattisgarh is a very talented place in terms of acting, with a special predilection for comedy, as against Rajasthan, which is very rich in music. I took up *Charandas* towards the end of the workshop in Bhilai, just tried out within four days with a very good actor called Ramlal who did the chor. This was towards the end of 1974. Then finally we had a show on the open-air stage of the maidan in Bhilai. It was a Satnami occasion. There are lakhs of Satnamis in this country and they've had quite a history from Aurangzeb's time, quite militant. Every year they gather in Guru Ghasidas's place near Raipur, thousands, a great mela. They sing and dance. Like most untouchables they are given a separate muhalla or area, not in the village. In that muhalla they're given a *chauraha* (crossroads), a chowk. In that chowk they have a white flag, the Satnami flag, which is kept on a pedestal. There is some little ritual every day.

It was a very rough version. Suddenly, when I was showing the skits on the open stage and the Satnamis were coming up on the stage again and again, I was inspired by them. Towards six o'clock, I said we have a play which is still in the melting pot, not quite ready and I'd normally never dream of showing it, but considering that this is a Satnami occasion and there're thousands of people sitting here and the play has something to do with Truth, which is the motto of Satnamis, I would like to dare to show it, knowing that you'll accept it with all its faults. And don't mind if I come in in the middle and change their positions. etc.

It ran for about 40 minutes. We called it *Chor Chor*. For songs I had this Satnami book with me and I just improvised by singing and asking them to repeat. And there was a big response for this rough, *kachcha* (raw) thing. Then I worked further on it, got the *panthi* dance party, choreographed them and was glad because 'Truth is god, god is truth' is their motto (*Satya hi ishwar hai, ishwar satya*). And this is a play about truthfulness and truth. It blended well together. So I included their flag, their dance, re-arranged it, got them to write my type of songs. The folk singer or poet generally writes in a reformist vein. Of course, some folk poetry is interesting, beautiful. But whenever it comes to that kind of thing, the folk poetry just doesn't have enough depth. Ganga Ram Sakhet was one poet, Swaran Kumar the other. I said, 'Look, I don't want to say that lying is bad, give it up, drinking is bad, give it up. I don't even believe that you can change a man, unless he changes himself. It doesn't help him that you're asking him to change. Habits are hard to shake off. So, I'd like you to say, that just as a drunkard cannot leave drinking, a liar cannot leave lying and a thief cannot leave stealing, truthful men cannot cease telling the truth. If habit is a vice and truthfulness becomes a habit, then that too is a vice. As vice sticks to you, so does habit.' The song worked, because I was very consciously working on the subconscious. I was also working unconsciously, but not so unconsciously. I said, death is coming; let us have the rumblings of the coming of death right from this point. So let us introduce the word Yama.

I first called the play *Amardas*. Amardas happens to be one of the gurus of the Satnamis, and they all protested that it can't be named after their guru. Then I called him some other Das, that was another guru. So finally I said Charandas can't be a guru and it was not. The original story has no name, he's just chor. At that time I didn't know the story except orally. Subsequently, it appeared in a collection of Vijaydan Detha's stories.

What happened was that Shyam Benegal with Girish Ghanekar (the son of the senior Ghanekar who used to be my boss years ago in Famous Pictures) assisting—now he's a director in his own right—and Govind Nihalani at the camera, pursued me all over Chhattisgarh, with *Gaon ka Naam Sasural*, covering many mandis—*marais*, they're called—melas and such fairs and marketplaces. A lot of footage was shot and *Sasural* was recorded. Copious, long interviews were taken with Bulwa, Ramcharan, me. All of it is lost. Great pity, because these were all young people at that time. They became history later. So he saw this improvisation and decided to film *Charandas* immediately, and *Charandas* the film was made for the Children's Film Society, before it was launched in Delhi. But he wanted a foil for the chor. I was doing the screenplay. I trusted his good sense as a cinema man—which I still do, of course, quite sincerely—and when he said children wouldn't take to a tragedy, I tried it on my daughter and she didn't like the story to end in the chor's death. So I produced a scene where Chitragupta, the munshi (bookkeeper) of Yama, Lord of Death, comes and Charandas steals his name from the register, and when he looks for his name he says it's not there. It's gone. He makes a paan of it and puts it in his mouth. He swallows it. Then there's great consternation because his name isn't there in the logbook, and the man is dead. Then Yama comes on his buffalo and gets down to examine it and Charandas rides the buffalo and runs away, stealing the buffalo, and what you see in the horizon in the evening is Charandas running and the havaldar chasing him. That's the end of the film. So he continues to steal even up there in heaven. Now this, plus a foil needed. Madan Lal was my choice for the actor, according to me, one of the great actors of Chhattisgarh. But Shyam didn't want Madan Lal, he wanted Lalu Ram. Lalu Ram was a wonderful singer, but not an actor. Whereas Madan Lal was an experienced actor, having been on stage for a long time. Lalu Ram was always singing and dancing on stage as a woman, not acting except for some very mechanical lines spoken. But he had this squint-eyed face. So I went by Shyam's judgement because he was a cinematic man and he saw it from the camera point of view and I thought he must be right. Lalu Ram did it well of course, because film acting is different, you can make an ordinary man act the way you want him to. And Madan Lal became the foil. He was dishonest, would keep lying.

This is the screenplay I had written. There was a court case and I played the judge. All this was in my own screenplay, my play ruined but I not knowing any better, loaded with these things, a foil, a donkey (I got four people to become a donkey), a court scene, all hilarious, enjoyed thoroughly by my wife Moneeka and some friends, and I then suddenly discovering that this is not my form. I don't need a foil, an actor can come on stage and simply declare that I'm a thief, my name is Charandas, that's good enough for the stage. So I cut the foil out. I made Madan Lal the actor; I cut out the judge scene, though I was acting in it and it was very funny and I enjoyed it. I cut out the posthumous scene, much to the dislike of Moneeka and others who said, no, no, it's nice. I said, yes, but I will stick to the story. Actually, I didn't even stick to the story. Vijaydan Detha, who related the folktale, is also angry. His chor gets killed, but that's not the end. The queen takes the guru as her consort and the guru accepts, because, in the story as written by Detha, in order to save face she proposes to the guru and the guru, who is very worldly, becomes her consort. That's the way the story ends. Vijaydan's argument is valid enough, that if you're showing present-day conditions, evil continues, hypocrisy continues, the raj must continue with all its corruption, nepotism, everything; your story is romantic. He may be right there, but I wanted a cruel end. I wanted to say something different. I had something different in my mind: on the subliminal level the effect of Yama, and I analysed it later, when it had a big effect, the word Yama coming so often in the sequence 'Give Death its Due', and then death coming really unexpectedly. People were stunned. Some didn't believe that he was dead, because I always used to get the actor to become very stiff. They thought it's a comedy and there'll be some trick and he'll come back.

I also had this other idea in my mind, that there's this man called Socrates who died for truth, and accepted it, but wouldn't budge from his path of truth. There was Jesus Christ—same thing. There was Gandhi, who also stuck to his principles, and died. Here is a common man—and that's why he must remain a common man—an unheroic, simple man who gets caught up in his vows and though he fears death, can't help it and dies. And the establishment cannot brook this. So for me, the tragedy in the classical sense was perfect because tragedy has to be inevitable. There is an inevitability to his death because he didn't go the convenient way of saying yes to the queen, which would be a way out. That way was barred, it was not an option. The queen is not simply a tyrant, but a politician. There is no way she can let him go free, because she entreats him not to tell anyone and he says, but I must tell the truth; and as soon as she knows that the *praja*, the populace, will get to know, she fears for

her position. As we have seen throughout history, such people are always eliminated. So the inevitability of it was perfect. That was my argument, that this
is, in the classical sense, a perfect tragedy. It makes you laugh till the last
moment and suddenly you're silent. You're in the presence of death. And if
you're receptive enough, there's absolute silence. Is it a tragedy? Yes. Is it a
comedy? Yes. Is it a comedy? No. Is it a tragedy? No. I don't know what it is.
It's difficult to put it in a category. And I think that's the secret of the success
of the play. To this day, I'm convinced that the death is the secret of its success.
And the ending of the original story, which also has a valid point, I don't know
if it would have managed to secure the kind of popularity *Charandas* has.

The very first night, it was a stunning experience in the Kamani auditorium. He died. Total silence. Strange silence. People got up, thinking, when
will the next line come? Disturbed. The restive, urban, Delhi audience was
moved. And then, before going out, they stopped, turned and then stood for
several minutes (because the anti-climax goes on for a long time, the whole
ritual of the deification of the chor, the last song), watching from the door,
uncomfortably. I learnt from Shakespeare to always end with an anti-climax;
in any case, this catharsis, to use a classical word, must be brought down somehow and I have something more to say through that ritual. I integrated the
Satnamis for that reason. Now nobody questions the end. I had something
more elaborate for death which I removed after the first few shows, and this
went on for several shows till there were no more dates in Kamani. So we
moved to Triveni immediately, and had twelve shows there. Then we were
booked for twenty shows in Haryana and after that it never stopped. From
1974 to now.

**Did the comic sequences come from actors' improvisations or from things
you've seen in other skits?**

No, no, most of it comes quite effortlessly to them, except that I was clear about the character of the thief. I did not want to romanticize or produce it in a heroic style, but to play him simply and produce a character who, because of his, let's say naïveté, ignorance, conservative nature, old-fashioned belief in vows, is so caught up in the web of his vows (which he really took inadvertently as a jest), that he doesn't think that he's going to really face death and when he's threatened with it, he cowers, cringes, supplicates and shows all the fears of the commonest man. But at the same time, he has a total inability to find a way out of it because he is caught up in a vow. He happened to have taken it. Having taken it, he faces the consequences. Madan did it exactly that way, I didn't have to hammer it in. Govind did it the same way. Deepak tended to be a bit flamboyant—but he can't help it. He wants lines, wants the gallery to respond. But in the end I said, try to show fear and agony, but just before the end, you attain peace, total peace. And then curtain. That he manages.

And you've received awards for *Charandas Chor*?

Yes, in 1982, we got the Fringe First award at the International Drama Festival in Edinburgh. The Scots newspapermen asked me, how come they were using their own language which we didn't understand a single word of, and yet we liked it, quite genuinely, so much that we wanted to not only give it the first award but also announce it before time; traditionally we don't announce it in the middle, we announce it long after the festival is over. And this time we had this strong impulse to announce it immediately. How come? And the audience was mostly white—very few Indians. I said, I found the actors so full of abandon, so totally lacking in any kind of inhibition in front of a white audience, they were totally confident that they were speaking a human tongue to a human audience who could understand it. They made no difference between this audience and the village audience back home. And there was no difference between their performance in the village where their language is spoken and the one here. And that confidence, that self-assurance and lack of self-consciousness, that enjoyment they themselves get, was almost contagious—that's what got you. I think this is one explanation; I know of no other. Probably I was right, because it does transcend the language barrier—I mean, for one thing it has a very strong visual language, and the story moves along simple lines and once you understand the vows it's quite easy to follow visually. But in the main I think it was because of the actors performing in that way.

I was doing things in Chhattisgarhi during 1970–73. But I didn't have a breakthrough until this time because I suddenly got the language of the body through improvisations before *Charandas Chor* and through other means at my disposal—my vocabulary of the visual language of the Chhattisgarhi players had increased and so had my confidence in using it. It was simply that. Otherwise, I could've gone on doing theatre in Chhattisgarhi and it would have remained obtuse to a lot of viewers and accessible only to a coterie of admirers. Suddenly we broke all barriers and people who'd never come to see Chhattisgarhi plays during those three years started pouring in. So *Gaon ka Naam Sasurual* and *Charandas Chor* must have had all these factors in it. I wasn't aware or conscious of it.

My long courtship of the Chhattisgarhi folk player from 1958, off and on, up to 1973, got a breakthrough in 1974–75. After all, what happened in all this time? Several things happened. One of them was what I just described. But many things, improvisations, my watching *nacha* and how they moved and why they couldn't be rigidly choreographed . . . the *nacha* itself is a form with two or three players, not requiring any intricate grouping, and they were just moving anyhow, anywhere, wherever they got a response from. And so it was difficult for me to get them to move with motivation on a line in a certain way, which is what I'd learnt in England. I had to unlearn all these things; I still choreographed them, but my method changed; I gave them all the freedom and then I brought all my authority to pounce down upon them and freeze it, crystallize it and that was the grouping, otherwise they'd never remember if they had to go right or left. So my methodology became perfected over these years and things became easier. I just work. And things begin to gel. But all these methods are at work even now, improvisations and many other things.

You see, I've learnt many things from watching *nacha*, although, of course, from *Mitti ki Gadi* in 1958, I'd come to a very simple kind of stage set, just a round *chabootra* (platform), and learnt to have the stage set functional, very economical so that we remain mobile, for artistic as well as economical reasons. The architecture, set design, were also affected by the kind of awareness I gained in regard to the importance of the actor related to space and the relation of time to space and to actor and to action. All these things, I think, gave me very simple forms, like a rectangular platform with just one tree, to which I came after a few shows. In the beginning, there was something like a curtain, with a temple or a queen's palace painted, on the platform—not the entire platform, just a little of it—and rolled up and down by an actor, visibly there. But I thought that was fussy, so I removed it during the shows and came to two bamboos and a little foliage piece, the branch of a tree connecting them, and through that, people used to pass. Then I got rid of even that, keeping only one bamboo, one branch, and it stayed at that. In other plays also, the bare minimum, absolutely simple.

Another factor is adaptability. I take plays to so many parts of Chhattisgarh and then perform in towns, proscenium, open-air, so we have to constantly adapt ourselves. Like *Hirma ki Amar Kahani* was really done in the open for the first show, in a railway stadium in Bilaspur, with the audience seated in the gallery; and we performed with a cast of seventy, several tribal parties participated, and they appeared to be enjoying dancing on the ground, on the grass, the sheer earth—and the dust being raised looked authentic, their feet felt firm and good, being used to earth. The actors who were playing the police-men, chasing people, enjoyed running and I enjoyed seeing them run, just run. It was a large space, about seventy feet. And then we had to come to Sagar, where the stage is twelve-fourteen feet. Then suddenly we came to Shriram Centre; that itself was quite an adjustment; so after one day's rehearsal we adjusted to that. I think this is one more factor which has given us flexibility, but the approach was such, the space was uncluttered by props and things, except the bare minimum, and the utilization of space was such that we could have people on three or four sides and still perform. So I think that is the rea-son you feel this kind of openness of space even in a proscenium.

The other point that comes to mind is that your plays are something in between a performance and a ritual; you feel like they're doing it for themselves, they're enjoying it, you're just an observer, it's not consciously showing something to the audience. But the level of communication is prob-ably taking place within the group itself, like enjoying a katha or oral tale, that the community shares, exchanges, develops—not performance for performance's sake. It's also a kind of celebration . . .

I think you're right, the ritualistic quality, the unselfconscious quality and cel-ebratory quality, it is all there. I have occasion to complain a hundred times about a hundred things, but never on stage. They're absolutely punctual, they get ready on time and long before the opening time, whatever the time of opening, they are there, absolutely professional in their attitude to the shows. Being groomed in Naya Theatre this quality got further sharpened. If 'professional' means virtuosity, an unselfconscious attitude and sheer excellence and deep involvement, they have it.

It appears, from the way you talk of working with the actors, that you use psychology to help them understand characterization better ?

Do I use conventional psychological methods? The point is, I use all the methods that I've learnt from them, and those I've learnt from myself and my studies. Sometimes, there is already an awareness. But I have to make them aware of their awareness. For example, the subtext of *Bahadur Kalarin* is a son's incestuous desire for his mother. They are aware of incest, but they aren't aware that incest can be analysed and dissected, reasoned out as an ailment, as a sickness. This was my Freudian analysis and they understood it when I explained in concrete terms how the mother must have been handling the child, right from childhood upto his teenage years, which is a very important, crucial turning point in a man's life, the threshold of adulthood. And then they brought to it all that sensitivity, and when I gave them their own examples, they brought in the mother's lover and worked on the other the improvisations. In *Good Woman of Schezuan*, I only tried out one scene as an improvisation, in the tobacco shop, when, one after the other a family of nine or eleven, including the little child and the grandfather, just come and start sponging off them, a cup of tea, no harm in one cup of tea, or one cigarette wouldn't make a difference, and helping themselves from the shop. The actors did it so effortlessly, so naturally—they are used to so much poverty and to sponging, they understand all about greed, the instinct to survive making them sly and clever— they have all that in them. They don't have to be taught the art of behaving like greedy people who are parasites on a family. So I said, we can do Brecht. But when it came to the aviation man, the pilot, with his dreams, talking about the aircraft with so much love and poetry—that they couldn't get. That was a problem. I had to tell them to forget the aeroplane, to think of the moon, a bird, a flower, whatever they love in their surroundings, in nature, in their village, whatever pleases them, and talk in terms of love for those things and only use the word 'aircraft'. And then Amar Singh, who was doing the role, brought all the beauty and poetry to the aircraft, imagining all these things. So I do feed them with these psychological impulses and methods.

I try to get the actor to relate himself to the reality around him, to his own experience; and knowing their experience as I do, I propel them towards that reality so that they can get the feel of what they are doing. So whenever I come across a stumbling block such as this, any difficulty, I create a kind of classroom situation in which exchanges take place. They narrate to me stories of incest and I analyse incest and tell them my way of looking at it; looking at a case of incest from a scientific point of view and a doctor's point of view and an analytical point of view, as a disease. They have the mental equipment to grasp it and to reproduce it in their acting. This is the method I use. In *Charandas Chor*, for example, I told them I wanted him to be a normal man who feared death. If I brought in heroics, it would fail.

Has there ever been an instance when they have come and asked to do a particular legend or a story?

No . . . you see, what they do in *nacha* is from what they know of Pauranic tales, most of them religious. Some secular story is concocted by them on a very elementary level, the evils of drunkenness or something like that, or of an unfaithful wife or husband, with song and dance and all those little subjects and scenes, or something reformatory—this is bad, don't do it; occasionally, a brilliant satire like *Jamadarin* about casteism but not beyond that. For that they needed some catalystic approach like mine.

Tell us something about your idea of the comic, because most folk forms have moments of comedy or elements of the comic which break the narrative, and almost all your plays have this element. You have used the comic in a very significant way; I'd say there's a structural similarity in the way the folk tradition uses the comic element and the way you use it in your productions.

Let us look at it like this: I find that there is a sad element present in most amusing moments. Molière's comedies have quite a few moving scenes, *Tartuffe* is an out and out comedy, but not without some sad elements. A clown is an instrument for making people laugh, but at the same time, there's something tragic about the clown, and I don't mean just Shakespeare's clowns. Charlie Chaplin is the best example. Chekhov, I don't know whether he wrote tragedies or comedies and therefore, we use the word tragi-comedy for Chekhov, amusing and yet very, very sad. *Charandas Chor*, you'll say, is an out and out comedy, right from the beginning till the very end, it makes you roar with laughter on many occasions, and then there is the unexpected death. In *Kalarin*, a tragedy, we've got many moments of the comic kind.

If you look for reality in life, you will find amusing moments in the face of death; you'll find amusing traits in the most serious of characters. And as a director you try to give it another dimension, a fuller form, closer to life, closer to reality, richer in its texture, appeal, plausibility and communicability to the audience. That is my understanding of the comic. And when I'm not dealing with an out and out, straight comedy, I'm looking for such relieving moments, if for no other reason than relief, but also because the porter in Shakespeare's *Macbeth* provides both, technically a relief, and at the same time, deepening the nuance and adding another dimension to the situation. So that's how I think you get the comic, but the presence of folk actors in my Naya Theatre helps me further, because they have an extraordinary predilection for the comic and the ironic, and they do it marvellously. They're such great improvisers and they know me by now, I know them by now, and on a mere hint they can come up and improvise in a very articulate and graphic manner.

Anjum Katyal has been involved with theatre publishing as an editor, writer, translator and critic. She was chief editor of Seagull Books (1987–2006) and editor of the *Seagull Theatre Quarterly* (1994–2004). The author of *Habib Tanvir: Towards an Inclusive Theatre* (2012) and *Badal Sircar: Towards a Theatre of Conscience* (2015), she has also translated Usha Ganguli's *Rudali* and stories by Mahasweta Devi and Meera Mukherjee. She is currently a consultant (publications) with Maulana Abul Kalam Azad Institute of Asian Studies, Calcutta, and co-director of Apeejay Kolkata Literary Festival. A published poet, she also sings the blues.

Prabha Katyal is a retired teacher who translates works from Hindi. She lives in Calcutta.

Javed Malick is an academic and freelance theatre critic. He is a reader in English at Khalsa College, University of Delhi, and the author of *Toward a Theater of the Oppressed: The Dramaturgy of John Arden* (1996).